Praise for

Son *of the* Old West

"The life of a Texas cowboy who ranged the wild frontier paints a broader picture of bygone times in the American West . . . Lively and detailed . . . Illustrations, vintage photos, and maps throughout the text add atmosphere and context to this stirring, multivaried life . . . A well-rendered cowboy tale that fleshes out a larger history of the Old West." —*Kirkus Reviews*

"Dozens of photos and other images bring the text beautifully to life. Perfect for biography, history, and western fans." —*Booklist*

"A veritable real-life Jack Crabb, Charlie Siringo claimed to have seen and done it all in the Old West. Even better, a lot of what Charlie claimed was actually true! In this engrossing book, Nathan Ward expertly guides us along Charlie's meandering trail, from Texas childhood to author of his own legend. At the same time, we are treated to a rich and fascinating portrait of the American West at its wildest." —**Mark Lee Gardner, Spur Award-winning author of** *To Hell on a Fast Horse: The Untold Story of Billy the Kid and Pat Garrett*

"Nathan Ward skillfully brings to life the enigmatic Charlie Siringo, a gypsy-footed cowboy, manhunter, and writer, who helped merge the Wild West of reality with the Wild West of myth." —**Michael Wallis, author of** *Billy the Kid: The Endless Ride*

Son *of the* Old West

Also by Nathan Ward

The Lost Detective: Becoming Dashiell Hammett

Ashes of My Youth:
A Tale of New York and the Wall Street Bombing

The Amateur: The Cold War Life of Rudolf Abel,
Artist & KGB Spy

Dark Harbor: The War for the New York Waterfront

The Total Sports Illustrated Book of Boxing
(co-editor with W. C. Heinz)

Son *of the* Old West

The Odyssey of
Charlie Siringo:
Cowboy, Detective,
Writer of the
Wild Frontier

NATHAN WARD

Grove Press
New York

This book is set in 11.75-pt. Stempel Garamond LT by Alpha Design & Composition of Pittsfield, NH.
The book was designed by Norman E. Tuttle at Alpha Design & Composition.

Published simultaneously in Canada
Printed in Canada

First Grove Atlantic hardcover edition: September 2023
First Grove Atlantic paperback edition: September 2024

Library of Congress Cataloging-in-Publication data is available for this title.

ISBN 978-0-8021-6366-0
eISBN 978-0-8021-6209-0

Grove Press
an imprint of Grove Atlantic
154 West 14th Street
New York, NY 10011

Distributed by Publishers Group West

groveatlantic.com

24 25 26   10 9 8 7 6 5 4 3 2 1

Once again with love for Katie,
who shared Montana and everything else
&
For my father, who taught me to love
a hard-riding story, leanly told

"Cow-boys"—a generic term including roving Texans, desperadoes, and horse-thieves.

—*Dallas Daily Herald*, 1871

If he had to spend a week of nights in some hurdy-gurdy dance hall, drinking and carousing with the gang, in order to get evidence against one of them, he went the limit, drank, gambled, shot out the lights and played bad-man—and then, suddenly he had his man in jail, and no one knew how it happened. . . . [Siringo's] experiences, compared with the adventures of Ulysses, Marco Polo and Benvenuto Cellini, make the latter seem as pallid as a Cooks' Tour.

—Henry Herbert Knibbs, 1927

Holy smokes and little fishes.
What a deceitful world this is.

—Charles Siringo

Contents

Book Two: Playing Outlaw

Book Three: Last of the Wild

Author's Note

No one wrote about Charlie Siringo's life as well (or as often) as the man himself. This is not a biography of the cowboy, writer, and detective so much as a portrait of the American West through which he traveled as such a compelling witness—from the birth of the cattle trail and railroad cow town to the violence of the mining wars and the Wild Bunch's long last ride. By the time he reached Hollywood, the lowly cowboy of his books had become the standard Western hero.

Prelude:
A Cowboy Adrift

The old man had not known it would be his last hunt when he set out from his desert ranch, taking his rifle and his horse Sailor Gray northwest toward the Jemez Mountains, in the fall of 1921.

They took a photo of him anyway, hat tilted back, hand braced on the rear saddle of his light-colored mount, as he forded the Rio Grande at Cochiti Pueblo. The hunting party then climbed into the hills that promised deer, turkey, bighorn, and bear, where a snow surprised the group, and Charlie Siringo slept with just a blanket on the powdery ground. He returned to his ranch with a cough that grew into bronchitis over the coming months. By the end of the following year he was sure he wouldn't hunt again.

When he first bought the place outside Santa Fe that would become his Sunny Slope, Siringo had dreamed of retiring to it for good and later rode behind his hounds after jackrabbits and coyotes over the cactus plains. Now high in debt and convinced he suffered from the pleurisy of the lungs that had killed his young first wife, he had to give up what was left of the ranch after thirty years. The last and hardest job was selling off his favorite saddle horses.

He raffled Sailor Gray for a hundred dollars cash but turned down a higher offer for the remaining horse, his brown eighteen-year-old, Patsy, fearing the animal, grown fat, might pass into "cruel" hands through a sale and be slaughtered. With Patsy nearly a decade ago he had retraced some of the Chisholm Trail route of his youth to see how much had been lost to barbed wire and the farmer's hoe; more recently Siringo had pursued fugitives with Patsy along the border as a New Mexico Ranger, where he saw a younger inspector, Bill Owens, shot through the lungs by a rustler near Abo Pass, returning fire as he died.[1]

Before leaving the Sunny Slope, he led Patsy out into the scruff woods they both loved, placed his revolver gently behind the horse's ear, and said goodbye. With the last of his sad tasks

Siringo rides his horse Sailor Gray across the Rio Grande on his final hunt, fall 1921. Riata and Spurs / *Author's collection*

done, he headed for the depot at Santa Fe and the train that would take him from his ranch.

Standing bowlegged in his boy-size boots, he looked leathery and frail, a small, desert-seasoned old man wearing a low-crowned Stetson and a white mustache, kerchief circling his tanned, lined throat. His brown eyes, often mirthful, were hardly merry as he boarded the train that December day, an undersize old gent moving to his seat, resting beneath his canted hat. After spending Christmas with an old friend in Douglas, Arizona, he traveled on to California to collapse in the house of his daughter, Viola. He arrived thinking he would die.

In San Diego he was nursed by Viola and her own teenage girl. Over several months in the house, his strength and agitation slowly returned, enough that he felt again like a cowboy adrift, once more in need of his own place. An old friend had once written Siringo from California about the film jobs to be had for men as skilled as he was at riding, roping, and shooting. By the spring of 1923, Siringo had left his daughter's for Los Angeles, where they were making stories about the West he had known.

Book One
TEXAS COWBOY

1

A Plain Damn Fool

He was an heroic, romantic figure in his day—but his day has gone.
The old-time cowboy of forty years ago is almost an exclusive motion
picture figure now.

—"The Passing of the Cowboy," *Los Angeles Times*, 1922

A number of Western films had come through Santa Fe's Paris Theater while Siringo lived there—*Hell's Hinges*, in which an entire town burned spectacularly down, sparked by a saloon gunfight involving a vengeful William S. Hart; breezier stuff, like the Tom Mix feature *Six Cylinder Love*; or another tough Hart picture, *Wolves of the Rail*, in which Mexican bandits attacked a moving train guarded by their conflicted former comrade. Such entertainments might be more romantic than life, but the riding and landscapes were a wonder even to a Westerner living among the desert mountains.

Real cowboying was no longer possible, so he'd headed toward the make-believe kind.

Other grizzled frontiersmen—from Emmett Dalton to Bill Tilghman and Wyatt Earp—had gone ahead of him to peddle their experiences to the movies. He came alone but was part of a migration of cowboys seeking movie work, some just for the winter but many cut loose from ranches collapsing around the West. In their chaps and hats and spurs, one columnist noted, there were "more real cowboys in Los Angeles right now than in any other one spot in the world."[1] To them, all work was honorable that wasn't on foot, and motion pictures offered a remaining hope of staying in the saddle.

Even as it quieted, the frontier was reenacted and revised, first in Wild West shows and rodeos and now in moving pictures, with the able help of its last working witnesses.

People reinvented themselves all over the West, in Siringo's case dozens of times. But unlike others hoping to sell their more fabled stories, since his thirties he had often kept stealthy and anonymous, adventuring under a series of personas not his own as a cowboy detective—C. Leon Allison, Leon Carrier, Charles T. LeRoy. He might have seen more of the West than most and met every bad man, lawman, outlaw woman, or cattle king worth knowing, but often not as himself.

He was known mostly as the man who had published the first cowboy autobiography, *A Texas Cowboy; or, Fifteen Years on the Hurricane Deck of a Spanish Pony*; as well as a detecting memoir that enraged the Pinkertons, *A Cowboy Detective*; and a short life of Billy the Kid, whom he had briefly known. Now he would become another retired cowboy in Los Angeles, a slight old Texan without a horse, fingers bent from the ranch work he no longer performed, selling his self-published books out of a satchel. One thing he retained was his silver-plated, pearl-gripped "old Colt's 45," which he would bring out for visitors on the least excuse.

By the time Siringo came to town in 1923, an enormous lighted sign was going up in sixty-foot letters spelling the name of a growing real estate development across the brushy hillsides, Hollywoodland.* The last time he had been in Los Angeles was

---

* Like the "land" part of its name, the lights from this "largest electric sign in the world" (once powerful enough to knock out nearby residents' electricity) did not survive the years. But the huge sign quickly became iconic—a car

the 1890s, before the first filmmakers visited California in 1906 and well before a young theatrical director, Cecil B. DeMille, arrived with a crew, rented a former livery barn at Vine Street and Selma Avenue, and made Hollywood's first three-reel feature, a melodrama of the West called *The Squaw Man*, in 1914.

DeMille had been pleased to find skilled cowboy riders drinking and playing cards at a place called the Water Hole, a simple gray frame building on Cahuenga between Sunset and Hollywood Boulevards, just blocks from his rented barn. (A number of these horsemen would ride as medieval Frenchmen in his Joan of Arc picture.) The Water Hole was more a café than an honest saloon but retained a brass rail and bar; cowboy patrons sneaked their whiskey and tequila from coffee cups. When a stranger entered, recalled the stuntman Jack Montgomery, everyone turned to determine if the newcomer was "Prohibition or free choice."[2]

As Siringo would discover, any cowboy arriving in Los Angeles was directed to take the streetcar out to the Water Hole to find old friends and learn the news. Some paid an extra nickel to bring their favorite saddle beside them on the trip. Of the Water Hole crowd, the movie gossip Louella Parsons reported, "These heroes of the horse operas are clannish. They talk their own lingo and let the rest of the world go hang. Always, any day you can see dozens of them in a small restaurant near Hollywood Boulevard, where they congregate to swap yarns and discuss their latest 'operas.'"[3]

Movie people needing cowboys knew to seek them out at the Water Hole, and in those early days before the Central Casting office, they also hired riders out of the Los Angeles stockyards at a day rate. Lucky ones might be picked up and shuttled

company advertised its brakes in 1924 by climbing the steep hill before the Hollywoodland roads were built and stopping short of the sign after rolling dangerously toward it.

to the enormous ranch at Universal City, stunt riding for one of the studio's many Westerns for five dollars a day plus a boxed lunch, far better than they had made as real cowboys.

Among Charlie's earliest friends in the city was George "Jack" Cole, a cowboy artist and son of Senator Cornelius Cole, whose Colegrove acreage became a part of Hollywood. When the younger Cole heard about Siringo pitiably moving from one lodging to another, he helped find him a place near a building his family owned. The man who managed the apartment house for the Coles lived next door, where he built a one-room cabin for Siringo in his backyard, at 6057 Eleanor Avenue. Charlie moved in, posting a sign above the door, "Siringo's Den," and turned the inside walls into what he called a "Rogue's Gallery" of tintypes showing favorite outlaws and lawmen he had known or hunted or people he merely admired, like Bill Hart.

Hart's long equine face and lanky form were familiar to anyone who went to the movies—tight-lipped and squinting beneath his broad hat, playing long-limbed frontiersmen like "Two Gun" Bill or "Square Deal" Sanderson, bad men like "Blaze" Tracy, or a self-made legend such as Wild Bill Hickok. Although he privately spoke in the Yankee patrician accent of the Broadway stage, Hart cut a charismatic cowboy figure on the silent screen, riding well and throwing a rope with conviction, flaring a match with one hand, or jumping his beloved pinto gelding Fritz through a window. Charlie had sent the screen Westerner an appreciative letter, and Hart's kind response credited the writer's old cowboy book as an inspiration, words Siringo would quote on the back of his new business cards.

From his little Hollywood bungalow, Charlie could now stroll over to the Water Hole. The existence of this cowboy haven walking distance from his new cabin made Siringo's life more bearable away from his desert ranch and horses. Along with his walk to the public library, Charlie made the Water Hole part of his daily routine, a place where he could hold court of an evening. Some of the bar's younger regulars had higher hats and shinier spurs than the cow folk he remembered, but the Western outfit Charlie wore did not make him an exotic figure. Everyone seeking movie work dressed the part before leaving the house, just as other hopeful extras crowded studio gates each morning gotten up as soldiers or shopkeepers or southern belles.

Set loose in bars like this one, Siringo had charmed his way into all manner of gangs. He could tell his Hollywood drinking friends about everything from trailing longhorn cattle up from Texas as a boy to playing cards with Billy the Kid or about how a blind old phrenologist once laid his hands on young Charlie's skull, declaring him fit to be only a newspaper editor, rancher, or detective. He had watched the Old West change, first as a Texas trail hand and later as a cowboy detective, had known the cattle trails in their prime, and had seen the creation of the wild cow town.

Siringo first outlined his ranching adventures in 1885 in *A Texas Cowboy*, which Will Rogers admired enough to call the "Cowboy's Bible." Though sold mainly by the "butcher boys" who hawked dime novels on trains, it had helped create the literature and spread the myth by which the world came to know the American West, with the humble cowboy as its hero instead of the cattle kings for whom he rode. There would be other books about his life. Except for his beloved first wife, Mamie, his greatest, most loyal friends in an often lonesome, dual life were his horses, Whiskey Peat, Damfido, Boney Part, Rowdy, Glen Alpine Jr., Beat-and-be-damned, Sailor Gray, and Patsy, who all got their thanks in his memoirs. "No other cowboy ever talked about himself so much in print," wrote the Texas folklorist and historian J. Frank Dobie, and "few had more to talk about."[4]

In his travels, "playing outlaw," Siringo had made unsavory acquaintances using many names, posing as a tramp in the Mojave or a Colorado silver thief, a machine oiler in an Alaskan gold mill, bronco buster, mining executive, union radical, or cowboy fleeing the law. He was a gifted and likable actor. While following the Wild Bunch gang he even romanced Butch Cassidy's Mormon sister and chased the Wild West to its last violent days. No one else in the Water Hole had seen what he had of the West, and scant few had outside it.* But when asked by an interviewer if his chancy life showed he'd been a brave man, he scoffed, "I was a plain damn fool, that's all."[5]

Going undercover as a tramp cowboy to locate a fugitive in 1889, Siringo applied for work as a bronco buster at a ranch outside Longmont, Colorado, where he suspected his man was hiding among some loyal family. The ranch's meanest outlaw bronc, which had tossed and stomped many cowboy applicants, was brought out blindfolded for Charlie's audition. As expected, a crowd gathered to see how quickly or spectacularly the bold stranger would be thrown. In his pocket, Siringo carried a photograph of his fugitive, wanted for attempted murder in an altercation in Helena—unless the victim died; from the saddle Charlie scanned the crowd that had assembled to see him get tossed. Among them, he recognized the dark-haired fugitive, sneaking

---

* The Water Hole was gone by 1929, when Lee Shippey wrote in the *Los Angeles Times*, "Still an occasional cowboy mopes along in the neighborhood of Hollywood Boulevard and Cahuenga in hope of meeting some other survivor" ("Lee Side of L.A.," *Los Angeles Times*, Nov. 8, 1929). Hopeful movie cowboys had learned to go to a drugstore and bar on the edge of the Columbia Pictures lots, an area eventually nicknamed "Gower Gulch" and referenced in movies and cartoons. These aspirants were literally "drugstore cowboys." In 1940, when one area cowboy shot another dead in a dispute over a woman, dozens of dispatches spread the word of the colorful Gulch.

a look around a door casing just before Charlie raised the gray bronc's blinders and rode out the bucking storm. Once the horse was spent, Siringo was offered the ranch job as promised but made his way instead to town to bring the news of his sighting back to his boss on the Denver train.

Such adventures in Siringo's memoir of his time as a Pinkerton, *A Cowboy Detective*, inspired Dashiell Hammett in writing his 1925 crime story "Corkscrew," in which his stocky urban Continental Op is sent to investigate some murders of Arizona cowboys and is thrown repeatedly from a devilish horse to gain acceptance.* If the hard-boiled American detective fiction of the 1920s was largely the classic cowboy story adapted to a city setting, then Siringo had carried it there from the Texas plains. In a cowboy tale, a skillful stranger of few words appears in a troubled community that needs him, then liberates the town from its threat (sometimes leaving it scorched) before moving on. Siringo had entered many dangerous towns as a detective and was often saved by his cowboy training; he wrote about both lives, bridging one genre to the other just as his own rough experiences had blended.

As an old man, after years spent ingratiating himself to outlaws, he said a reckoning was probably due: "When the final call comes, I shall have to take my medicine, with Satan holding the spoon." Of the many characters Siringo had played among the desperadoes, the role nearest his heart seemed to be the Texas stranger buying rounds, the sociable cowboy with a dark Lone

---

* The pulp magazines Hammett wrote for in the 1920s published both Western stories and detective fiction, and the Siringo-inspired "Corkscrew"—a cowboy story with a city detective as its hero—split the difference. The Op asks the cowboys for a mild horse and of course receives the opposite, proving his worth by gamely taking his beating by being repeatedly thrown. A realistic fictional detective would not have had the skills that Siringo brought to the job.

Star past and a rich father who paid his bar bills. "He never for-
got the lure of the grasslands of the balmy coast ranges where he
first earned his spurs," wrote J. Evetts Haley, who met Siringo
at the end.[6] But Charlie's own immigrant father had not lived to
help him out of any of the considerable trouble he found; from
Red River to the Rio Grande, Texas had raised him.

2

A Fatherless Boy

Am I not a queer conglomerate—a sweet-scented mixture indeed!

—Charles Siringo, *A Texas Cowboy*

Texas was so large that Siringo once made a long ride from the Panhandle ranch that employed him down to pick up a herd at Goliad, on the lower Gulf coast, only to be seen as a Northerner. An older cowhand watched the exotic visitor rope for an afternoon, then declared Charlie pretty good "for a Yankee."[1]

He was in fact the slender son of a man he could not remember, an Italian who had made his own long journey so his children could be born as Texans. When Antonio Siringo set out, emigrant guidebooks promised "rolling land, something similar to parts of New Jersey," but with high, luxuriant cotton. In Texas, "smiling prairies . . . invite the plough," one guide explained,[2] and while a New England farmer might slavishly serve his livestock year-round, in Texas "the cattle are the slaves of the owner."[3] In fact, these animals wandered the plains, largely indifferent to their masters. Writers of such early books were often eastern literary men who had not seen the God's country they conjured. But their hyperbole was matched by the discoveries the emigrants made once launched toward paradise.

Waves of would-be Texans answered the call, traveling south in wagons across the Red River, overland out of southwest Louisiana, or arriving by boat at Gulf coast ports, as Antonio Siringo did. "An unusual tide of emigration is now flowing towards Texas," wrote a reporter watching loaded vessels dock at Matagorda Bay in 1851. "Each of the Southern States . . . as well as England, Ireland, Germany, are contributing an annual swarm to complete the medley."[4]

In Matagorda, at the mouth of the Colorado River on Texas's mid-Gulf coast, Antonio found the young woman he would marry. Bridgit White had arrived from Ireland with her parents and siblings and some Irish stained glass to distinguish the windows of their plains farmhouse. Charlie later joked that his parents met during a hurricane before marrying on October 12, 1852, in Matagorda, a place with 2,214 residents (more than half of them enslaved, three others freedmen).*

The Siringos secured their own small ranch on the Matagorda Peninsula, what was then a seventy-five-mile coastal strip between the bay and the Gulf of Mexico. Here the couple joined the Texas story of upheaval and succession: new immigrants making a home in a German section called Dutch Settlement, set within a former French colony that had long belonged to the Karankawa people, who first made a captive of the conquistador Cabeza de Vaca, after he unfortunately came ashore in the region in 1532.

But while some colonists had arrived in Texas already wealthy, as planters and slaveholders, humbler immigrants like

---

* In the fall of 1853, the town proposed an order banning Mexicans from the county. "They have no fixed domicil," explained the *Indianola (TX) Bulletin*, "but hang around the plantations, taking the likeliest negro girls for wives" (*Bulletin* quoted in [Marshall] *Texas Republican*, Oct. 8, 1853, p. 2).

Antonio came to farm and perhaps ranch, adding cattle once they had settled and seen the loose herds. It is not known what brought him all the way to the peninsula, but he must have heard or read that the South Texas plains were lively with mustang horses and wild cattle with long twisted horns. There was not yet an established market for beef, as there was for cotton, but Texas longhorns could be sold for their hides or tallow to make candles or soap. Antonio would live just long enough to realize what Texas would be increasingly about. He registered a brand first for himself and later in the name of his first child, Catherine, hoping to claim some of the free longhorns for a herd of his own. Perhaps seeing how it was growing as a port, Antonio also bought a business lot in the town of Matagorda in 1854.[5] Then he died, months after the arrival of the couple's son, Charles Angelo, soon called Charlie, born February 7, 1855. Antonio's passing left Bridgit alone to raise their two children and manage the small ranch. The couple had been married almost three years.

In April 1856, an exotic, strong-smelling cargo anchored off Matagorda shortly before it disembarked at Powder Horn wharf in nearby Indianola. Interest in the ship's strange holdings had built before it even left the port that February, some of the animals sent as gifts from the viceroy of Egypt. It was the fruition of a request first made to Congress by Secretary of War Jefferson Davis several years earlier. His report had declared that imported camels and dromedaries were needed in the tablelands of Texas, New Mexico, Utah, and elsewhere for the "transportation of supplies and for the services of troops stationed along our new frontier and operating against the predatory and nomadic Indians." The *Louisville Daily Courier* echoed the idea: "Even the completion of a railway from the Atlantic regions to the

Pacific would but increase the necessity" for camels to "distribute supplies and transport troops to vast regions which the railway could not touch."[6] Davis certainly hoped his plan would aid slaveholders to settle across the southwestern territories.

A crowd was fascinated to watch the first thirty-three camels, which had spent months rolling and pitching at sea, brought finally ashore to lumber gawkily through Indianola on their way to a pen built for their arrival. Many were nearly hairless from the deprivations of the voyage, seeming huge and ungraceful until they trotted, and their strange bodies suddenly made more sense. Correspondents sent from New Orleans and Nashville explained to their readers the distinctions between one- and two-humped camels and that there were fighting breeds as well as others that were purely pack animals; they investigated the milk, which one reported was "in no way distinguishable from cow's milk, and we do not wonder at the fondness which the wandering Bedouin has for it."[7]

A group of Arab keepers had accompanied the camels through the sometimes turbulent crossing, making an equal impression on Texans when they arrived in their "Bedouin costume." But managing the beasts on land turned out to be an infuriating challenge for locals not raised to it, and after only a few weeks, two frustrated camel handlers named Kauffman and Rey came to a deadly altercation. Rey, identified as "principal handler," fired four shots into Kauffman, later "found in the night with his throat cut from ear to ear."[8]

Horses and mules did not welcome the imported animals but seemed to hate the smell of them and refused to trail together. In fact, rules of the road were soon established in Texas, since "neither horses nor mules can endure the sight nor smell of the camel. Indeed, camels are not allowed to travel the highways in the daytime, and if a train of these animals is loaded with freight for Virginia City, it must not enter the streets until late at night, when no horses or mules are abroad."[9] Though originally imports to the continent themselves, the equines won the contest against the musky invaders.*

Young Charlie learned to make his own adventures, often provoking his overburdened mother into using her strap or swinging her wooden "mush stick" at him when he neglected chores such as finding driftwood to burn under her washpot.** "Crowds of cow boys used to come over to the Peninsula from the mainland and sometimes have occasion to rope wild steers in my presence," he remembered in A Texas Cowboy. The sight inspired him to ride his stick pony over the nearby beachfront, swing a fishing-line lasso at scuttling sand crabs or the flying shadows of seagulls, any unsuspecting thing that moved.[10] He wore a long shirt his mother had made for him out of flour sacks until he went to school at age four, in the fall of 1859.

That October, a long-bearded, wrathful figure, the abolitionist John Brown, launched a violent operation he had spent much of the summer making vague plans for in a rented farmhouse near Harpers Ferry, in what was then Virginia. With a force of men kept hidden on the farm, he meant to seize the nearby federal arsenal and its ammunition, then inspire a rebellion of the enslaved on area plantations (something like Nat Turner's 1831 slave revolt that killed fifty Virginians), arming his recruits and hopefully drawing others to his growing band as it moved south. Between October 16 and 18, Brown's men did seize two bridges and the federal arsenal, but his call for slave rebellion went unanswered. Ten of his militiamen died in the fighting with

---

* Congress declined to renew funding for the camel experiment in 1858.

** Mush is a dish made from cornmeal that is beaten with a stick before being boiled in cow's milk.

federal troops overseen by Colonel Robert E. Lee; seven more were executed later, including Brown.

Brown's "servile insurrection" proved as divisive as it had been unsuccessful. "Slavery drives John Brown to madness, and then hangs him for that insanity," mourned an Ohio newspaper, while Texas writers railed against his "villainous and treasonable plot." Around the country, a rash of meteor sightings occurred that summer and fall, from a "fireball and shooting stars" over Pittsfield, Massachusetts, in August into the cool of the hunting season in the Northwest, where a man saw a "dazzling light" along the barrel of his gun before a meteor fell loudly to the ground.[11] After Herman Melville watched John Brown hang that December, he came to consider him as of a stormy piece with the year's atmospheric disturbances, "the meteor of the war."

Each day, young Charlie followed his sister, Catherine, barefoot for the mile to the schoolhouse, sometimes delayed by his investigations along the beach. One time, following a crab to its hole, he investigated too closely and had his nose and lip clamped by its claws; he arrived late and bloodied at school and was spanked. The schoolhouse was run by an Illinois man far from home named Mr. Hale.

In April 1861 came the Confederate attack on the US garrison at Fort Sumter, South Carolina. Teachers with classes of over twenty students were at first exempt from Confederate conscription. But the schoolmaster Mr. Hale felt the call to return north to serve, and may also have heard about the hangings of Unionists elsewhere in Texas, preferring to die in a blue uniform. One year into Charlie's formal education his teacher broke up the school and left for home. Siringo was left "doing nothing and studying mischief" as the war approached.[12]

* * *

In order to join the Confederate States of America, Texas state senators had to fire their young state's most celebrated hero, Sam Houston, the tall, square-jawed leader of the Texas Revolution and first president of the Republic of Texas. Houston had won the last election of his career in 1859, barely becoming governor despite opposing secession from the Union, which he predicted would bring disaster.

Before coming to Texas in his thirties, Houston had already lived a whole other political life and had spent several years living among the Cherokee. Born in Virginia in 1793, he moved with his family to Tennessee, where he was a veteran of the War of 1812 and was a protégé of Andrew Jackson, under whom he served. After becoming Tennessee's young governor, he left the state in response to a marital scandal after his wedding night in 1829, which, out of either honor for his young bride or embarrassment, he refused to discuss.

There followed for Houston several grieving years, living and drinking among the Cherokee in the Arkansas Territory, his second time dropping out of white society: he had first run away across the Tennessee River to live with the Cherokee as a teenager, when he was given the name Raven. This time he was called Big Drunk, and with reason.

Houston eventually emerged from his second Cherokee period to become unofficial ambassador to the tribal nations for President Jackson (who had also already begun the massive relocations of Native peoples known as the Trail of Tears). This allowed Houston to travel on Jackson's behalf while also serving his own ambition to organize the Texians (colonists living in Mexican Texas) into leaving Mexico, noting many of their grievances in letters back to Jackson. For the Texians, besides withholding taxes for lack of services from the Mexican government, the fight for independence coalesced around what they considered their American inalienable rights, including their freedom to be slave owners.[13]*

Houston was appointed major general of the Texas army in the fall of 1835 and at first proposed destroying the Alamo Mission, whose defenders were largely volunteers beyond his authority at the time they dug in. After the grievous losses there and in the massacre of Texian prisoners of war at Goliad, Houston secured his reputation with the final eighteen-minute raid at San Patricio on April 21, 1836, attacking as the Mexican soldiers rested in camp and capturing General Antonio López de Santa Anna shortly after. Houston was twice elected president of the new Republic of Texas and, after statehood, became one of its two original senators.[14] By the 1850s, though still a slaveholder, he remained a Unionist opposed to the idea of a separate Southern nation. Elected governor of the state in the eruptive year of 1859, he refused to swear an oath to the Confederacy and was deposed from office in March 1861, weeks before the attack on Fort Sumter. Texas joined the secession, and the ruination he predicted soon followed.

Siringo had lost his school months after the bombardment and surrender of Fort Sumter. War visited the Gulf coast, and as a boy in 1862, he separately encountered troops from both armies camped near his family's ranch or drilling on the beach where he played; the Union volunteers bribed him with hardtack, a welcome break in his wartime diet of "fish, oysters, corn-bread and sweet potatoes. Coffee was made of parched corn and sweet potatoes."[15] The two companies fought to a standstill, according

---

* "What the Americans in Texas feared was not the failure of Mexican officials to enforce the law," H. W. Brands has written, "but the possibility that they *would* enforce the law—in particular that portion of Mexican law forbidding slavery" (H. W. Brands, *Dreams of El Dorado* [Basic, 2019], 106).

to Charlie, who could hear the distant guns. A number of bodies washed ashore, including one whose uniform and clothes were gone, identifiable only by "J.T." inked on his wrist.[16]

Union boats fired shells over the houses of Dutch Settlement toward Fort Caney. The Siringo family scavenged wrecks along the coast, collecting what became their tableware from the old hulk of a Spanish vessel. "During the war several ships were driven ashore by the Yankee gunboats," he wrote. "The folks at the 'Settlement' would get all the plunder."[17] Until the middle of the war, Matagorda was a favored point from which Confederate boats tried to slip the Union blockade and bring Texas's remaining cotton to market.

Like many of the state's immigrants, Bridgit Siringo had learned to side with the Confederacy; Charlie grew up reciting doggerel about Abe Lincoln riding a mule and Jeff Davis astride a noble steed.* But in the spring of 1863, when residents of the peninsula were ordered to set their cattle loose on the mainland to keep them out of the hands of hungry Union soldiers, Bridgit handed over the rest of her small herd but argued for the right to keep one milk cow to feed her children. This cow would be even more important than she knew. "Often when I would be hungry and afraid to go home for fear of Mother and the mush stick," Siringo recalled, "[Browny] would let me go up to her on the prairie calf fashion and get my milk."

Charlie's best friend and partner in "devilment" was Billy Williams, their specialties "riding the milk calves, coon hunting and sailing play-boats" on the bay shore.[18] Old women of the settlement told the devilish boys they would be hanged before they were twenty-one. Billy's father, John, was almost hanged by

---

* "Jeff Davis is our President / And Lincoln is a fool, / Jeff Davis rides a big gray horse / While Lincoln rides a mule" (Charles A. Siringo, *A Texas Cowboy* [Penguin, 2000], 64).

Federals for stealing Union horses to supply the Confederates. A
general let him go as "too old" to be further danger. Spared hanging and having survived a close call with some landing cannon-
balls, John Williams found another way to die. Discovering an
unexploded cannon shell near his home, he carried it back with
him and set it in his front yard for entertainment. Thinking he
had emptied out most of its powder, he brought a burning coal
from the fire and lowered it inside the shell with tongs, expecting to see a mild sparkler effect, but instead was blown up in
front of his entire gathered family, their dog, who was maimed,
and Charlie, luckily watching from behind a tree. Now Billy was
fatherless too.

Between seventy thousand and ninety thousand Texans
fought in the disaster Sam Houston had predicted, which left
one-fourth of all "able-bodied" Texan men dead or wounded.[19]
Texas fought even after the Confederate surrender at Appomattox, winning the Battle of Palmito Ranch, near Brownsville on
May 13, 1865. During the Civil War, the "total slave population
of the state . . . increased by 35 per cent," noted the Texas historian T. R. Fehrenbach, as thousands of enslaved people were
"sent South by worried owners in Louisiana and Arkansas" to
hedge against their possible freedom. At war's end, the news of
their emancipation was muffled at best in Texas, until the arrival
of Union general Gordon Granger and his soldiers, who read out
General Order Number Three—the Juneteenth proclamation—at
Galveston on June 19, 1865, making official that Union authority over Texas was restored, the acts of the Confederacy "null
and void," and slavery abolished. General Order Number Three
reaffirmed the freedom of more than two hundred thousand
enslaved Texans months after Lee's surrender and two years after
Lincoln's Emancipation Proclamation.[20] Some freedmen now

established their own communities, and many hired on as cow-boys on the South Texas plains. Recalling the time of the great livestock drives, the Texas cattleman George W. Saunders estimated that perhaps a third of the thirty-five thousand cowboys riding during the height of the trail drives from Texas had been Black or Mexican.[21]

When the fighting finally ended, local men joined the "cow hunt" to retrieve the peninsula's cattle from the mainland, where they had been hidden from Union soldiers but had multiplied and grown wild across several hundred miles. The initial job took months to complete. Charlie and Billy were still judged too young for cattle work, so they practiced lassoing and riding wild yearlings around the peninsula. With his older sister now at school in Galveston, Siringo's adventurous days left his mother alone with the work of the ranch; after he sneaked into his bed at night having once again skipped his chores, Bridgit would appear in the dark room with her mush stick.

An adolescent Charlie, about the time he joined the cowboy ranks.

A Cowboy Detective / *Author's collection*

When Charlie had just turned twelve, he finally got his tryout as a cowboy. His mother sometimes took in boarders for extra money, as landlocked Texans often liked to escape to the shore for the hottest months. In the spring of 1867, a man named Faldien rented rooms in the Siringo house for his family to spend the summer. A drover,

Faldien needed to stash his loved ones somewhere breezier and less prone to mosquitoes while he returned to his ranch for the spring roundup of his longhorns. He asked Bridgit if Charlie, who seemed keen on all things cowboy, might come along and learn to run cattle. As the boy was desperate to go and contributed little to the household as it was, she consented, making Charlie a cowboy at last.

3

Mavericking

The "cow-boys" of Texas are a peculiar breed . . . as distinct in
their habits and characteristics from the remainder of even the
Texas population as if they belonged to another race.

—*Galveston Daily News*, 1873

The life Charlie Siringo was entering, of the distinctive
Texas cowboy running cattle from the back of a mustang pony, had been created out of the remains of a
Spanish ranching culture. The longhorn cattle roaming much of
South Texas in Charlie's time were hybrid descendants of livestock from old Spanish missions and abandoned Mexican ranches.
They were a lean, ill-tempered breed that often sheltered in the
native brush, traveled at night, and favored soft prairie grasses.
To capture them, early riders would force a nighttime stampede
until the herd was spent.

Even domesticated livestock on the open range was known
to "stampede to freedom" and return to the wild, while free cattle reproduced so rapidly on the Texas coastal plains, "their number doubled in size every four years."[1] The 1860 census reported
3.5 million head of cattle in the state, one-eighth of the number
across the country. (Modern estimates put the number as high as
4.5 million.) Spanish ponies introduced to North America had
also scattered and developed in the wild ("mustang" comes from
the Spanish for "stray"), transforming the way of life of those

Native peoples who mastered them, enabling quick raids and escapes as well as hunting from horseback.

The humble job of the *vaquero* had also begun with the ranches of New Spain, as mounted servants tending to the ranchero's horses and watching for rustlers. When North American colonists began to come in large numbers to what was still Mexico, the vaqueros would capture and tame wild horses to sell to them. "The horse-catchers—or 'vaqueros,' as they are called—are famous riders," wrote one Texas newspaper:

> and to see them capture a wild mustang is better than to go to circus. The vaquero puts a Spanish saddle on a tame horse, and starts out to see what he can find. In front, on the high pommel of the saddle, he hangs in large coils a leather rope, about a hundred feet long, called a lasso. . . . The vaquero has not long to wait, for there are droves of horses cantering or walking about over the swells and hollows of the prairie, with here and there a smaller group looking on, or watching a battle between two horses who wish to be captains of their bands.[2]

Texians learned from vaqueros to gradually abandon their own saddles in favor of high-horned saddles for roping and adopted their lassos and spurs as well. The open-range method of ranching—letting cattle and sheep roam on unfenced lands—they learned from the Mexicans. The American cowboy, wrote Philip Ashton Rollins in 1922, "obtained from Mexican sources all the tools of his trade, all the technic of his craft, the very words by which he designated his utensils, the very animals with which he dealt."[3]

The term "cowboy" (often styled then as "cow-boy") in the modern sense was first used here during the Texas Revolution,

according to David Dary, when Anglo-Texans hoping to feed soldiers after the victory at San Patricio gathered cattle from Mexican ranches whose owners had fled across the Rio Grande. But
"cowboy" did not become more common until after the Civil
War, when the great migration of Texas longhorns to market was
underway, sending thousands of these riders northward.[4]

The interaction of Texas longhorns with vaqueros and cowboys would determine the course of Charlie Siringo's life. He
was twelve that spring of 1867 when he became "a full-fledged
Cowboy, wearing broad sombrero, high-heeled boots, Mexican
spurs, and the dignity of a full-grown man."[5] (Not until he was
living in Kansas in his late twenties would he be forced to hold
up his pants with anything but a vaquero's sash.) Until now, his
experience with lassoing had been playacting with Billy Williams
or roping calves at home to hold them back long enough for his
mother to complete her milking.

Charlie rode out in a wagon with Faldien's cook to a place
called Big Boggy Creek, near Lake Austin, where the crew was
to retrieve some vacationing cow ponies and ready them for the
job of the roundup. The boy saw his first wild boar hunt, which
bloodied the dogs, and soon learned about branding as a fully
waged cowboy making ten dollars a month. With the Texas
economy in ruins after the war, the first large-scale cattle drives
north had been launched the previous year, in 1866, and it was
easy to see all that remained plentiful to sell on the landscape.
"The country was literally covered with wild mustangs and
long-horn cattle," Charlie remembered. "The unbranded cattle
were public property, and our object was to 'Make hay while the
sun shined' by putting Mr. Faldien's brand on as many cattle as
possible."[6] He also improved his lassoing, as cattle needed to be
roped and thrown before the hot brand was applied. A name was
used to refer to these thousands of unclaimed animals roaming

the Texas mainland: mavericks. Among the various Texas tra-
ditions he grew up with, Siringo hailed from the birthplace of
mavericking.

Samuel Augustus Maverick was a flesh-and-blood man who had
first come to Texas from South Carolina during the year of the
revolution, 1835. Though a latecomer, he became a signatory to
the Texas Declaration of Independence. He moved his family
and enslaved workers from San Antonio to a farm in DeCrow's
Point, near Matagorda Bay, in 1845, before the Siringos arrived.
Mary Maverick, weary of stifling summers inland in the Colorado River bottoms, recalled that her husband "decided to take
us to the Gulf Coast, where we could enjoy sea bathing." Once
there, she pronounced the peninsula "a dreary, sandy flat," but
the swims and ocean sailing were as promised.[7]

Sam Maverick was a Yale-educated attorney who came to
Texas hoping to be a land speculator more than a cattleman,
arriving in Matagorda with just nine cows. But in 1845 he came
to own four hundred steers in lieu of a debt payment from an
overextended neighbor, Samuel Nathan Tilton, whose farm,
Tiltona, he would buy two years later. The evidence of Maverick's inattentive ranching was soon wandering the peninsula.
"Within a year or two the residents of the coastal region began
referring to every unbranded head as 'one of Maverick's,'"[8]
wrote David Dary. "Maverick" naturally evolved into "Mavericking," referring to the branding of supposed strays as one's
own.

The naming part seems less in dispute than how Maverick's
cattle came to wander unclaimed. Several origin stories compete, the most popular being an account blaming an enslaved
man called Jack, who had worked for the defaulting neighbor

Tilton and was left as caretaker of Sam Maverick's new herd. Sam's son George Madison Maverick later described Jack and his family as "nominally slave, but essentially free,—especially, free to be shiftless,"[9] an attempt to shift responsibility for his father's long-running indifference to his herd onto a man who was by definition largely powerless. It was Sam Maverick himself who ignored his cattle year after year.

After he had moved back to San Antonio in late 1847, Maverick received distressed letters about the cattle he'd left. Jack asked one rancher to write to Maverick for help rounding up his herd, which was becoming increasingly wild, and for permission to marry a woman named Elizabeth, "who belongs to Miss Ward." In the spring of 1853, Maverick received a plea signed "A friend to Justice" from a concerned cattleman: "Send someone to look after your stock of cattle immediately or you will not have in eighteen months from this time one yearling nor calf." Hearing that two of his own branded calves may have been Maverick's originally, a prospective buyer scolded, in an 1856 letter, "I am surprised that this has not happened more frequently, so little have your cattle been attended to."[10]

From San Antonio, Maverick answered: "By last night's mail I have word that my negro boy is driven away, and his life threatened." Maverick had essentially turned his back on his herd and its guardian.[11] Later, in 1856, he was grateful to finally sell the four hundred that could be rounded up to A. Toutant Beauregard. (The number of cattle matched his original purchase after more than a decade, showing that many unbranded calves had disappeared or been claimed by other ranchers, who had little fear of an enslaved caretaker.) Whatever his name later came to mean, Maverick never became a "cattle king" or even invested in cattle after selling his original herd.

Though born just after Maverick's controversial time on the peninsula, Charlie Siringo regarded him simply as a de facto range thief, "a chicken-hearted old rooster, who wouldn't brand nor ear-mark any of his cattle. All his neighbors branded theirs, therefore Mr. Mavrick [sic] claimed everything that wore long ears."[12] Once others adopted the custom of mavericking, a Texas farmer wrote bitterly to a newspaper in the 1880s that an "unsuspicious 'clod-hopper'" might let his cattle out to graze and find they had changed owners when they returned, as "cattle men multiplied and replenished their herds at the expense of farmers who had only a few cattle and could neither watch them by day and night, nor hire some person to do it for them."[13]

However passive its origins, mavericking nevertheless became a process by which a number of Siringo's early friends and employers would build ranching fortunes. But as Siringo would unfortunately learn, there were different levels of aggressive mavericking, some of which could be deadly for the violator.

Siringo's cowboy debut was cut short after only a couple of hard, exciting months with Faldien's men in the spring and summer of 1867. He was sent home with typhoid fever, which swept Texas coastal communities, and was "laid up for two months. . . . Everyone thought I would die." But no sooner had he recovered his strength than a second tragedy occurred that took him even farther from the family's small ranch: his mother accepted the marriage proposal of a Northerner named William Carrier, whom Bridgit had no doubt met during the weeks Charlie was happily away cowboying. After they married that August, Carrier insisted his new bride sell her land and several dozen cattle and return with him to the property he claimed to have up in Michigan. Carrier would become the first legal father figure Siringo had really known.

The family said goodbye to Texas and their small herd (including Browny) and the Matagorda Cemetery, where Antonio Siringo was buried. Whatever he had heard about "Yankeeland" during the war, Charlie was about to see it firsthand on the family's misadventure with William Carrier. "Now," Charlie wrote, "the real misery of a boy began."[14]

4

River Cities

Leaving Texas proved to be a bad idea almost immediately. The steamship the family boarded at Indianola, the *Crescent City*, struck a brig that had been drifting rudderless for some time. After towing the brig and its hungry passengers to Galveston, the *Crescent City* crew had repairs made to their own vessel before the family continued on, hoping to switch steamships at New Orleans for Saint Louis. But first William Carrier made his way to the ship's barroom, flush with his new wife's cash.

The gamblers aboard were happy to meet a man who could not stop drinking or walk away from a losing streak. Carrier did not need to be built up and cold-decked by professionals in order to fall apart on his own. Over the days and nights, money from the sale of the Siringo property and cattle was handed around the barroom of the *Crescent City*, and on the final leg of the trip, Carrier begged his wife for the chance to redeem himself with the last of her savings, her "hard times" stash of gold coins from her stocking. Charlie saw the broad, brown Mississippi on this journey but mainly remembered his new father giving away their money to sharpers and barkeeps before they reached Saint Louis.

Unlike Huck Finn, who finally runs away from a father who is an abusive drunkard, Charlie was dragged off with his troubled new father. The Siringos had been modest landowners and proud Texans, but they arrived in Saint Louis needing to pawn Bridgit's feather mattress and pillows in order to rent some shabby rooms. The jobs Carrier could find in Saint Louis were chopping wood or shoveling snow or coal that winter. For a while, he brought home regular pay, then left steadily more of it at the bar each night, before eventually departing "for parts unknown." That left the boy to make what money he could, learning quickly that he could count on his new father even less than the one he had never known.

Ten dollars then miraculously arrived by letter from Carrier, coaxing Bridgit to the new place he landed, twenty-five miles away, in Lebanon, Illinois. Bridgit, Charlie, and his sister briefly reunited with Carrier there before he lapsed again, seriously enough to draw the intervention of neighbors one loud, ugly night, when a crowd came to the house and announced he could "skip or be hung" by morning. Whether or not the crowd had chased him off, Charlie never saw Carrier again. The Siringos were now free of the cause of much of their troubles, but their income came just from Charlie's sawing wood or shoveling coal and the chores his mother did for a nearby boardinghouse.

So the following September, Bridgit and Catherine returned to Saint Louis to hunt for better work, leaving Charlie doing odd jobs. He worked one very long day for a carpenter grinding tools on a stone wheel, then took a farm job that was interrupted by recurring fever and chills from what he called "ague." Charlie records he had separate cases of typhoid fever and ague several months apart, but it seems just as likely he had malaria from the start, with its recurring fevers.* Feeling poorly, and having not heard from his mother or sister, he bought a satchel and a railroad ticket to the city.

When he reached East Saint Louis, he was afraid to buy a meal for fear he could not pay for the ferry's final leg. Wandering alone, he began learning skills that had little to do with running cattle. The first night he spent inside an empty dry-goods box, recalling, "I did not sleep well, and when I did sleep it was to dream of snakes."[1] Soon he would pawn his Bible for a mince pie and think nothing of it.

Charlie roamed Saint Louis for days asking for work before a passerby in the Eighth Ward took pity and found him a job as a bellhop at the famous Planters House Hotel, on Fourth Street adjoining the county courthouse. Siringo fell in with the other boys working the hotel's three hundred rooms, making ten dollars a month plus daily tips, far more money than in his stint as a cowhand. A bantam-size boy, he showed an early predilection for getting in fights with people he saw as "bullies." Despite the anger he must have felt over what had happened to his family, he lasted almost a year at the Planters, until sometime in the fall of 1870, when a fellow bellhop called him a liar, leading Charlie to jump the boy and get slapped by the desk clerk, Mr. Cunningham. Siringo quit on the spot, packed his satchel, and collected his remaining pay, eighteen dollars, from the hotel proprietor before storming out with no plan except to buy a pistol and return to settle things with Cunningham.

He found a gun shop and bought a pearl-handled five-shooter, but luckily discovered a carnival game on the street outside—the player merely had to toss a ring onto some knives to gather up

---

* He also may have had childhood seizures that he outgrew, as he cautions the critical reader in the last line of *A Texas Cowboy* that he had "fits" as a boy. Much of frontier medical history is murky and self-reported.

St. Louis's Planters House Hotel, where Siringo worked as a bellhop before his temper ended his tenure.
Missouri Historical Society

easy prizes. He spent some of his last hotel money on the ring-toss con, becoming so disgusted with himself he thought better of shooting his boss. Now broke, he stole aboard and then begged his passage on the steamboat *Bart Able* to New Orleans, hoping to work his way at least partway to Texas. He was given a job of sewing torn grain sacks but fell through an open hatchway and badly injured his back. When the ship made a brief stop at the landing in Memphis, he lost his pistol and valise key, tricked by some grifter kids he met near the docks, who robbed him with his own gun. He was both penniless and physically unable to work the rest of his way home when the *Bart Able* put him off in New Orleans.

Siringo was stranded on the levee, sleeping on cotton bales and living off dropped rotting fruit, getting refused by ship captains he interviewed about free passage to Texas. Sitting stiff-backed on an old stove at the foot of Canal Street, he was wondering about his next move when he was spotted by an older shipping agent for the Red River Line, William R. Myers. The man hired Charlie to help his wife at their house in the Iberville district, promising that at the end of a month he would secure the boy's steamer passage on to Galveston. Bringing him home on the Canal Street trolley, Myers presented the hungry urchin to his wife for a bath and a steak dinner. Now almost fifteen, Charlie may have longed to see his real mother, but he had survived more than a year on his own when William Myers took him in. A month after his arrival, though, the older couple, with no children of their own, proposed Charlie stay on with them and go to school and, after graduation, into business.

5

Shanghai

Siringo had by now made quite an accidental study of the larger Mississippi towns. New Orleans was the oldest and most exotic; if you had to leave Texas for a big city, it was a comfortable and lively place to land, having French airs but still the South. His new benefactors bought him some fancy clothes, including "peaked-toed gaiters," as Mrs. Myers said the high-heeled boots he asked for would make him look like a "hoosier." When Charlie wore his new clothes outside, the neighborhood boys took him for a "dandy," and he soon dirtied his outfit in a street fight down the block while the Myers couple watched like proud new parents.[1]

The Fisk School was a respected public academy where his new guardians hoped he could make up for his uncompleted Texas education.[2] He soon rebelled, though, rapping another boy in the nose for calling him a liar and pulling away his hand when his teacher tried to cane him. (No doubt Siringo had seen enough of his mother's mush stick by this time.) After his teacher sent for the principal, Charlie fled the building. Considering how he would later live such a variety of falsehoods while "playing

outlaw" as a cowboy detective, the charge of lying was a powerful trigger, bringing out what he called his "tiger blood" as a boy.

Having fought his way out of the public school, Charlie was
next sent to a private one to study German, French, and English
and become generally more polished for a business future. The
event that finished him this time involved yet another "bully,"
a larger boy named Stemcamp, who accused him of lying as the
boys were all gathered on the green for recess. Charlie found himself fighting on all fours beneath the other boy, taking punches
to the face; he produced a small pearl-handled knife, a recent
gift from the lady of his new house, "Miss Mary," and stabbed
Stemcamp "just below the groin." As the boy leapt and screamed,
Charlie cut into his back for good measure, then ran off, certain he had killed him. Stemcamp eventually recovered from his
wounds but never returned to the scene of his goring. In later
years, communing secretively with outlaws, Charlie could easily
see how his own life might have tilted in another direction had
the stabbing ended differently.

Fleeing the bloody scene, he left his indulgent new parents behind to sneak aboard a northbound packet, survived a
cylinder-head explosion while sleeping in the engine room, and
then walked off at Saint Louis to search again for his mother. At
the farm across the border in Lebanon, Illinois, where the family
had last been together, no one had heard from her. He worked
long enough as a field hand to collect pay, then returned to his
New Orleans family and their steak dinners.* He even briefly
returned to school, after William Myers somehow convinced the
headmaster to take him back. In 1870, the census taker listed a

---

* Siringo claims to have returned by leaping aboard the *Robert E. Lee* just in
time for its famous Mississippi race that June against the *Natchez*, which would
not be impossible, just lucky timing.

fifteen-year-old named "Charles Seringo" at the Myers house, "occupation: at school."

The other schoolboys welcomed him back as a dangerous hero before he once again defied a teacher who refused him permission to leave class and investigate a large fire nearby. Charlie walked out anyway, this time for good, and when the fire had died down that night, he walked to the levee and stole aboard a Morgan steamship from New Orleans to Indianola. He hid all the first night until the vessel was safely at sea and polished brass railings in the sunshine after he was discovered.

It was a stormy voyage once they were on the open water, but out there he knew the captain would not turn around and put him ashore. He was going home, two years after William Carrier had first dragged him north. In that time he had lost all track of his family and briefly gained new parents, washed out of two schools, and refused a career in business. There was no longer a family ranch waiting for him in Texas, but as the ship drew near, he wrote, "I shouted down in my heart: Back at last to the Lone Star state; the natural home of the cowboy and the long-horn steer."[3] Charlie had a few hours while the ship put in at Galveston for repairs. He went and stood at the gate of an uncle he had long heard about but never met. Not wanting to feel beholden to a stranger, or even a relative after so long away, he returned to the boat as it left for Indianola. Once the port came into view, he thought he recognized some of the boys lingering on the Indianola wharf. He stepped off as a worldly young river man.

It was hard to imagine the imperious cattle king "Shanghai" Pierce working for any man but himself. "I'm not going to wait until I'm dead to have a monument raised for me," Pierce once informed a journalist, and he built himself a lifesize granite-and-marble tribute.[4] Arriving in Hot Springs, Arkansas, one time

without a reservation, he was
enraged to find the hotel full;
loudly inquiring whether or
not it was for sale, he wrote
the manager a $15,000 check
for his half interest before
retiring upstairs to his very
expensive rooms.[5]

Like many Texas cat-
tlemen, Abel Head Pierce
had come from elsewhere
to brand his fortune on the
plains, arriving from the
smallest state in the Union;
born in Little Compton,
Rhode Island, in 1834, he
had been briefly schooled
there before being sent to
Virginia to work for a mor-
alizing, Bible-quoting uncle

Rhode Island transplant Abel "Shanghai"
Pierce, a ranching mentor to young Charlie,
ambitious as he was loud.
USGenWebsites.org

he came to despise. Hearing about the epic possibilities of the
Lone Star State, he stowed away on a Texas-bound schooner
when he was almost twenty, but was too tall to stay hidden for
long and so he loaded passengers' baggage after being discovered.
Finally arriving in Matagorda County in June 1854, the runaway
apprentice met an older fellow New Englander, a longtime ship
captain turned rancher named Richard Grimes, whose son, William Bradford "Bing" Grimes, put Pierce to work splitting rails
on the family's large property, Tres Palacios.

Abel Pierce was now a lean six feet four inches tall, and
local people compared him to a long-necked Shanghai rooster.
"Shanghai" Pierce he became, lanky and confident and famously

loud. (Pierce claimed, convincingly, to have no indoor voice.) He learned ranching very fast and was a foreman for Grimes at twenty, when he led a cattle drive through Louisiana.

W. B. Grimes resented the arrangement his fellow rancher John Foster had with the Morgan steamship line, monopolizing the cattle-shipping market from Indianola to New Orleans. So Grimes opted to move his stock overland in 1854 and chose Pierce to lead the experimental drive. His route covered some unsuitably swampy country for cattle, but Pierce managed, even keeping vivid travel notes for his boss of his longhorns' progress picking their boggy way to New Orleans: "My steers were nice, fat slick critters that knew how to swim, but they were used to a carpet of prairie grass. They were mighty choosey as to where they put their feet. . . . Purty soon over there in Louisiana they got to balancing theirselves on logs in order to keep out of the slimy mud."[6]

Pierce was too ambitious to work for anyone else very long, claiming hundreds of mavericks under his "AP" brand while working for Grimes and even having ambitions to marry Grimes's own sister, Frances Charlotte, which Grimes discouraged. Pierce continued to gather his own wild cattle, showing, wrote one of his future cowboys, "what could be done in those days, with no capital, but lots of cheek and a branding iron."[7]

Pierce's brother Jonathan joined him, though shorter and quieter and less comfortable aboard a horse. Jonathan Pierce began doing bookkeeping for Grimes, and the brothers had branded their own sizable herd when the Civil War came, depleting their holdings as Shanghai sold beef to feed the Confederate cavalry in which he served. After Appomattox, the Pierce brothers found their remaining cattle gone and had a falling out with Grimes when he tried to pay what he owed them with worthless Confederate scrip. The brothers at first meant to collect and ship wild cattle to market rather than breed them, but Abel eventually built an empire from the many scattered mavericks roaming South Texas. In 1871, the same year the brothers founded El Rancho Grande with partners, a sixteen-year-old cowboy named Charlie Siringo came to work for them, fresh from his adventures in the river cities.

Upon returning to Texas, Charlie had spent some weeks with his godfather, Mr. Hagerty, in Indianola, starting work in the largest of the packinghouses or "beef factories" outside town, where slaughtering and tanning of wild cattle were done. Typically, Charlie did not later reference any ghastliness associated with the work, no blood-slick floors or stink of death. Instead, he remembers how, as a sixteen-year-old boy would, he used his first month's pay to buy a pistol and much of his second toward a pair of "star-topped boots." A biographer speculates Charlie may have picked up his first Spanish from Mexican co-workers who did much of the slaughtering, also acquiring his fondness for the red vaquero's sash he later wore. He remembered it as the place he learned to love the Mexican card game *monte*.[8] (As a boy from southeast Texas, however, it is hard to think he wouldn't have known a little Spanish already.)

After returning to Matagorda and the peninsula where he was raised and seeing the old family ranch he left two years before, he was hired at the beginning of April by Tom Nye, who was gathering cowboys to staff up the Pierces' new spread, El Rancho Grande. It had been conceived as a roaming collection of branded steers but now had a headquarters twenty-five miles northwest from the town of Matagorda, near Tres Palacios River, and a range extending hundreds of miles. By the 1880s, when a railway crossed his enormous property, Shanghai Pierce would have three depots built along it, Borden, Shanghai, and Pierce.

The ranch employed about fifty cowboys when Charlie arrived, a number of them African American, most notably Neptune Holmes, a powerful man with a necessarily tough demeanor who traveled with Shanghai Pierce, carrying his gold and silver on a packhorse for trailside purchases of "beeves." Another Black cowhand, Jim Heller, later remembered how much young Siringo still had to learn: "He was happy-go-lucky and usually out of luck. He could let more horses get away with the saddle on than any other cowboy in the country."[9]

Before he could hope to get up the cattle trail to Kansas, Siringo had to help brand many mavericks for the ranch, later claiming the operation was so large they branded twenty-five thousand mavericks and calves that first season.* At the ranch's company store, his credit was stretched thin by his purchase of a complete outfit from saddle to spurs. Thrilled to rejoin the ranks, he wrote to William and Mary Myers in New Orleans that he had "attained the desire of my life by becoming a full-fledged cowboy in the Lone Star State."

---

* While this may have been possible, the branding record for a season cited by David Dary (*Cowboy Culture*, [Kansas, 1981]) is eighteen thousand by the King Ranch.

6

Shorthorns

One day in the spring of 1871, Shanghai Pierce returned from Mexico trailing several hundred wild ponies, stolen or "wet" horses bought cheap that had swum the Rio Grande. On these spirited mustangs, Charlie would soon learn a hard skill he practiced well into his detecting days, riding a pitching horse until it became a dependable mount. As part of a group of new cowboys, he took a sailboat to Palacios Point, in southwestern Matagorda County, and arrived at a camp run by the ranch. There, twenty young cowhands would spend their days getting thrown by ponies they were gradually civilizing. "Of course," he boasted, "I naturally became an expert at riding 'bad' horses and roping 'wild' cattle."[1]

His skills with feral cattle were soon honed during several dangerous weeks along the Navidad River, capturing hundreds of "mossy horns"—longhorn cattle named for the fine moss seen on the horns of some from living in the brush. These animals fed on the plains grasses by night and returned each morning to the thickets, where cowboys could not follow and swing their lassos for roping the brutes. Instead, the men were forced to raid before sunup, when the animals would be too well hidden. Tom

Nye, who had hired Charlie and others staffing the ranch, spent a month overseeing the gathering of a herd of timber cattle for a client of the Pierces named Black, a blacksmith from Wichita who was a new investor in longhorns.

Wild cattle that refused to move with the herd and kept returning to the brush the cowboys might make docile by sewing their eyelids shut; after about two weeks, when the thread had decayed enough for the eyes to reopen, the animals were less likely to stray. The trail hands spent stormy nights in their saddles, watching the nervous group they had assembled, or otherwise slept in shifts on bedrolls on the ground. But to Charlie it was the only life worth having.

Black, the smithy client, brought from Wichita an outfit of inexperienced Kansas boys (what Texans called "shorthorns") to take charge of his semi-wild herd. Nye turned over the eleven hundred head, uncertain whether the herd would arrive intact guided up the trail by these shorthorns, largely unfamiliar with the Texas landscape or its surly longhorns. Shanghai Pierce learned the truth later, when he ran into Black back at his forge in Wichita, and the smithy complained that most of his cattle had never reached Kansas. "They crossed Red river into Indian Territory," Charlie later mocked in his first autobiography, "with nothing left but the 'grub' wagon and horses."[2] Some of the willful mossy horns had returned to their home range, where Pierce was happy to sell them a second time in the spring.

Siringo, who had the gift of being likable unless crossed, seems to have gotten along well enough on the ranch for his fellow cowhands to pull him out of most trouble. As a young man he lashed out more from his volatile nature, his "tiger blood," than from prejudice, grousing that one early foreman "wouldn't allow me to rope large steers nor fight when I was on the warpath."[3] Whatever they privately believed, the work of cowboys demanded cooperative skill, especially on drives, in which they rode and ate as a group for months.*

While rounding up steers in Colorado County to bring to Richmond, Texas, for shipment, something happened that would earn Siringo a nickname he later found useful. After swimming cattle across a swollen stream, he was standing barefoot in the grass waiting for his clothes to dry when a rattlesnake bit his left foot. He smashed and cut up the snake with his bowie knife. Though his foot swelled so

An artist's imagining of Siringo as a young cowboy.
A Texas Cowboy / *Gutenberg.org*

much "I couldn't wear my boot for a week," he survived. Afterward he earned a reputation for tossing his knife at rattlers when they appeared in the grass or among the rocks along the trail, sometimes throwing from the saddle. His fellow cowboys who borrowed his blunted blade called him "Dull Knife" (after the great Cheyenne leader), a name he would later adopt for a secret

---

* On the whole, Siringo remembered African American cowboys he worked with equably—sometimes recalling them from fights but more frequently ticking off his cowboy debts: to a Black rider called Lige, who interfered once as Charlie was about to be shot; to Jim Keller, who loaned him a saddle on the Grimes ranch when young Siringo's own pony galloped off; and to a cowboy known as Jack who saved Charlie after a mount rolled and twisted him in his own lasso.

Kansas newspaper column and while competing undercover in a Denver rodeo.

The Pierce brothers sold their interests to their ranching partners, Allen, Poole and Company, for $110,000, and Charlie then worked under Wylie Kuykendall, a personable man powered by strong coffee and constant puffing on a black pipe. He was married to the Pierces' sister Susan and called "Mr. Wylie" by his cowboys out of respect. According to Siringo, he had already quit the ranch once and returned to work before leading a group on a branding expedition in Jackson County, Texas. There he was discovered putting his own brand on some superior steers; to help keep the secret of his side business, he encouraged his young crew to brand their own mavericks, building a "nest egg" that would wander and fatten.

Siringo was now launched as a young "mavericker." From here on, he kept a small iron tied to his saddle, heating it on a small cow-chip fire on the prairie when he was riding alone, planting a brand ("A.T. connected—the T on top of the A")[4] on the ribs or shoulder of the longhorn he was claiming. "I put my own brand on quite a number of Mavricks . . . which began to make me feel like a young cattle king," he recalled. "The only problem was they were scattered over too much wild territory and mixed up with so many other cattle. When a fellow branded a Mavrick in those days it was a question whether he would ever see or realize a nickel for it."[5] Wylie Kuykendall was fired in the fall of 1872 when his own mavericking was discovered by the new owners. Charlie quit soon as well, after one trip with the new boss that left him less than impressed.

Having worked nearly two years at the ranch, Siringo went to settle up at the Rancho Grande store in December 1872. A man called "Hunky-dorey" Brown stacked up silver dollars to show what he had earned. Allen, Poole and Company owed him

$300, Hunky deadpanned, setting up the cruel punch line, but Charlie owed the ranch $299.25, leaving him 75 cents, enough for a bottle of peaches and some stick candy.*

He went back to the competition, W. B. Grimes's Tres Palacios ranch, where he found work looking after Grimes's dozens of stock horses, riding over a fifty-mile grazing area to mind their progress. This job also allowed him the solitude to brand what mavericks caught his eye. But he soon quit to live a few miles from the Grimes ranch at the pious home of another rancher, Horace Yeamans, a veteran of the Mexican-American War living on Cashs Creek, who tolerated no swearing.

When winter storms in 1872–73 pushed scores of hungry steers to the water's edge at Matagorda Bay, Siringo began skinning and selling the hides of dead cattle, partnering with Yeamans's son Horace Jr., a boyhood friend. The money seemed excellent at first that hard winter, when "Cattle died by the thousands . . . the country being overstocked."⁶ It was what they called a "skinning season." Many cattle would bog down in the mud and freeze, a number of them in Turtle Bayou near the Yeamans place. Hordes drifted down during cold northers and sleet storms, and "Often a boggy slough would be completely bridged over with dead and dying cattle, so that the ones following could walk over dry footed."⁷ Sometimes Siringo also killed strays rather than wait for them to die (a breach of range rules perhaps, but he knew firsthand that not all the cattle that entered Grimes's slaughterhouse wore his brand).

While living with the reverent Yeamans family, Charlie was especially inspired to clean up his language while "casting sheeps eyes" at Horace Jr.'s younger sister Sally. But he was truly taken

---

* Siringo says $300 "or whatever the amount was." It may have been a less rounded figure but no less dramatic a rip-off by the ranch.

by her fourteen-year-old cousin, the daughter of Matagorda's sheriff, who came to stay a month. After the young cousin returned home, Charlie invented errands for visiting her such as registering brands in Matagorda, and he would imagine her waiting for him as he wandered and had adventures, but events would prove he had overestimated the depth of the girl's feelings.

A family friend from the peninsula had heard from Charlie's sister, Catherine, and he learned from her at last the address of his long-lost mother in Saint Louis. Flush from his skinning season, he sent twenty-five dollars to the mother he had not seen in several years and bought himself a new saddle.[8]

In 1860, a young engineer named Theodore Judah calculated that the Donner Pass, infamous for the grisly fate of a group of snowbound westward travelers in 1846, was the suitable point for taking a railroad through the Sierra Nevada. At the time, a stagecoach across the country could take six months, and traveling by boat around the horn of South America about the same; the shortest route, breaking up two voyages with a crossing of the Isthmus of Panama, had its own feverish hazards, as Judah would learn. His idea would eventually get rail passengers across the country in a week. He began gathering investors—the famous "Big Four," Leland Stanford, Charles Crocker, Collis Huntington, Mark Hopkins—and went to Washington. The country was at war, and the proposed route would cross hundreds of miles where no towns yet existed (although Native tribal lands did). But federal loans were secured from Congress with passage of the Pacific Railway Act of 1862, facilitating the collective dream of cheap homesteads and cross-country trade.

"Now time and space are in the race!" quipped one sign at a torchlight parade in San Francisco celebrating the railway's announcement. (Another poster warned, presciently, "Little

Indian Boy Step Out of the Way for the Big Engine!")⁹ Some
imagined the line as a long race along one longitude chasing bison
toward the western sunset. In Washington, Abraham Lincoln's
secretary of state, William Seward, saw the strategic purpose,
that with West tied to East, "disunion shall be rendered forever
after impossible."¹⁰ Ground was broken in Omaha, Nebraska, by
December 1863.

To create a transcontinental line, two separate railways
were to race to their meeting point, the companies being paid by
the government for every mile of track finished, the completed
route snaking from the edge of Iowa across Nebraska, Wyoming,
Utah, and Nevada to California. But the Central Pacific Railroad, working from west to east, would run into the high passes
of the Sierra Nevada, needing to be tunneled, and cross deserts
for 690 miles, while the Union Pacific hammered its way east to
west over the Great Plains for 1,085 miles. The venture had little
precedent in railroad building, which was still based largely on
eastern rail achievements.

As it went west, the Union Pacific created its own small,
sinful towns of tents and shacks that entertained its largely Irish
immigrant (but also freedmen, Mormon, and war veteran) crews;
the workmen were met at each region in which they laid track
with newly set up saloons, brothels, and gambling halls. Some of
these towns lasted, while many winked out once the brief good
times moved on. (Other railroads were also receiving federal
land grants and loans out West during the period the transcontinental was being built, the government gambling on the towns
established on acreage along these rail lines.) Although crossing a landscape less physically challenging than that faced by its
counterpart, the Union Pacific passed through many tribal lands,
and multiple violent attacks were made on its surveyors and train
crews in hopes the railway could be stopped. In 1866, General

Grenville Dodge, who had surveyed much of the route before serving in the Union Army in the war, took charge of the railway and brought the project home.

Theodore Judah had quickly grown unhappy with the business practices of his investors (who would later renege on their government loans) and hoped to buy them out. He was on his way to Washington, taking the long route his innovation would replace, over the Isthmus of Panama, when he contracted yellow fever and died, in November 1863, a month before the groundbreaking. Without him, the Central Pacific had a hard going at first, slowed by the daunting granite rock faces of the Sierra, which would require thirteen tunnels by the end. With fewer Irish workers than needed in San Francisco, construction supervisor Charles Crocker had been convinced to bring in a test group of fifty Chinese workers from the California goldfields, some of whom had mining experience.

With the project stymied in the mountains, one of the men suggested a method used in the gorges of the Yangtze River; sending for reeds, the men wove baskets from which they hung while drilling holes into the rock face for placing powder, eventually using nitroglycerin, which was dangerous to handle but smokeless when it blew, speeding up the tunnel clearance. Soon more laborers were summoned direct from Canton, and some ten thousand Chinese were working in the Sierra Nevada by 1867, earning the same daily pay as their counterparts but enduring eleven-hour days instead of ten. Realizing their worth to the project, the Chinese workers demanded higher pay and the right to work where they pleased. The partners stopped deliveries of food to their remote camp, starving the men back to work.[11]

After negotiations with Washington about a meeting point, on May 10, 1869, came the famous joining of the rival rail lines in Promontory Summit, Utah, and the hammering of the golden spike, celebrated across the country with fireworks and cannon blasts. (Although the project's completion was "in large measure" due to the Chinese, Charles Crocker acknowledged, the Chinese workers weren't part of the commemorative picture).*

The completion of the line would be transformative for the West and for the country as a growing power in the world. (Railroad commerce eventually, by the 1880s, forced the creation of time zones for all Americans.) But for the Texas cattlemen hoping to bring their herds east to market, the table had already been set three years earlier by Joseph McCoy.

The trail drive Charlie would eventually follow to Kansas was a recent and revolutionary invention. And the cattle migration it made possible introduced the cowboy to Northerners (and later the world). Before the railroads expanded west, Texas ranchers had made their own ambitious routes to California and Missouri, searching for markets for their multiplying stock, the journeys long and hazardous, with steers often lost to raids or stampedes. In early 1853, the English-born Illinois rancher Thomas Candy Ponting and his Indiana partner, Washington Malone, went to Texas, where they bought longhorn cattle and drove them through Missouri, wintering the herd until spring, when they delivered 150 longhorns to the railroad at Muncie, Indiana, bound for New York. The cattle were brought by ferry the last leg into Manhattan, where they understandably impressed the newspapers.

But Ponting's accomplishment could not be easily replicated until after the war, when there was a shortage of beef in the North and an oversupply especially in Texas, where cattle had grown wild and much farmland lay ruined. The challenge was in

____
* For the 145th anniversary, in 2014, a Chinese American photographer, Corky Lee, reenacted the Promontory Summit portrait including descendants of the Chinese railroad workers.

somehow getting longhorns, each worth four or five dollars, to the East, where beef was valued at ten times that.

In 1866, after being grandly shown the door by representatives of several bigger railroads, a young, goateed Illinois cattle merchant named Joseph McCoy talked a man from the Hannibal and Saint Joseph line into helping him establish a railroad siding and cattle market at Abilene, Kansas. This was an outpost of log buildings when McCoy found it, a "very small dead place," whose mayor made a side business selling pet prairie dogs to eastern visitors.[12] But the town was surrounded by miles of plains grasses cut through by the necessary rivers for watering cattle, and it was served by a railway. When the freight agent agreed to ship cattle to Chicago (through Quincy, Missouri) rather than to Saint Louis, it helped make Chicago the meatpacking capital it would become, where livestock were delivered, slaughtered, and prepared for shipment east.

With money from his family, McCoy built up much of the town of Abilene himself, including constructing the aspirational Drovers Cottage for the coming cattle trade. The result was the prototype for the Kansas cow town, which could be put up wherever a cattle trail met a railhead. Instead of ranchers bringing their own herds north, the growth of the Kansas markets would bring professional trail drivers, or "drovers," whom McCoy welcomed with his hotel. "If any one imagines that the life of a ranchman or cow-boy is one of ease and luxury," he would write in 1877, "or his diet a feast of fat things, a brief trial will dispel the illusion, as is mist by the sunshine." McCoy had connected the North and South, and the Texas ranchers with the East Coast markets.

Perhaps 260,000 head of cattle trailed up toward Kansas and Missouri in 1866, the year before McCoy's Abilene experiment debuted. But less than half reached their intended destinations, as "bands of armed men calling themselves jayhawkers, red-legs,

bushwhackers, guerrillas, or some other name waylaid many."[13]
The desire of many Civil War veterans to keep fighting against
perceived enemy invaders, combined with local farmers' real fears
of "Texas fever" borne by traveling alien cattle, meant disaster for
many Texans, as "armed mobs met the herds with all possible
violence" in Missouri, southern Kansas, and Arkansas—where
some drovers were tied to trees and flogged.[14]

But in 1867, some 35,000 head made it up from Texas to
McCoy's new market at Abilene, enough that their surprising numbers slightly depressed the price of beef; the next year
it was 75,000, and in 1869 as many as 350,000 reached town.
Two years later, when Siringo luckily joined Shanghai Pierce's
Rancho Grande, some 600,000 head of Texas cattle traveled to
new railheads in Kansas, fattening over the winter before being
shipped in specially built cars to new stockyards in the growing
slaughterhouse capital, Chicago.[15] A Topeka newspaper bragged,
"The cattle family, as well as the human, cannot help fattening in
Kansas."[16]

As the beef market grew, so did the rail line and string of
cattle towns it made possible—Abilene, Dodge City, Caldwell,
Coffeyville, Ellsworth, Wichita—many dividing their down-
towns between blocks of practical stores for locals and commercial strips for arriving Texans, ready to drink and lose money and
otherwise cut loose in bars with familiar names like Alamo or
Lone Star. From Leavenworth to Dodge City and Baxter Springs,
a cow town was not complete without a Lone Star Saloon for its
seasonal revelers, while even Abilene's children walked to school
along Texas Street. A reporter embedded with a cowboy crew in
the 1870s captured the spectacle of "Texas Herdsmen" hitting a
cattle town like a pack of sailors: "The saloons guzzle him with
whisky, the gambler plies him with keno, faro, and monte. The
dance-house surfeits him with the charms of the raw-boned and

blear-eyed beauties of the frontier . . . and the keen-eyed clothier tickles his uncultivated fancy with an apparel as gaudy as that of a monkey in a sideshow."[17]

Much of a lawman's job in a cow town was protecting against the rowdy excesses of cowboy invaders, the end-of-trail antics Charlie had long hoped to join. Among their many recreations, cowboys on a spree might hoist citizens from the street into a saloon and demand they buy drinks for the group. This game preceded Abilene's most infamous gunfight on an early October night in 1871. According to the town's newspaper, the drunken cowboy band had even tried to carry the city marshal into a saloon for a round. Unfortunately for them, the marshal was James Butler "Wild Bill" Hickok, the charismatic gunfighter, scout, lawman, horse thief, and noted poker player, who had arrived in Abilene months before, appointed after the town's first marshal was killed in the street.

Marshal Hickok stares down an Abilene photographer, 1870.
Kansas Historical Society

In Abilene, Hickok often kept an eye on his town from a card table at the Alamo Saloon. He had shoulder-length hair that newspapers liked to linger over almost as much as the Colt Navy revolvers he wore walking the town or the pistol pocket he had specially designed for retrieving a weapon from under his vest if a challenge disturbed his poker.

On July 21, 1865, Hickok had been in what is often called the first recorded one-on-one gunfight—quick draw, as opposed to European-style gentlemen's dueling—when he and a man in a white linen coat named Davis K. Tutt fired at each other across some seventy-five yards of Springfield, Missouri's public square. Tutt, who had taken Bill's pocket watch against his poker debt, moved first, according to some witnesses, then grabbed his breast after the shots were fired to announce, accurately, "Boys, I am killed."[18] After the facts of the shooting made the local paper, Hickok's name was introduced to a public hungry for other stories of frontier violence, true or not. Hickok was happy to oblige his growing myth, particularly in an interview filled with tall tales he fed to the journalist Henry Morton Stanley, who more famously found Dr. Livingstone near Lake Tanganyika in Africa a few years later.

On the outside wall of the Bull's Head saloon in Abilene, a virile animal was painted shockingly intact. It amused visiting cowboys but outraged townspeople, despite the many live bulls that passed naked and intact through their streets each season; bearing a shotgun, Marshal Hickok had supervised the alteration of the animal's phallus earlier in 1871, warming his ongoing feud with one of the bar's owners, the Texan Phil Coe, a gambler with a gunfighting reputation of his own, though not on Hickok's level at either cards or pistols. The two men may have also shared an interest in the same woman in Abilene.

Phil Coe was still hot over his bull's alteration when, on the night of the cowboy spree, October 5, 1871, the group, disappointed that a nearby county fair had been rained out, turned to bullying townspeople for drinks. Hickok appeared in the lamplit street to speak to the crowd; Coe fired two errant, furious shots at the marshal from roughly eight feet away, the first passing through Hickok's open stance, the second harmlessly piercing his coat. Although said to favor accuracy over speed, Hickok reacted "quick as thought," according to an Abilene reporter, drawing both his guns to shoot Coe twice through the stomach as well as wounding others in the crowd who showed their weapons.[19] When a shadowy figure came around the corner, drawn by the gunfire, Hickok expertly killed him through the smoke and darkness, only to learn it was his friend, city jailer Mike Williams, coming to his aid. Phil Coe died after several days of suffering, claiming he had originally fired at a wild dog, but Hickok grieved the death of Williams.*

Cow towns often peaked quickly. Kansas farmers filled the empty tillable spaces and got quarantine laws passed against the trampling Texas herds, altering the trail routes and affecting which towns thrived, as the "dead line" moved and the railroad built westward. In the case of Abilene, though ably protected by Marshal Hickok, the town decided it could manage without the seasonal spike in crime that came with the cattle roundups, preferring its growing year-round population of farmers over the seasonal drovers. Hickok left Abilene months after the accidental killing of his friend and would never again battle with guns, although he did shoot targets onstage, playing himself in a production with "Buffalo Bill" Cody called *Scouts of the Plains.*

Just four years after its debut, town officials posted an advertisement canceling the coming Texas cattle season. Abilene's inventor and by then mayor, Joseph McCoy, bitterly called the move a failed attempt to "blackmail" the drovers into higher prices; they instead delivered their herds elsewhere, skipping Abilene altogether. The town's decision was ruinous for its many

---

* Fresh from playing Hickok on-screen, the actor William S. Hart re-created the shootout onstage for members of New York's Lambs Club in 1923, claiming Coe had tied and shot a dog outside the saloon, wanting to draw the animal-loving marshal out to his death.

businesses that depended on the cattle trade; Abilene's Drovers Cottage, which had just been expanded to one hundred rooms, was disassembled and carried down the line by flatcar in 1872, to be put up at Ellsworth, where it was soon full once again.[20]

Siringo had just missed the brief rise and decline of the first Kansas cattle town. For several years he ached to go up the famed Chisholm Trail before he was finally hired on at nineteen to help gather a herd for the Muckleroy brothers, in the spring of 1874.

7

Chisholm

The cowboy is little understood except where he works and plays, and of late the term has been so misplaced that every frontier ruffian who carries a six shooter and rides a horse is so dubbed, even if he never "rounded up" a steer in his life.

—*Ellsworth* (Kansas) *Messenger*, 1884

By the time Siringo joined the Chisholm Trail, it was the most familiar and heavily traveled of the routes to the northern markets, fed by many inlets that gathered toward Austin. Its main trunk ran from Red River Station, at the northern Texas border, northward through what was called the Indian Territory (the catchall term for an evolving area of land the US government reserved for relocating displaced Native peoples). Only a section was based on the actual wagon road once laid out by the pioneer trader, guide, and mediator Jesse Chisholm, son of a Cherokee woman and a man of Scottish descent. The trail's exact route had grown fluid over time, detouring as needed around new settlements or quarantine lines. In 1868, when Joseph McCoy was still printing trail guides and placing advertisements to lure Texas drovers to his new cattle junction, he hired a surveyor to straighten the Chisholm Trail to veer toward Abilene.[1] The Western Trail weaved toward Dodge City, while the Goodnight-Loving Trail (named for ranchers Charles Goodnight and Oliver Loving) led to Cheyenne. The oldest major cattle trail, the Shawnee, headed toward Kansas City and Saint Louis.

Starting in the early spring of 1874, Charlie was part of a crew bossed by Tom Merrill that spent a month gathering some eleven hundred mossy-horn steers along the Navidad River in Jackson County, Texas. The clients were Jim and Charlie Muckleroy. Once the cattle were road-branded and pointed north, Siringo was one of three Texans who came with the herd to join an outfit that included "shorthorn" Kansan recruits not yet savvy with longhorns or with breaking horses. The drive would eventually be sabotaged by weaknesses among its cowboys.

Many things might spook cattle: a low roll of thunder (frequent in the South Texas spring), someone shaking out an empty slicker, the clatter of a frypan, flash of a bull's-eye lantern, or a wolf's keening howl. Keeping watch on storming nights, weary nighthawks sometimes rubbed tobacco juice in their eyes just to stay alert, but once a panic had really got going, it took a hard-riding group with reasonably fresh horses to head off a blind charge, gradually turning the leaders until the herd circled back, like a snake eating itself, or riding until the cattle exhausted themselves before hunting for the missing. Spooked cattle circled to the right, remembered the Texas rancher Charles Goodnight: "If any old trail driver ever heard of a herd milling to the left, I would like to hear from him."[2]

Charlie had already spent a tiring month on night guard readying this herd before it was given over to the Muckleroys. Weather agitated steers early in a drive before they could be "trail broken," and when thunder threatened their first night on the trail, the cattle began to drift before the men caught up and sang "melodious songs" to quiet them.[3] Under rumbling skies, cowboys traditionally rode guard in a circle, whistling and singing around the herd, which could be soothed equally by Methodist hymns and minstrel tunes, trail ballads about the death of

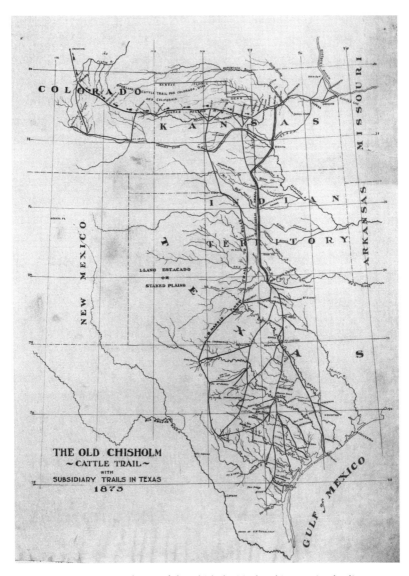

A railway company's rendering of the Chisholm Trail and its arteries, leading drovers to Kansas, 1873.

Kansas Historical Society

a cowboy or a lost love, and didn't seem to mind when riders altered lyrics.*

Unfortunately, Siringo was not riding with a veteran group. Later on the same night, after they had sung the restive herd to sleep, a full stampede broke out, started by a "long-legged fellow" named Saint Clair; he had got himself temporarily separated from the drive, then followed the sound of cowboy singing back to camp and loudly reappeared in the early hours. The cattle broke into perhaps a dozen mini-herds veering in all directions. In the morning, after a long chase, Saint Clair was found sleeping on the ground.

Siringo loved trail work, even the sleepless night herding. But when Jim Muckleroy asked him and another Texas boy, Henry Coats, to gentle some wilder horses for his less experienced crew, they demanded to be paid extra for their trouble. "Before reaching Austin . . . I rebelled on account of having to break wild ponies for other cowboys who were poor riders."[4] Their negotiating position seemed strong until Charlie suddenly "got the bounce," cut loose in Indian Territory well short of the Kansas border to make his way home. The other Texans as well as the trail boss were fired a little farther on, and replacements hired. No one had liked Jim Muckleroy, who was now bossing his herd, and even his own nephew Patrick quit in disgust when Siringo was bounced. The two youngsters would miss out on a cowboy spree once the herd was delivered.

Siringo had liked the other Muckleroy brother, Charlie, and befriended young Patrick, who was near his own age. After

---

* Many trail songs were a collaboration over time, no longer having one single author. One of the best known, a ballad called "Lasca," was widely performed by William S. Hart (before his movie days) in the 1890s, at one point credited to a Texan, Thomas P. Ochiltree, then claimed by a visiting Englishman who brought the song home. Like other trail recitations, it may have been the work of many cowboy Homers.

Siringo's firing, Patrick convinced him to ride the train back with him to his father's house in Columbus, Texas, on the Colorado River. Siringo ended up staying there for three weeks, spending time with Patrick's two sisters, his disappointment in the trail drive soothed by Mrs. Muckleroy's apple cobblers. After much drinking in town with Patrick and his friends, he was feeling "light in the pocket" and wondering how he might finally get home, when he lucked into meeting a cowhand he recognized from the Pierce ranch, Asa Dawdy. He was in Columbus loading some stock into railcars and had planned to pasture his own horse there while he traveled on with his cattle to Galveston. But he was happy to let Charlie take his pony home for him the seventy-five miles south. Charlie spent his last dime on a glass of lemonade and rode off. Up in Kansas, the Muckleroy brothers delivered their herd without him, short three hundred head.

On his return, Charlie sought work again with Grimes, but all the rancher could offer was a solitary job cutting cordwood two miles from the ranch at his "wood camp." After two weeks working alone, felling and splitting live oaks and taking long breaks to hunt raccoons or turkeys, Charlie settled with Grimes for the timber he had cut and moved on to a new scheme of his own: after learning that a factory hand named John Collier had a boat for sale, he finagled a devious horse trade.

Siringo's volatile horse, which he called Satan, was unrideable by anyone but himself and so could not easily be sold to an average rider. But he did exchange his interest in several brands he had bought from other cowboys for a safe, weak-legged old gray mustang from Horace Yeamans. He delivered the pony to Collier after dark for inspection, since Collier meant to ride out the next morning. Once the animal was accepted for trade, it came up lame a few miles into its new owner's journey, but Siringo had by then gained his pleasure boat, outfitted as a schooner and renamed the *Bloodhound*. Siringo had been exposed to sailboats growing up near the water, and he sailed over to Matagorda Peninsula, where he bought melons cheap and then sold them to eager employees coming off shift at Grimes's packinghouse.

He shuttled melons and later oysters and some passengers across Matagorda Bay, stopping at least once to spend his profits playing monte. The ferry business led to a bolder idea, to carry his boat inland and trade tobacco, jewelry, and oysters with the Black settlers living along the Colorado River. To get there, he had to pay to drag his schooner by oxcart on rollers several miles overland to avoid a long raft of driftwood clogging the Colorado's mouth. He hired a "gentleman of color" named Anthony Moore for help securing the oxen to pull his boat across the five prairie miles from Wilson's Creek to the river.

For his trading business, Siringo had unfortunately chosen an older partner called "Big Jack." Like Charlie's departed step-father, Jack kept pretty steadily drunk, dosing every fifteen or twenty minutes. While Anthony Moore was out trying to hire an extra yoke of oxen to complete the *Bloodhound*'s overland crossing, Siringo traveled to Deming's Bridge to collect his mail. When he returned, Big Jack had made off down the river in a stolen skiff with much of their merchandise, which he unloaded on the cheap. Charlie found only his loyal dog, a stray he had picked up, waiting for him. Without goods to trade or money to hire the extra oxen to continue dragging his schooner, he sold the *Bloodhound* where it lay to Anthony Moore, leaving it shipwrecked on the prairie.[5]

Although he sometimes imagined himself a rising cattle king "wallowing in cash," Siringo found it hard to manage his scattered range holdings, and as the schooner venture showed, money did not generally stick to him, apart from what he gained through opportunistic branding and skinning (and occasional killing for skins). The latter practice had been noted by others, however, and got him targeted by an angry rancher who sent a man out one night to kill him.

One April evening in 1875, Charlie was smoking by the fire of his camp near Cashs Creek in Matagorda County, when he was visited by Sam Grant, a Black cowboy with a reputation for paid killings. He appeared on horseback and asked innocently to examine Siringo's gun, lying beside him on the ground.

After turning the pistol over in his hands, Grant placed the weapon farther from Charlie's reach, asked why he didn't have "a good one" like his, then, as if to demonstrate, aimed his aged Colt Dragoon at Siringo's heart and pulled the trigger. Sitting by the fire, Charlie had fortunately not changed his position since Grant appeared. He still had his left leg drawn up in front of him, level with his heart, so the pistol ball entered his kneecap instead of his chest.

Almost as lucky, one of Siringo's friends, a Black cowhand known as Lige, came riding suddenly through the trees, causing Grant to lose his nerve before he could fire a second shot. Seeing Siringo's new visitor was carrying a rifle, Grant pretended he had fired by accident, then rode off, his job uncompleted, after pledging to send back the doctor from miles away at Deming's Bridge. Strangely, the failed assassin kept his word, and Dr. A. M. Pelton was able to ride to Siringo before sunrise, remove the ball, and save his knee. Thirty-five years later, Siringo learned more about the assassination attempt from his friend Nolan Keller, who had worked for "a certain wealthy cattleman, who . . . hired Sam Grant to kill me, on account of my boldness in branding mavericks and killing stray bulls for their hides."*

---

* In *True West* ("When Siringo Was Marked for Death," by Stony Nagel, Dec. 1970), Stony Nagel suggested rancher T. C. Jones had feuded enough with Siringo to have a strong motive.

Hearing later about the shooting, Jonathan Pierce offered
to put up Siringo at his house on the old Rancho Grande and
to pay him to shepherd the Pierce children, riding together to
their schoolhouse each day. Charlie accepted, once he was up on
crutches, and even opted to stay for the lessons, his fourth and
last time in school, until an inevitable conflict developed with
the red-headed young schoolmaster, who, feeling his authority
challenged, threatened to whip him, "so as to convince the other
scholars that he wore men's size pants."[6] Once Charlie showed
the schoolmaster his knife, the whipping was abandoned, and the
teacher returned to the day's lesson. At the end of school, Siringo
got the children home and then rode away from the Pierce ranch
on his horse Boney Part, crutch tied to his saddle.

Siringo visited with a rancher named Sam Allen and then
rode on to Houston to look up his mother's sister Mary and her
husband, James McClain. Houston was having the Texas State
Fair, and Charlie lost some money playing monte before putting
his full mind to finding his aunt, whom he did not remember ever
meeting but who had long ago sent him white breeches. He found
her boardinghouse near the Union Depot and accompanied her
husband, a Confederate veteran, back to the fairgrounds. There
James McClain introduced Charlie to a spectral historical figure
he barely recognized, Jefferson Davis, who was not the hero on
a gray horse he had imagined as a boy. He moved on, spending
two weeks with his uncle Nicholas White in the "Island City"
of Galveston, then headed slowly back to Tres Palacios, carrying the gift of his uncle's wartime Spencer carbine.* After weeks
spent mending his wound among various family members, he

---

* Charlie says variously that the rifle had put a number of Yankees "to sleep"
and also that it had been taken from a dead Yankee soldier. It could be both.

returned to find a letter at the post office from his mother, saying that she was coming.

Charlie's own dutiful letter about his "accident" (his shooting by Sam Grant) had reached his mother in Saint Louis, along with some money. She vowed to come and care for her long-lost cowboy and had been waiting for him at the home of their friends the Morris family near the mouth of Cashs Creek, although she felt poorly.

His first grateful instinct was to build his mother a house and not let her slip from his sight again. He sold some mavericks, and the two pooled their money, which he sent along with the Morris men to buy him lumber when they left for Indianola in their schooner on September 15. An ill wind literally began to blow, growing into a historic hurricane by the next day: "The wind blew fearfully, and as night came on the situation was awful," wrote a survivor. "Screams from women and children could be heard in every direction. The water was six feet deep in the streets. About two o'clock Friday morning the wind veered to the northwest; the waves then became chopped and ruin and destruction came, houses washed away or tumbled to pieces."[7] Churches and the Masonic lodge were swept away along with many houses. A prisoner freed to save him from drowning may have escaped, only to perish in the storm.

The big storm of 1854 that struck Matagorda County when Charlie's mother was young had scattered her family home, along with its Irish stained glass, across the prairie. Now she had returned from Missouri in time to see a more destructive hurricane that would wash away much of Indianola.

About ten o'clock at night, the high winds pried the roof off the Morris house, and rain poured into the rooms. Charlie had to

carry his mother as well as plot an escape for Mrs. Morris and her
children, spending much of that night battling water and high
wind: "I picked Mother up out of her sick bed and jumped into
the foaming water, which was more than waist deep. . . . Mrs.
Morris and her two little girls and two sons followed suit. It
required all my strength to hang onto Mother and to keep the
Morris family from drowning."

The wind from the west was blowing the group inevitably
toward Tres Palacios Bay, but Siringo thought they could brace
against the flood current by reaching "an osage hedge of large
trees" a few hundred yards away. "I decided to face the wind
and tide to reach that haven of safety. Hence my little crew were
drilled to keep only their heads above water and their feet in the
mud—leaning their bodies towards the wind." With his mother
still limp in his arms, the group inched toward the sanctuary of
the trees. "It took nearly an hour to reach it, then we were saved."[8]
By daylight they saw the bay shore lined with drowned cattle.

On September 21, the Morgan steamer *Harlan* arrived from
Indianola at Galveston, which had also been ravaged by the
storm (although faring better than it would in the epic hurricane
of 1900). With its flag at half-mast, the ship carried written pleas,
including one from Indianola's district attorney, W. H. Crain:

> We are destitute. The town is gone. One tenth of the popu-
> lation are gone. Dead bodies are strewn for twenty miles
> along the bay. Nine tenths of the houses are destroyed. Send
> us help for God's sake.[9]

Several hundred people had died in Indianola, but although
blown over with their capsized schooner, the Morris men had
somehow swum to safety in the storm. After his return home,
the elder Morris moved his house to the head of Cashs Creek,

not that far from where Charlie had been shot by Sam Grant. Siringo began work building his mother a shanty nearby, "so she wouldn't get lonesome while I was away," using scrap lumber bought "on tick" from Jonathan Pierce.[10] Then, again needing money, and seeing his mother reasonably set up near kind neighbors, he joined his second drive up the Chisholm Trail, for thirty dollars a month, in the spring of 1876. He told her he'd return in the fall.*

---

* Indianola would rebuild in smaller form, but was effectively wiped out by a subsequent storm in 1886.

8

Wichita

After night has thrown its misty mantle of gloom over Wichita, the
city undergoes an entire transformation; those business houses which
have been thronged the entire day with the staid and steadier portion
of the population, close their doors, and the store-keepers depart for
their homes or boarding houses.

—*Leavenworth* (Kansas) *Times*, 1873

By 1876, it was Wichita's turn to raucously arrive. Until
recently a trading post on the Chisholm Trail, it had,
since the railroad's appearance, a regular population
of about twenty-five hundred; at high season the young cow
town had grown rowdy enough to need its many new saloons
and dance houses, along with its police force, which had just dis-
missed Wyatt Earp. With the growing Texas cattle trade would
come, warned the *Wichita Eagle*, the "rough-scuff that hang on
the borders of civilization and infest all of our frontier towns."[1]

Siringo finally started up the cattle route to Wichita, thanks
to W. B. Grimes and his young trail-driver friend from the Pierce
ranch, Asa Dawdy, whose chatty, easygoing manner would soon
be tested.* Dawdy was leading a group of twenty-five riders, six
fresh horses per man, plus a cook, herding twenty-five hundred

---

* Siringo spells the name "Dawdy" in his first book and "Dowdy" in another.
Biographers are divided over which spelling to adopt, but a thirty-year-old Asa
Dawdy appears in the 1880 census, living at his father's house in Matagorda. He
also later ran a successful saloon.

mossy-horn cattle for Grimes. Starting in April, he hoped to make the Kansas cow town in three months, crossing hundreds of miles and multiple rivers at all levels of flooding. The journey would have the usual challenges of a large drive, including the threat of raiding tribes as it crossed the Indian Territory, as well as one well-meaning blunder.

The open beauty of the plains became terrifying in spring-time lightning storms; feeling a charge in the air, those men who carried pistols might toss them out of fear, while on some nights, electricity could flash on cattle horns, brims of men's hats, or tips of their horse's ears before striking nearby.[2] Hailstorms, too, were more violent on the plains, forcing cowboys to jump off and uncinch their saddles for cover from the pelting stones.[3]

After traveling northwest to the outskirts of Gonzales, Texas, near where the San Marcos River meets the Guadalupe, Dawdy decided to give his men a hard-earned break. He had all his steers packed inside a large public corral, hoping his crew might have a night's rest from watching for stampedes. The enclosure was round, built to accommodate smaller groups, so that agitated cattle could mill safely in a circle until tired. But Dawdy's large herd strained the live-oak log-and-rail corral to its limit; a sudden storm whipped up around midnight and sent a panic through the tightly packed steers. Siringo woke to see them break through the rails near where he was sleeping, boots on and reins loose in one hand; "I hardly had time to mount my pony, which saved me from being trampled to death," he wrote.[4] The cattle burst out still so squeezed together that Charlie claimed he saw the wedges of broken rail across their shoulders as they ran.

Unlike his cowboys, Asa Dawdy had undressed for bed and left his night horse tied to a wagon wheel. Startled with the others, he rode out through the rain barefoot and in his under-clothes, nearly severing a toe when his horse galloped into a tree. While the men regathered the cattle, they found some with injured legs and cracked horns from the breakout. When the drive finally continued north, twelve of the twenty-five hands peeled off for home as they passed through Austin, the capital city on the Colorado River. After Austin, for the next nearly six hundred miles to Kansas, the Chisholm would be at its fullest, Charlie noted, "one continuous roadway, several hundred yards wide, tramped hard and solid by the millions of hooves which had gone over it."[5]

New settlements encroached on the hallowed trail as they approached Fort Worth, where the Texas and Pacific Railway had recently come. A number of watering places were blocked off by settlers, some using the harsh novelty of barbed-wire fencing, recently invented. "We paid no attention to fences, but shoved the herd right through," Charlie recalled. When the barbed wire clung to the cattle and provoked a stampede, "the big and little 'hoe men' ran out to sick the dogs on us. Some of these dogs bit the dust," shot by angry cowboys who saw the Chisholm Trail as "too sacred to be scratched with plows and hoes."[6]

As they reached the Red River, the traditional crossing point out of Texas, a prodigious rain was flooding its banks; some twenty other drives of various sizes had paused ahead of them, camped along a crowded half-mile stretch of shore. All were awaiting a visit by the state cattle inspector from Red River Station before entering the tribal areas of the Indian Territory, once the river eased.

The stranded cowhands spent much of two nights singing trail songs. The state inspector appeared on the second night to explain the details of his next morning's process of tallying what each outfit owed for crossing, at ten cents per head, and cutting out any cattle showing different brands that had joined their herds along the route. One of the trail bosses, hearing these

Cowboys have their hard-earned dinner in Indian Territory, while their horses wait, reins tossed before them, 1883.

Riata and Spurs / *Author's collection*

details, invited the state inspector to join his men for coffee when he appeared early next morning at their campsite, the river now passable and clear. After accepting the drover's hospitality before the start of what looked to be an exceedingly busy day, the inspector found himself abducted, tied up, gagged with a handkerchief, and left in a plum grove; the cowboys even shaved a prankish message into the coat of his Kentucky mare, sent cantering home.

This greatly impressed Charlie, who felt for the unlucky inspector, but was more troubled by something else he saw that day. As the outfits took advantage of their free passage (skipping out on inspection fees that might have been $250 for Grimes's herd), and their cattle entered the river, the cowboy yelling drew perhaps one hundred full-blooded Durham steers out of the brush to join the Grimes outfit's line of mossy horns. These traveled on mixed together with the Grimes herd and would be added to his profit when sold altogether in Kansas. To Charlie, the owner of the Durhams had needed the money more.

In the Territory, there were more rivers to cross and frequent visits by "roaming bands from the Comanche, Kiowa, Kickapoo, and Wichita agencies," who would ride into camp when the cook was alone and begin "eating all the cooked grub" or demand beef from other trail drivers in exchange for safe passage, threatening night stampedes if denied, causing panics "among the hundreds of herds passing up the trail at this season."[7]

Approaching the Kansas line, Dawdy managed to get his wagons across the surging Salt Fork of the Arkansas River during another hard rainstorm. But it was rising fast as he rode back to meet the rest of his herd, the quick-moving water a half mile across and dangerously full of driftwood. Not wanting to be cut off from the wagons, the group attempted the hazardous crossing, with Henry Coats riding lead and Dawdy and Otto Draub on left point. Siringo and "Negro Gabe" shared right point as the lead steers entered the water without complaint, bringing the other cattle behind. Henry Coats's lead horse then refused to swim in the current, falling over in the deeper water. As Coats nearly drowned, the steers turned back in fear toward Gabe and Charlie, whose shouts and waving could not stop their brutish retreat. Back on land, the cattle refused to reenter the rising river.

The men made a camp, where for seven miserable days they waited around a fire for the water to subside, chasing stampedes during nighttime storms and hunting strays. One night, Charlie and Gabe sneaked away to make their own fire to roast some meat and afterward parch in its hot ashes an ear of yellow corn they had found. "Gabe contended that God had dropped this ear of corn there for our special benefit," Charlie wrote. It was the only break from meat in their week's diet.[8] On the seventh day, while out searching for more stragglers after a nighttime storm had caused yet another stampede, three of the men spotted the white tents of the US Army on the far side of the swollen Wild Horse River. The soldiers were on their way to Wichita and offered to share what they could from their supply wagons if the Texas cowboys would come get it.

Dawdy nominated Siringo to swim across with his pony Yankee Doodle to collect the provisions. Once there, he stuffed as many government biscuits in his belt as he could fit, while soldiers whipped other hard biscuits across the narrowest bend in the river to Dawdy and another man, Hastings. Siringo then filled a washtub with vital supplies such as coffee, flour, and the all-important salt, and he and his horse swam back alongside it, arriving considerably downstream but a hero to the hungry men, who had lived for days on unsalted beef. They soon were drinking coffee with bread they had improvised by cooking dough on sticks. It would not be the last time Siringo was saved by the bluecoats he was raised to hate.

The drive resumed, and by July 4, 1876, they were camped on the Ninnescah River some thirty miles outside Wichita, where Grimes had come by train to check on his arriving stock. They might have known that day was the national centennial, but news of the recent slaughter at Little Bighorn of soldiers and scouts with George Armstrong Custer's Seventh Cavalry was still steaming down the Missouri toward Bismarck.

While Grimes's stock fattened over that summer, Charlie discovered a pair of young New York sisters to admire on their family's nearby quarter-section farm. The excuse for his visits was trade: bringing wagonloads of dried cow chips (for fuel in that treeless country) to exchange for the family's cantaloupes and watermelons. Eventually his flirty cowboy chatter became tiresome to the sisters, and he was turned out. He then grew lonesome; with the drive ended, his cowboy chores were haunted by thoughts of the Texas girl he imagined still waiting quietly for him back home—the Matagorda sheriff's daughter whom he had met in the house of her cousin, Charlie's skinning partner Horace Yeamans Jr. Having nothing to think about except "my best Texas girl—the only one on Earth I loved," Charlie decided to write her to "see where I stood."[9]

At least a month passed before a letter arrived with the supply wagon from Wichita. The cowboys from camp brought him the envelope, addressed in a young girl's hand, which he excitedly opened when he came off herd. It turned out she had not been waiting for him but had married his boyhood Matagorda friend Billy Williams, whose father had once blown himself up lighting a Union cannonball in his yard. Further, she had thought all this time that Charlie liked her only as a friend. He was crushed, "I wanted someone to kill me—so concluded to go to the Black Hills—as everyone was flocking there then."[10]

Not a few were dying on the way. In September 1874, two years before the events at Little Bighorn, men from Custer's Seventh Cavalry had reported discovering gold in the Black Hills, in what was then the Dakota Territory. It seemed to confirm what had long been rumored and spurred an invasion of prospectors north into treatied Lakota lands. As stories of gold circulated, some hopeful miners had died en route.

Before he could set off prospecting, Siringo sneaked away with another trail hand to get a proper drunk on and lose his sorrow for a few days in Wichita's vice district. The cowboys spent all the first day getting barbered and buying new clothes and boots at Wichita's New York Store. Then, in outfits they had been assured were stylish, they headed for the town's lively nighttime section and what was supposed to be the "swiftest of the joints" in Kansas, Rowdy Joe's.

In Texas they had long heard of Rowdy Joe's dance hall and its sometimes deadly rumpuses on the other side of the Arkansas River in West Wichita. Now all that stood in the way of their night of pleasure was a one-legged man collecting tolls on the river bridge. With their drinking well underway, Siringo and his well-dressed friend tried to gallop through and beat the fare, howling and shooting over the toll taker's head when he emerged from his shanty. As they crossed his bridge, he scattered buckshot at their ponies' hooves.[11]

On the far side of the river, Siringo would not have found Rowdy Joe himself, who had escaped Wichita after shooting his neighboring competitor, Edward "Red" Beard, described by a Wichita paper as "a jolly, rollicking man," in November 1873. The "proprietors of the two dance houses," the *Leavenworth Daily Commercial* reported, "both being mad from the effects of distilled poison, and armed with revolvers and shotguns, waltzed into a deadly melee."[12] After jumping bail, Joe (Joseph Lowe) was reported killed the following year by Sioux while trespassing for gold in the Black Hills, but he had actually gone south to resettle with his equally high-spirited wife, Rowdy Kate, in search of new "hurrah" towns.

But even without Rowdy Joe or Red Beard presiding, there was plenty of vice remaining in Wichita for young cowboys in a hurry to lose their drive money; monte, keno, faro, poker, or chuck-a-luck could be played nightly in a large hall, accompanied by a brass band. What one adventurous reporter called "resorts of the vivacious" lured lonely young Texans into soft-lit parlors where "gaily attired females thumb and drum upon pianos, and in dulcet tones and mocking smiles invite the 'boys' in, and night is commenced in earnest."[13] For the two trail hands, night commenced at last.

Siringo stayed around the cow camp until late into the fall, well after much of the crew had taken the train home to Texas. As the first snows fell, he still had not bought winter clothes when he finally quit the Grimes outfit to go find gold of his own with a fellow cowboy named Collier. Each had recently secured his own excellent horse, Charlie's was a racer named Whiskey Peat.* However deadly it might have been to enter the Black Hills, Charlie was still heartbroken enough from his recent letter to risk it. The two men returned to Wichita to settle up with Grimes.**

One who had made the trip into the Black Hills that summer was Wild Bill Hickok, traveling to the grubby Dakota mining camp of Deadwood in early July, in a caravan of gold seekers that included the frontierswoman Calamity Jane (Martha Jane Cannary), who would later claim to have briefly been his wife. Hickok had left his legal wife running a brothel in Cheyenne on the prospecting excuse, but the call of the saloon poker table proved stronger than the lure of panning cold streams, and he began to take the camp's money instead. Fictional tales of Wild Bill's violent encounters, and occasional death, had continued to appear around the country since he'd left Abilene.[14] Deadwood was beyond the law, a rough gathering of prospectors and outlaws on Lakota lands, where he could be left largely alone as he neared forty.

But even his revolvers could not save Hickok when his back was turned on the morning of August 2, 1876. After relieving

---

* Siringo sometimes uses the Irish and American (Whiskey) or Scottish (Whisky) spelling for this horse's name, sometimes also "pete" or "peet" rather than "peat."

** In his 1981 biography of Siringo, Orlan Sawey sees the mining expedition idea as driven by a heartbroken, suicidal wish: "When he received the letter bearing the bad news, Siringo, considerably wrought up, decided to go to the Black Hills, scene of a recent Gold Rush, where, he was sure, somebody would kill him" (Sawey, *Charles A. Siringo* [Twayne, 1981], 48).

a bitter, drunken character named Jack McCall of his money at cards, Bill gave McCall a coin and told him to "go get breakfast." This lordly act of kindness set McCall's many churning grievances into action, and he returned hours later to Nuttal and Mann's saloon, where the great Wild Bill still sat at the poker table, his back and mane uncharacteristically to the door despite his better judgment, as his seat had been the only one free at the game.

"Jack McCall walked in and around directly behind his victim," reported the *Black Hills Weekly Pioneer*, "and when within three feet of him raised his revolver, and exclaiming 'Damn you, take that!' fired, the ball entering the back of the head and coming out at the centre of the right cheek, causing instant death." Word spread by three o'clock, when the *Weekly Pioneer* reporter reached Nuttal and Mann's: "We found the remains of Wild Bill lying on the floor. The murderer, Jack McCall, was captured after a lively chase by many of our citizens."[15]

After settling with Grimes late in the fall, Siringo and Collier had burned through the last of their pay on another bender in Wichita, leaving them unable to outfit a Black Hills prospecting trip. The men drifted a hundred miles west toward the Medicine River instead, latecomers in search of winter work. Collier took a job in Kiowa, Kansas, while Charlie, broke and still in summer clothes, drifted southwest until he found riskier employment at the camp of Gus Johnson, spending a month moving his longhorns south into the Indian Territory for winter grazing on a tributary of the Cimarron River.

With his pay from Johnson, Siringo outfitted himself to try fur trapping nearby but was not suited to it. His first lodge, which he made out of long poles and dry grass, tindered to flames after he lit his fire; he then gathered his surviving belongings and returned to the Johnson camp for a night before making a new lodging, a "3 by 18 mansion" dug in the bank of a stream, finished with a sod roof and a better chimney.

The Johnson herd he had moved south for grazing now passed over his dugout as a snowstorm began. Charlie was trapped and nearly killed when a red steer stepped through his snow-covered roof and appeared, "tumbling head first," above him.[16] Trapped, he was "fixing to turn my wicked soul over to the Lord" when he saw a square of daylight and struggled out from beneath the beast.[17] He then dumped his pelts and rode out of the "God-foresaken country"—originally aiming for Kiowa but diverted in a sleet storm toward Texas, southeast along Eagle Chief Creek and the Cimmaron River, to reunite with the Chisholm Trail. Quicksand prevented his crossing the Cimmaron, so he camped between two sand hills and "made my bed in a tall bunch of blue stem grass."[18] While out harvesting snow for drinking water the next morning, he turned his back on his campfire long enough for the flames to jump to the high grass, frying his leggings, saddle blanket, and the slicker holding his matches. Rescuing his saddle and Whiskey Peat, tied to a tree that had begun to burn, he headed south. Along the way, a kindly passing teamster gave him some pants and a blue coat, before he wandered into a "crowd of Chickasaw Indians who bantered me into a horse race."[19]

Whiskey Peat, surprisingly, retained his speed on the journey despite coming through sleet storms and two close fires. Charlie won a Chickasaw pony in a bareback contest, then wisely resisted calls for a second race against a larger mount. He carried on with his two horses, staying overnight at a ranch on the Washita River. There he traded his new pony before following the river until he found his grateful way to Erin Springs, in the south-central part of the future Oklahoma.

In Erin Springs, Siringo met Frank Murray, an Irish immigrant and farmer who had married into the Chickasaw nation, making him what was called a "squaw-man." As Charlie arrived, Murray was hosting a dance for local Chickasaw women and their white husbands and families. Charlie danced until dawn with a number of "Indian maidens." "'Squaw-men,'" one disapproving reporter explained, "are white men who have married squaws, and draw rations for their wives and live because of these annuities."[20]

It seemed an enviable existence, judging by Murray and other Anglo men he met, especially Smith Paul, the wealthy old farmer he found farther on in the town of Pauls Valley. Now ninety-two, Paul had come to the life he enjoyed on a wagon train from North Carolina as a young man, marrying a Chickasaw woman and starting his first family. Old man Paul owned most of the fertile surrounding valley, Siringo observed, and had followed the custom that "any Chickasaw Indian, or squaw-man, held title to all the land that he could keep under fence," as long as he wasn't closer than a quarter mile to a neighbor's fence.[21] Before Siringo left him in the spring, the "husky old man" would marry a sixteen-year-old girl and start anew.

Charlie finished the winter breaking broncs for Paul at $2.50 per pony and became "plum loco'ed" himself by a Native woman he met, almost smitten enough to marry her. But he lost his nerve, worried that living as a "squaw man" might somehow later disqualify him from becoming President of the United States, which his schoolbooks had taught him every boy had a chance to become.[22]

9

"Stinkers"

Mr. W. B. Masterson is on the track for Sheriff, and so announces himself in this paper. "Bat" is well known as a man of nerve and coolness in cases of danger.

—*Dodge City* (Kansas) *Times*, Oct. 13, 1877

By May 1877, a drive of mixed stock belonging to Captain George Littlefield was traveling up from Gonzales in the direction of Wichita. Charlie joined the outfit as the herd of thirty-five hundred cattle reached Saint Jo, Texas, on the Chisholm Trail, for what proved another rough journey through storms, over Indian Territory, and across many cresting rivers; he was nearly crushed once while swimming amid the herd when it turned back halfway across, saving himself by walking the broad backs of the struggling steers. "Often these milling bands would drift a mile or two down the stream before we could get them strung out again," he remembered. A log raft was built to get the mess wagon across the rough currents, but after swimming the Cimmaron River, the drive was soon stopped and diverted by fresh farm settlements, "fool 'hoe men'" claiming the grazing country west of Wichita. The Littlefield outfit turned northwest instead toward Dodge City.[1]

On July 3, the herd rumbled into Dodge, which that summer was becoming the "Bovine Capital of the World," boasted the *Kansas City Times*, with "upwards of one hundred thousand head of cattle in the immediate vicinity."[2] Dodge had been plotted out only in 1872, when the railroad reached what had been a buffalo hunters' camp near Fort Dodge.

From here, the Littlefield drive was to continue northward to Oglala, Nebraska, but Siringo cashed out in order to see the Fourth in "the toughest cattle town on Earth," curious how many of Dodge's sixteen licensed saloons he could visit before heading back to Texas.[3] He ran into a cowboy friend named Wes Adams who was just as eager to cut loose. The young cow town was having its first official Fourth of July celebrations, but except for some afternoon horse races, Charlie and Wes probably did not notice many of the festivities through their drinking haze.

Of Dodge City's many brothels, the best known was the Red Light, often credited for the term "red-light district" for its doorway's crimson glass, through which light shone rosily by night.[4] Another thing Dodge had plenty of was buffalo hunters, the shaggy, often blood-smeared antagonists of the cowboy, who called them "stinkers." The city remained a headquarters for supplying the hunters, who sent thousands of hides east each year. The buffalo men were pungently distributed among Dodge's bars, bawdy houses, and gambling halls.

Dodge was a collection of new frame buildings and a railroad, a "noisy cattle mart" in season, surprising one tired eastern reporter arriving blearily late one night to see it still "thronged with swaggering, swearing cow-boys and oily confidence men. . . . Any of our companions that might be bent on sport could need no special beckoning, for all the billiard halls, concert saloons, and keno dens, the lamp still held out to burn."[5]

Despite Dodge's recent reputation as a wide-open gunfighter town planting dead duelists in its Boot Hill, Wyatt Earp and W. B. "Bat" Masterson had reduced the city's body count in their first two years as lawmen here, often holding cowboys'

firearms while they were drinking on the more respectable
north side of the city's "Dead Line," which roughly followed the
new railroad tracks. The lawmen had also been paid for arrests,
not for killings, bringing down the number of shootouts with
drunken Texans, whom they "buffaloed" and dragged to jail
instead. Dodge may have been as wicked and violent as its reputation but not as prone to deadly gunplay as Western fiction
would have it. For one thing, the railroads had an interest in at
least a minimum of safety in these towns, which is what Earp
and Masterson had tried to maintain in Dodge.* (The lawless
mining camps were another matter.) But Dodge still experienced
a fair amount of brawling and noisy, pointless shooting. Siringo
missed by days Earp's return to Dodge from Deadwood, but he
certainly encountered Bat Masterson.

That summer of Siringo's visit, Masterson was just twenty-
three and had recently returned to law work, convinced by the
new mayor, James "Dog" Kelly, to take up the undersheriff's
badge again. A handsome, mustached figure, six feet tall, with
dark hair and blue eyes, Masterson had done a fair amount of buffalo hunting with his two brothers, who now helped him police
the streets of Dodge. He roamed the town with his cane, wearing
a bowler hat and two pearl-handled pistols, a "man of nerve and
coolness," as he worded it, who "knows just how to gather in the
sinners."[6] His cane and limp had come after taking a bullet in the

---

* "In effect," Allen Barra has written, "after Earp's arrival Dodge City ceased
to be Dodge City" (*Inventing Wyatt Earp* [Carrol and Graf, 1998], 405). Richard White (*Railroaded* [Norton, 2011], 660) has also shown figures proving
Dodge's deadly reputation was exaggerated compared to the homicide percent-
ages of mining camps such as Deadwood, or New York City, during this same
period: "Those towns such as cattle towns that disarmed young men lowered
the rates of personal violence considerably. Those towns such as Bodie [CA]
and Aurora [NV] that did not disarm men tended to bury significantly more of
them." (*Railroaded*, 332)

"A man of nerve and coolness," young Bat Masterson called himself.

AmericanCowboyChronicles.com

groin and hip in a shootout in Sweetwater, Kansas, shot by a rival for a woman named Mollie Brennan, who died trying to intercede.[7]

After a law was passed making it illegal to carry concealed weapons in Dodge, visiting Texans continued to "run the town," shooting out windows and firing in the air from their horses before riding out to nearby cowboy camps. The 1877 season that took Charlie to Dodge (along with more than two hundred thousand head of cattle) also brought cowboys like A. C. Jackson, who made the occasional loud spectacle, drawing the ire of Masterson (and a reporter): "Like all true sons of the Lone Star State, he loves to fondle and practice with his revolver in the open air. . . . The programme of the Texas boy . . . is to come to town and bum around until he gets disgusted with himself, then to mount his pony and ride out through the main street, shooting his revolver at every jump."[8]

Had Jackson been on foot, Masterson would have clubbed and hauled him off. But Jackson knew to stay in his saddle as he fired, drawing a crowd each night before galloping back to camp. One September night, as he turned to spur another of his escapes, Masterson unholstered one of his pistols and shot Jackson's horse, followed by a round from his brother Ed. After racing beyond city limits, the loyal animal bled out and collapsed. Jackson walked the last part back to camp before he could be caught.

The popular Lone Star Dance Hall and Saloon was half owned by Masterson, who drank and played cards there and occasionally served as bouncer. On the July evening when Charlie saw it, the Lone Star was filled with a rivalrous mix of cowboys and stinkers and the "free-and-easy girls" for whom they competed. One thing the hunters knew well was knives and the expert work of separating bison hides from their pulpy carcasses. Animated by some suspect frontier booze, around eleven o'clock, Siringo's friend Wes Adams picked a fight with several buffalo men, who may or may not have insulted him, intending to show "the long-haired buffalo hunters that they were not in the cowboy class," according to Siringo, and having no apparent plan if the hunters rose to his bait except for the backing of his scrappy fellow cowboy.

Wes held his own until the blades came out and the fight whipped round the room, drawing in other cowboys on principle. One of the hunters cut Wes in the back with a skinning knife, and Charlie helped him fight his way to the door. From behind the bar, Bat Masterson used up beer glasses winging them at Charlie's head, the misses crashing in glass splinters off the nearby wall. By the time he ran out of glasses to hurl, a dozen cowboys and hunters were battling in his saloon. Masterson came out from the bar raging with an ice mallet, which he swung on "a big Dutch cowboy" with no hand in starting the fight, blood flying as Bat struck the cowboy's face.[9] Siringo and Wes Adams had worn their Colts into the bar, but when guns were pulled they were used for clubbing, in a brawl that cracked the skull of Jim White, the long-haired boss of a crew of buffalo hunters, for one.[10] Had anyone fired a shot that night, Siringo recalled, a number of drunken brawlers would have gone to Boot Hill.

The pair reached their horses, tied just outside the Lone Star, and started riding toward the town limits just as one of the city police, possibly Joe Mason, appeared.* Chasing him back into a doorway and shooting off their pistols, they rode about a mile east to the stockyards, where, after lying him down on his stomach, Siringo lit matches to inspect Adams's knife wound. A deep, semicircular cut beneath his shoulder blade revealed the hunter's twisting skill; his clothes were blood-soaked, and the skin separated. Siringo would have to sneak into town and bring back needle and thread to stop the bleeding.

Years later, when Pinkerton superintendent James McParland introduced them, Masterson told Siringo that his men had lain in wait all that night on both sides of the road, hoping to kill the pair of troublemaking cowboys if they returned to Dodge. Though still more than a little drunk, Charlie somehow had known to enter another way, by traveling south in an arroyo until he met the railroad track, which he followed into town before kicking on the door of the drugstore to rouse an "old Dutchman," who appeared in his nightshirt and sold him needle and thread, sticking plaster, and a candle for his surgery. Then he returned the same way to his patient.

Pushing the wound painfully down by sitting on Wes's back, he still could not close the skin together to sew it, using sticking plaster instead. The pair then slowly mounted up again and carried on for eighteen miles to the D. T. Beals cattle yard, with Siringo holding his weakening friend on his mount the last part of the ride. The two arrived after dawn; Wes passed out from the bleeding but would survive. They rested among the herd.

---

* Dodge City had overlapping law enforcement: a countywide sheriff and undersheriff as well as a citywide police force. Later in 1877, Bat successfully ran for sheriff and his brother Ed took charge of the Dodge City department.

Although one of them was now in no condition for it, both men signed up with the Beals Cattle Company for an unusual drive. It was not a regular herding job back down the trail. Instead, Charlie would be accompanying twenty-five hundred steers into a part of his home state long known for its buffalo herds and the Native peoples who hunted them, "the wild Panhandle of Texas." There, David Beals intended to establish a new ranch, bringing down thousands more cattle once he had claimed a range for them.[11] On the way, Siringo would learn to have even less respect for the stinkers he had bloodied in the Lone Star Saloon, once he saw how easy it was to shoot a buffalo.

10

Panhandle

The eastern and southern sides of this great table-land are gashed and seamed by a succession of canyons and arrogors, the raggedness and grandeur of which are beyond description.

—*New York Herald*, 1874

S iringo would remember David Beals fondly as his favorite boss, "an honest, broad-gauge cattleman." A manufacturer of shoes and boots, from North Abington, Massachusetts, Beals had come west first intending to make footwear for miners, until he saw the opportunities in cattle ranching. He sold some businesses in 1873, secured eastern partners, and started his first ranch near Granada, Colorado, keeping herds along the Arkansas River. While the cattle raising was good, Colorado's recent statehood was attracting too many new residents for Beals's liking by 1877.

Feeling the area becoming overstocked, Beals decided to move much of his operation down (including from his cattle yard outside Dodge City) to the still-wild Texas Panhandle and start a new ranch in the High Plains above the broad area of table-lands the conquistadors had named the Llano Estacado (Staked Plains), an arid plateau that bridged New Mexico and Texas. Even the boosterish *Immigrants' Hand-Book* for 1875 had called the Staked Plains "the only uninhabitable portion of Texas,"[1] while the Panhandle was long traveled by Comanchero traders bartering with Plains tribes in remote spots such as the Valley of the Tongues.*

But a recent visitor had found much to admire in the Panhandle wilderness, starting with the Prairie Dog Town Fork of the Red River, noting sandy prairie bounded by occasional hills; plains covered in gamma, buffalo, and mesquite grasses; tributaries lined with cottonwood and hackberry; some promising black loam soil in the uplands; and the deep, rock-rimmed system of canyons of the Palo Duro, "a vast chasm with vertical walls of earth hundreds of feet in height, inaccessible except in a few points."[2] The first Panhandle cattle rancher, Charles Goodnight, would learn the canyon's access points from an old Comanchero and discover that sheepherders had entered the Panhandle ahead of him.

Ranching in this wild part of Texas had been made possible by two events: the forced relocation of Native peoples and the continued killing of plains buffalo by professional hunters, which peaked from 1874 to 1878. "The buffalo is fast being exterminated," announced the *Dallas Weekly Herald*. "Where he roamed in countless numbers only a few years ago now lie millions of bones." Where Charlie was headed, the federal government had proved unable to enforce protections promised in the 1867 Treaty of Medicine Lodge, which had assigned Cheyenne, Arapaho, Kiowa, Comanche, and Plains Apache to reservations in the southern part of the Indian Territory (which now included much of the area that would become Oklahoma) and specified their remaining hunting grounds. Others had previously moved to the "territory" over the years to keep ahead of white settlers advancing westward.

---

* Into his old age, Siringo liked to flash the talking hand symbols he learned on the Great Plains called "Indian sign," a common language developed by Native Americans to bridge differences in tribal languages and dialects, especially useful in trade.

Despite the latest treaty, the government could not keep out professional buffalo hunters nor provide much supplement to the tribes who depended on the decreasing herds. In the summer of 1875 alone, a group of sixteen hunters reported killing twenty-eight thousand plains buffalo for their hides, leaving the skinned carcasses, for which there was no market; by 1876, there were at least two thousand working buffalo hunters in Texas alone, more than the total number of buffalo twenty-five years later. The tribal relocations combined with the depletion of the buffalo created what the western historian Howard Lamar has called "a faunal void," into which the ranchers moved.

Quanah Parker was the tall son of a Quahadi Comanche man and a white woman named Cynthia Ann Parker, who had been famously abducted as a young girl and raised her own children as Comanche, then was liberated by force by Texas Rangers and returned to a white society she barely recalled. Quanah Parker's Quahadi band of Comanches refused to move to their reservation in the early 1870s, still living by hunting and vengeful raids across the Texas border while eluding US troops. But it was clear that the greater threat to their way of life was not the army they repeatedly evaded. As a leader at a Ghost Dance in 1874, Parker was convinced to shift tactics from raiding settlements and skirmishing with cavalry to attacking his direct rivals for the plains bison, the hunters killing his herds. Quanah Parker crossed into Texas along with a medicine man called Isa-Tai, who had guaranteed victory as well as invulnerability to bullets, leading a party of nearly seven hundred Comanche, Kiowa, Southern Cheyenne, and Arapaho warriors.

After singing a song to prepare themselves for battle, they attacked at dawn on June 27, 1874, riding toward a cluster of buildings not far from the ruin of an old hunters' trading post called Adobe Walls, deep in the Panhandle just north of the

Canadian River.* As there had been a nighttime storm, many
of the twenty-eight buffalo hunters (including Bat Masterson)
and one woman had been driven inside to sleep but were alert as
the attack party approached, working to repair a ridge pole that
had snapped. While far outnumbered, the fortified hunters were
nevertheless armed with some of the heaviest and longest-range
guns in the West.

As they tried to run their ponies against the doors, warriors
and their mounts were picked off from hundreds of yards, one
hunter's legendary shot said to have unhorsed a rider nearly a
mile away. Quanah Parker was shot from a doorway as he galloped toward it on the first day; he recalled the moment years
later for a magazine writer, throwing "a great sprawling hand
over his breast" as he spoke of it.[3] After five days, Parker's group
abandoned its plan to lay siege and starve out the hunters, and on
July 1 they rode away on their remaining horses. (Siringo visited
the Adobe Walls scene not long after he came to the Panhandle in
1877 and saw that "skulls and bones of dead Indians still lay on
the ground.")[4]

Cavalry forces led by General Philip Sheridan were dispatched to put down the uprising and force the tribes to return,
an operation called the Red River War. After failing to rout the
buffalo hunters, Quanah Parker and a smaller band held on
through a hard winter and spring as soldiers burned villages and
supplies, before surrendering in the summer of 1875, retreating
finally to the reservation. The Red River War would not end,
though, until the tribal removals were complete, after the Fourth
Cavalry regiment led by Colonel Ranald Mackenzie raided

* A previous nearby engagement, often called First Battle of Adobe Walls,
had taken place in November 1864, in which a US Expeditionary Force led by
Kit Carson fought a very large army of Comanche, Kiowa, and Plains Apache
before withdrawing.

Native encampments in Palo Duro Canyon on the morning of September 28, 1876, killing three people along with hundreds of the tribes' ponies, trapping the horseless survivors in the canyon.

In the spring of that year, the Texas rancher Charles Goodnight had crossed the Red River and drifted sixteen hundred of his Colorado cattle to the rock rim of another part of Palo Duro Canyon, roughly 120 miles long and ranging from six to twenty miles across.* Goodnight was born in Illinois in 1836 and moved with his family to Waco, Texas, at age ten, where he learned the frontier life. In addition to his part in blazing two famous cattle trails, he had created the first chuck wagon for his daring 1866 drive from the headwaters of the Brazos to Fort Sumner, New Mexico.

Near a spring close to the site of the future town of Canyon, Texas, was the path an old Comanchero trader had suggested Goodnight use to get his herd down the steep Native trace into the Palo Duro canyon in 1876. Goodnight's mule-led mess wagon had to be dismantled and carried down the seven-hundred-foot slope, his stock moving single file past red cedars and sandstone. Once the trail widened, Goodnight saw hundreds of buffalo grazing on either side; shooting rifles in the air to scatter them, he replaced a wild herd with his own cattle on the canyon grass.

He wintered his stock on Turkey Creek, protected from northers by the Palo Duro's walls, before establishing a headquarters for his JA Ranch (given the initials of his Scots Irish investor, John Adair). "Nature had fenced his range," Siringo observed. "There was only one place in the canyon where cattle could climb out, and a few rods of stone fencing fixed this."[5]

---

* His earlier partnership with the cattle driver Oliver Loving has been turned to literature by Larry McMurtry, in his Lonesome Dove series.

With the removal of the Native peoples, ranchers could claim as much of the free range as they could cover with their cattle and find dependable water nearby. Goodnight's JA would soon be followed by the Panhandle outfits of Tom Bugbee, Beals and Bates, H. W. Cresswell, George Littlefield, and Mose Hays. "These beautiful solitudes have been the battle grounds of the Pan-handle," the *Galveston Daily News* reported soon after the ranchers arrived, "but now you can see peacefully grazing in these valleys once so dangerous to red and white, thousands of sheep and cattle."[6]

Within days of his brawl with the buffalo hunters in Dodge in July 1877, Siringo was traveling down to the Panhandle with an establishing herd led by David Beals's Bostonian partner, W. H. Bates, called "Deacon" for his air of New England propriety. Siringo accompanied Bates while Beals stayed behind to buy more cattle to stock their new territory. After the drive crossed the Cimmaron River into the area known as No Man's Land or the Neutral Strip (now in Oklahoma), they saw their first buffalo herd. Bates selected Siringo for a hunt.

In the restless West at this time, a proper New Englander called Deacon could give a lesson in bison hunting to a rough young Texan born to Europeans, imparting skills the Yankee had recently gained while ranching in Colorado. Once they were within a mile of the grazing herd, the two men tied their ponies in a gulch and "walked afoot out on the open flat, straight towards the wooly animals." At about a hundred yards, "we raised our Sharps 45 caliber rifles and fired," Charlie recalled. "Two young animals, a bull and a heifer, dropped over dead. Now the whole herd began bawling and milling around the fallen beasts."

No stranger to cattle stampedes, Siringo expected the same from buffalo, and was anxious to "run back to my pony."

Bates, however, answered that buffalo were "harmless unless wounded, when they became vicious. . . . On reaching the edge of the milling herd, he pulled off his hat and began shooing them out of his way. At first, they seemed to pay no attention to him, but finally they started away on the run." They would run at the sight of a horseman, Bates explained, but ignore a man approaching on foot. (Many hunters crawled on their bellies from downwind to approach stands of buffalo, sliding their heavy rifles across the grass.) But the buffalo's nature clearly made it easy to slaughter "by the thousands."[7] While in camp later on the drive, Charlie saw another passing herd and impulsively rode out to try roping a bison calf, drawing a charge from its mother and learning firsthand that even a calf could not be thrown like a young steer. He ended up having to cut the roped calf's throat with a rusty knife when he found he had forgotten his hunting tools in his haste.

After the drive with Deacon Bates camped near Blue Creek, he rode ahead with Charlie to the spot where the LX Ranch would be established, on a tributary of the Canadian River:

> Mr. Bates selected the site for the home ranch on a little creek about a mile east of Pitcher Creek. This was to be the center of the future LX cattle range, which was to extend twenty miles up the river and the same distance downstream, twenty miles south to the foot of the Llano Estacado, and twenty miles north to the foot of the North Staked Plains. This constituted a free range of forty miles square. Thousands of buffalo, deer and antelope were roaming over the plains.[8]

While scouting, the men had seen the nearest outpost to the LX, a small settlement called Tascosa, named after the nearby

Altascosa Creek ("boggy creek"), which drained into the Canadian River. Growing from a Native camp in a cottonwood grove to a settlement for New Mexican sheepherders and a center for open-range trading and cowboy vices, Tascosa would be a future county seat, with an Upper Tascosa for hotels and a Lower Tascosa, or "Hogtown," for the usual cowboy recreations.[9]

But when Charlie saw it, Tascosa was still just a half dozen families of Hispanic sheep ranchers served by a general store, Howard and Rinehart's, and a blacksmith. It had no post office yet, but one visitor recalled that roughly every three months, "Old Dad Barnes, an antiquated old-time cowboy . . . ambled up and down the valley on a has-been mustang, picking up letters for Dodge City at fifty cents a letter, and retrieving answers at the same price."[10] According to Siringo, the general store kept three barrels of whiskey and "half a dozen boxes of soda crackers," but as cowboys from the new outfits increasingly made their way to Tascosa, buying out the store's liquor stocks, saloons and dance halls soon began opening.[11] As the town became larger and rowdier, it was visited by well-known gunfighters and lawmen and required its own Boot Hill. One of Charlie's friends from the LX, Jim East, would later patrol the town as sheriff of Oldham County and open his own saloon.

Once all the LX cattle from Colorado and Dodge City had been merged on the free range, Charlie started out at one of a number of signal camps posted about every twenty-five miles, this one south of the main ranch, "reading sign" for evidence that LX cattle had wandered and then retrieving them. Some had mingled among passing buffalo. Cattle were not swift enough to keep up with running buffalo but were suggestible herd animals that would trail them far out onto the Staked Plains. Sent to turn the strays back, Siringo sometimes followed cattle tracks mixed among those of a buffalo herd. Minding cattle on the free range of the Panhandle was not like chasing mossy horns through the brush and thickets.

Not long after Charlie's arrival, a young doctor from Saint Paul, Minnesota, named Henry Hoyt came to the Panhandle in 1877 and was told he was the first medical doctor to settle in the area and would find plentiful work with a local smallpox outbreak. In Tascosa, he successfully treated a young Mexican woman's full-blown chicken pox with a paste he smeared over her body made from water and gunpowder. But when cases of smallpox and chicken pox subsided, young Dr. Hoyt found there weren't enough gunshot wounds to keep in business; with but a handful of women yet in the area, little prospect of many babies to deliver either. Low on funds, the doctor applied for work at the largest area employer, the sprawling LX Ranch, training to be a cowboy under a young man named Siringo.

Hoyt had mostly outfitted himself for his new work, except for the all-important rawhide *riata* for roping, an item the Minnesota farm boy had not encountered. Siringo brought him out, and together they "took a large cowhide that had been stretched and dried, trimmed off the legs and corners until it was circular in shape, and then with a sharp knife cut it into a long strip one-half inch wide, by going around its circumference."[12] Four long strips were scraped clean of hair before each was rubbed with tallow until soft for braiding. Once the riata was finished, Siringo taught Hoyt how to throw it, a lassoing skill that would serve the doctor even during his future army postings but first got him assigned to range riding.*

---

* More than fifty years after leaving the LX, the men would reunite in California, with Hoyt serving as Siringo's doctor.

Despite carrying the cautionary nickname of "Outlaw Bill," William C. Moore was hired the fall after Siringo arrived and quickly became general manager of the new ranch. He brought with him to the High Plains the novel long riata (seventy-five feet) and single-girth saddle of California ranching, as well as a natural ability to lead cowboys.[13] He had already been manager of the Swan Land and Cattle Company of Cheyenne but had fled after killing a Black coachman, ultimately reaching the Panhandle. Siringo judged him both a criminal and a highly effective manager of men, whose ranching excellence outshone his notoriety

"Outlaw Bill" Moore, the LX's skilled and notorious ranch manager.
Riata and Spurs / *Author's collection*

as "Outlaw Bill," getting him hired across the West. According to Charlie, Moore showed a predilection for setting aside cattle for his private herd, rebranding LX steers for his own ranch.

That first year on the High Plains, Siringo witnessed one of the great sights of his crowded young life, while camping fifteen miles south of the main ranch at Amarillo Creek, where his mission was to shoot and scare buffalo away from the LX range: "The main herd of buffaloes migrating from the north passed a mile west of us. For three days and nights there was a solid string of them from a quarter to a half mile wide—sometimes in a walk and other times on the run. During daylight, we could look to the northward, across the Canadian River breaks, a distance of about thirty miles, and see this black streak of living flesh coming down off the north plains."[14]

It would have been almost the last time a group that size could have been seen together.[15] Of the herds he saw traveling south, he wrote, "not over half of the wooly beasts ever returned . . . slaughtered for their hides, worth one dollar each, at the south edge of the Llano Estecado."[16]

By the time Quanah Parker returned to the Panhandle seeking buffalo in the fall of 1878, he had to settle instead for beef cattle. Parker came with a group of several dozen Comanche as well as bands of Kiowa, Apache, and Pawnee, bitterly driven by hunger from the reservation, many of their families accompanying the expedition. Finding no buffalo herds, the hunters discovered Charles Goodnight's cattle instead, on what was now his JA Ranch, and began killing beef as a consolation. Line riders spotted the slaughter, and Goodnight rode to meet his visitors, who interviewed him (through an interpreter) at the center of an angry circle.

"Don't you know this country is ours?" one of the men demanded, to which Goodnight neatly answered that the ownership question was between Parker and the state of Texas, and if they were found to own the land, he promised to settle with them. According to his later remembrance of Quanah Parker, Goodnight told the men he was not Texan himself but from Colorado and promised that the hunters could slaughter two of his cattle every other day until they found some buffalo. But the animals they remembered hunting did not appear.[17] The tribes remained camped around Goodnight's ranch until the following spring, when the last returned with a detachment of the Tenth Cavalry.*

The same fall of Quanah Parker's arrival on the Panhandle, a group of horse thieves came to squat on Charlie's ranch. In addition to drifting after wayward cattle for the LX, "reading sign" across the Staked Plains, Siringo was assigned to trail rustlers. His time working for Beals helped to reveal his talents for man-hunting, and Bill Moore would later assign him to a posse that went after these thieves when they returned to New Mexico. But the rustlers made colorful company at first.

---

* While obviously benefiting from the bison's decline in the Panhandle, Good-night later helped save the species with the starter herd he raised with his wife, beginning with orphaned calves they adopted.

11

Squatters

Peace to William H. Bonney's ashes.

—Siringo

By the fall of 1878, Charlie was a wiry young LX fore-man when he discovered a gang of strangers one evening playing cards beneath a stand of Texas cotton-woods. One of the men was boyish, gaunt, and downy-lipped, front teeth slightly jutting, brown hair curling down his neck, at ease wearing a holstered Colt revolver. Charlie learned from the cook that the stranger was the killer known as Billy the Kid, along with some "warriors" from Lincoln County, New Mexico.[1]

Siringo was just returning from the ranch's first cattle drive north. He had ridden out after the herd once it was already on the trail, hoping to overtake the eight hundred steers in time to see them shipped by rail from Dodge to Chicago, a place he very much wanted to see. On the trail, he and a fellow rider were shaken by the sight of a large passing Cheyenne raiding party; Siringo broke into an empty house, abandoned because of news of bloody attacks, and found the evening's beef soup still sitting in a pot. After helping themselves, the cowboys reached Dodge, full of nervous evacuees asking for word of relatives, but there was no sign yet of the LX herd he had been chasing. The drive had luckily been steered off the normal route in search of water.

Once the steers reached Dodge, the cowboys divided them in two shipments, with Siringo escorting the first half on the train to Chicago.

It was his first time performing the duty of an actual cowpuncher, as he and two other hands moved along the walkway above the cattle cars, carrying a lantern for looking through the slats and using a long pole with a spike in the end to keep the steers "punched up when they got down in the crowded cars." The cattle were fed and watered in Burlington, Iowa, and the cowboys visited that "swift" city for fun. But when the train later stopped for coal during a sleet storm, the men did another check, spying for prone cattle, then running back along the top from the engine to reach the caboose before the train lurched forward; leaping car to car, Charlie slipped on the ice in his boots and just caught the foot plank's edge to save himself from falling to the tracks.[2]

Once the herd was delivered in Chicago, he cut loose but felt his bowed legs and high-heeled boots raised prices in each store he visited and among the bootblacks who followed, calling him "Texas Ranger." After an expensive dinner at the famous Palmer House with his boss David Beals, he checked into the more modest Irvine House and spent enough over several days, including a rare and expensive visit to a dentist, that he needed to return to borrow from Beals. Then he took the train back to Dodge, where his favorite horse, Whiskey Peat, was stabled and waiting. (Being away from Whiskey Peat, Siringo would remember after his time in Chicago, was almost as hard as having "sixteen jawteeth pulled.")[3] The two rode the trail home to Texas bearing a box of Cuban cigars.

There Siringo found the rough squatters on his range, scruffily at rest between exploits, transporting a group of pilfered horses from New Mexico that they meant to sell in the Panhandle.

Among the rustler gang was the young gunman known to some simply as the Kid. Named William Henry McCarty by his Irish mother, he had lived as Henry Antrim or "Kid" Antrim until recently, when he started going by "William Bonney." Born in New York in 1859, Billy and his brother had followed their widowed mother, Mary McCarty, on a hardscrabble tour of America—Indianapolis, Wichita, Denver, Santa Fe (where Mary married Henry Antrim in 1873), and Silver City, New Mexico, where she died of consumption and Billy was first arrested at sixteen. He fled to Arizona, then another crime sent him back to New Mexico, where he fought with the Regulators in the Lincoln County War of 1878. Part of his lore was that he had killed a white man for each year of his short life, leaving Apache and Mexicans off his death tally. The real total was probably much lower.

With a widowed Irish mother of his own, Siringo found the Kid, or Billy, surprisingly companionable despite his dark reputation. Charlie was just in his early twenties, the Kid almost nineteen and nearly his size; each commanded the respect of a group of tough men. Neither had known his own father very long, and each endured a stepfather he resented, though Billy suffered his longer.

Siringo became acquainted with the other young outlaws who rode with this man-child across the Southwest, taking horses and cattle and rowdy comforts as they found them, killing when challenged or merely annoyed, escaping small-town jails when caught. The men camped on Charlie's range and reported for meals when the mess bell rang as if they worked for the LX, but still he found the gang good company.

After a few friendly days of cards and drinking, target shooting, and enjoying the Cuban smokes, Charlie let Billy keep the meerschaum cigar holder he had bought for himself in Chicago;

in return, the Kid signed and gifted him a bound novel he was carrying. Some writers claim it was Cervantes, picturing the Kid escapading around the Southwest with *Don Quixote* in his saddlebag. Whatever the novel was, Siringo did not manage to keep it to the end of his life.*

The gang had recently killed a sheriff and his deputy back in Lincoln County, New Mexico, before they had stolen the horses from the Seven River Warriors (their enemies in the Lincoln County War) and headed to Texas to sell them. When he rode into Tascosa, the Kid was leading a handsome Arabian sorrel racehorse, Dandy Dick, ridden by the sheriff of Lincoln County, William Brady, on the April day he was killed.[4] In addition to regularly stealing livestock from the Mescalero Apache, the gang was also taking Panhandle cattle to rebrand, traveling the three hundred miles between Tascosa and White Oaks, New Mexico, to steal and resell. Henry Hoyt, the underemployed doctor who had learned cowboying from Siringo, befriended Billy in Tascosa, reporting that he had "clear blue eyes that could look one through and through." The region had "not a semblance of government or law . . . consequently it was the Mecca for the outlaw, the gunman, and his kind."[5] When the young doctor finally left the Panhandle for New Mexico, it was on that same stolen Arabian, Dandy Dick, signed over to him by W. H. Bonney.

One of the Kid's cohorts in camp was a lean, square-jawed Texas gunman named Henry Brown. When the rustlers moved on from the ranch later that fall, not all wanted to return with the Kid to New Mexico, where they were wanted men. The group

---

* There is a remote chance the book burned up in a fire at Siringo's son Lee Roy's house. But, according to J. Frank Dobie, in his introduction to the 1950 edition of *A Texas Cowboy*, when Charlie's remaining books were sold by his daughter Viola to Dawson's Book Shop in Hollywood in April 1940, the sale catalog made no mention of either Cervantes or the outlaw.

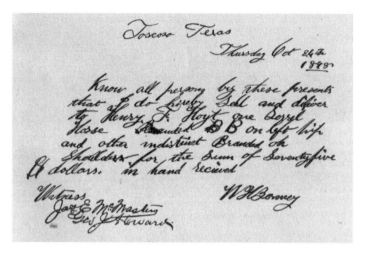

A letter from William H. Bonney himself, selling the Kid's stolen horse to Charlie's LX friend (and later his physician) Henry Hoyt, in 1878.

Riata and Spurs / *Author's collection*

dispersed, but Tom O'Folliard continued loyally on with Billy. Henry Brown traveled with another of the gang, Fred Waite, across the northern border into Indian Territory to hide out with Waite's Chickasaw family and so escaped the shooting fates of O'Folliard and the Kid. Much as he seemed to admire the Kid, Siringo would never see him again, but he met up several years later with Henry Brown.

In the fall of 1880, a posse of cowmen was assembled out of several Texas Panhandle ranches that had lost stock to the Kid and finally had had enough. Siringo was sent by Bill Moore from the LX Ranch, given a wagon, and instructed to choose some fighting cowboys and join the expedition into the New Mexico Territory to find missing LX cattle and, if possible, take part of the capture of Billy himself and share the bounty. Once across the border, Siringo went to Las Vegas, New Mexico, to buy provisions while the others camped along the Pecos River in Anton Chico. Killing time waiting for a feed shipment, he lost the supply money playing monte, but a sympathetic merchant allowed him to charge the lot to his ranch.

He then drove a full wagon to rejoin the posse at Anton Chico, where Billy and his latest gang had recently crept into town at night to steal more horses. Siringo's outfit headed toward the new gold-mining town of White Oaks, forty miles northeast of Lincoln, and there the company met Pat Garrett, the lanky former buffalo hunter, whom Billy called a "long-legged son of a bitch." The newly elected sheriff of Lincoln County, Garrett knew all parties well and was going after the Kid (and the reward fee) in earnest and with the patience of an experienced hunter.

Garrett took a dim view of amateur posses, a "whirlwind of lunatics" he called one group of would-be heroes.[6] Siringo and Bob Roberson of the Littlefield ranch decided to loan several of their men to Garrett's cause and carry on after their missing cattle, their primary mission. They rode through a snowstorm, passing the smoking stump of a road ranch where Billy and his gang had fought a battle with lawmen several days earlier, killing a deputy sheriff named Jim Carlyle. After marching through the dark, the Kid's gang then stole new horses and saddles. Carlyle's possemen then torched the ranch hideout to prevent the rustlers' return.

Late on the night of December 19, 1880, Garrett and his men (including six loaned from the Panhandle posse) lay in wait for the Kid's gang to appear on the snow-covered road near the old Indian hospital building in Fort Sumner. They knew that Manuela Bowdre, wife of one of the gang members, was staying nearby and was a likely first stop for their night on the town. Hearing Garrett's command in the dark to raise his hands, Billy's friend

Tom O'Folliard (who had visited the LX two years earlier with the Kid) reached for his pistol. Garrett and posseman Lon Chambers shot O'Folliard, his horse bolting as he screamed from his wounds. "Don't shoot, Garrett," O'Folliard pleaded before he died. "I'm killed." Garrett's men lifted him down and discovered he had been hit just under the heart. The other men had escaped during the shooting.[7]

On a freezing night days later, Garrett trapped the Kid's gang inside a windowless old sheeperder's dwelling outside a place called Stinking Springs. Surrounding the rock and adobe building at three in the morning, Garrett's men opted not to risk a gunfight inside the dark stone house but waited in the cold until Charlie Bowdre appeared in the doorway in the predawn. He was holding a bag of feed and wearing a sombrero, cutting a figure very like the Kid himself, who was rumored to be sporting one. Garrett killed him where he stood. Bowdre managed to blurt "I wish . . . I wish" as he faded.[8]

Billy had already pulled his pony inside the cold rock house, and after the shooting of Bowdre, the rest of the gang meant to pull in their tied horses as well and mount up for a dramatic gallop out the open doorway. But, according to the recollection of cowboy and lawman Jim East,[9] the possemen had shot through two horses' tethers before another mount being tugged inside was shot dead in the entrance by Garrett, blocking Billy's escape in a grisly checkmate. The remaining men had spent days without food, water, or heat, and so Garrett cooked a fragrant meal of bacon and beans nearby and waited for them to surrender. The men could be heard trying to dig gunports into the windowless walls, but it was useless; the Kid reluctantly gave up the standoff and a white kerchief on a stick emerged from the chimney. Garrett delivered his prisoners first to Fort Sumner and then Las Vegas, New Mexico. After he was sentenced to be hanged, Billy returned to Garrett's custody at the Lincoln County jail, which was really Garrett's office on the second floor of the courthouse.

The Kid had been captured, but emanations of the outlaw followed Siringo and the remaining possemen all the long way home to Texas. They spent a night in the rock house at Stinking Springs where Manuela Bowdre was widowed by Pat Garrett, noting the marks where the gang had tried to dig gunports before surrendering, and they camped and rested their recovered stock in the place known as Los Portales ("the porches"), a natural limestone ledge near an alkaline lake and freshwater springs southeast of Fort Sumner. Charlie admired the three-sided stone corral the rustlers had used to hold stolen livestock, and he slept beneath the rock overhang the men called Billy's Cave.

The Kid would escape from the Lincoln jail in April 1881, killing his two guards while Garrett was out in White Oaks collecting taxes. Siringo may have been personally conflicted about shooting the Kid, whom he had liked in person, or simply had wanted to finish his mission retrieving LX cattle. While Garrett returned to his manhunt, Siringo and company carried on searching for their steers.

He had yet to join Pinkerton's, but Charlie was already thinking like a natural detective, playacting undercover to get information, adopting the part of the Texan on the run from trouble, his default alias in his future life. Approaching one old witness who had seen a herd of clearly stolen livestock hurried past, he scribbled a kind of lineup of fictitious brands surrounding that of the LX, which the old man identified. He found some LX hides at the slaughterhouse of rancher Pat Coghlan, "a large, portly looking half-breed Irishman" known as the "King of Tularosa." Siringo wrote, "I introduced myself as having been sent from the Panhandle after the cattle he had purchased from the 'Kid.' He at first said I couldn't have them, but finally changed his tone, when I told him that I had a crowd at White Oaks, and that my instructions were to take them by force if I couldn't secure them in any other way."[10]

On his way toward White Oaks after stolen steers, he received some directions from a seeming stranger that were overly precise. It was a setup by rancher Coghlan. Charlie's mule was shot out from beneath him on the mountain trail. The assassins had just missed him, and Siringo and his bleeding mule carried on after his cattle.

Weeks after the Kid's celebrated escape, Siringo brought some of his recovered steers back through Sunnyside, New Mexico, seven miles outside Fort Sumner. He carried his rifle into a store where he meant to buy feed as well as a missing screw for his Winchester. Reports of Billy's escape had just reached the town when Charlie entered, a leathery young cowboy, wild from the trail and rifle freed from his saddle, sending two employees out the back of the building in a panic. The proprietor nervously explained, "Well, I'll be damned! We thought you was Billy the Kid. You look just like him."

He soon tested the resemblance at a Mexican dance in Fort Sumner with Manuela Bowdre, the much-admired widow of Billy's associate recently killed by Pat Garrett. Mrs. Bowdre, whom Siringo called "a good-looking young Mexican woman," had once shared a house with the Kid and her husband, drawing the kind of talk that followed a woman who lives with outlaws. Charlie and the widow Bowdre danced until almost dawn, when he accompanied her to the door of her room, anxious to be invited in.[11] "I tried to persuade her to allow me to go inside and talk a while," he remembered chastely. "But she insisted that her mother would object." Instead, he "bade her good-night." If she had been interested in carrying their passions inside, Charlie learned from her months later, she had a good reason not to: hiding in the dark, just beyond the locked door and recognizing Charlie's voice, was her secret guest, the Kid himself, armed and waiting.[12]

After seven trying months, the group the New Mexico newspapers called the "Panhandle boys" returned triumphantly with their recovered herd of several thousand cattle. Upon arrival, Charlie learned that the manager, Outlaw Bill Moore, had left the LX to tend to his own ranch affairs. David Beals nominated Siringo to take over Moore's duties, but other partners judged him too "wild," and he was denied the position.

A month after Siringo's homecoming, Pat Garrett surprised Billy the Kid for the last time, on the night of July 14, 1881, in Pete Maxwell's house in Fort Sumner. Fortunately for Garrett, he had cowboyed on the Maxwell ranch during his own early days in New Mexico, before having a falling-out with Pete, and knew well the abandoned officers' quarters where Pete still lived and the Kid was said to rendezvous with Pete's teenage sister, Paulita Maxwell. It was probably Billy's love for Paulita that had brought him back to Fort Sumner despite being a widely wanted man.

Pat Garrett, the relentless manhunter who killed Billy the Kid, then defended his actions against "credulous idiots" in a classic book.
Riata and Spurs / *Author's collection*

With two deputies outside in the dark, Garrett stole into Pete Maxwell's bedroom. He woke Pete and was speaking softly to him in his bed, sitting beside Maxwell's pillow, when a hatless stranger in stocking feet appeared in the doorway, holding a revolver and a butcher knife, demanding, "*Quién es? Quién es?*" ("Who is there?") He had come over to Maxwell's house from one of the adjoining buildings, hoping to cut himself some beef to cook for his midnight supper, and spotted the dark silhouettes of the two deputies watching outside. But these would be his last words. Garrett recognized the figure approaching the bed as the Kid, and Pete confirmed, "That's him." Garrett fired.

The Kid still held his Colt but failed to shoot back. Garrett fired a second bullet that missed, but his first had been to the heart and ensured the Kid would join "his many victims." The following day, Billy's body was washed and freshly dressed and buried in the old post cemetery in Fort Sumner. A stave from a picket fence was used to mark the site, and a passage from Job read over him. He had lived a long ragged life for twenty-one. Siringo would write about Billy in five of his books, including a life of the Kid, spending more words on him than on any other person save himself.

Readers who had never been west of Hoboken nevertheless learned to lionize distant frontier figures and their murky violence: after the shooting, reports appeared that a jar had turned up in New York containing the Kid's trigger finger, with which he had killed his victims (as well as possibly signed Siringo's book), and that people paid to see the floating finger on the chance it originated on their young hero's hand; the outlaw's alleged skeleton also went on tour, drawing true believers as well as the ghoulishly curious and Southern newspaper editors who worried about "bogus Billies": "Worshippers of the hero can never know of a verity that they are not paying for a sight at some ninny who never murdered a man in his life—some soft person from the East, may be, and even, perhaps, some Sunday-school superintendent."[13]

No part of the Kid seemed to have remained buried, despite the angry denials of the man who put Billy in the ground, Pat Garrett: "Some presuming swindlers have claimed to have the Kid's skull on exhibition, or one of his fingers, or some other portion of his body, and one medical gentleman has persuaded credulous idiots that he has all the bones strung upon wires."[14] According to Siringo, who was not a witness, Garrett finally had his outlaw dug up to count all his fingers, but this is probably not true. Garrett knew where he was. After seeing eight fanciful dime novels about the Kid appear, and driven by rumors that he had killed Billy in a "cowardly" manner, Garrett undertook his 1882 chronicle of the manhunt, *The Authentic Life of Billy the Kid*, with his journalist friend Ash Upson, aimed largely at the "credulous idiots."

After rehearsing much of the familiar lore of the Kid's outlaw career, Garrett's narrative abruptly switches to a steely, first-person manhunt story: how many desert miles the sheriff had chased Billy on horseback, the number of Winchester shots traded, the dimensions of the outlaw's cave hideouts, straight through to the fatal night waiting in the dark bedroom, the bootless outlaw holding a revolver and a butcher knife and demanding, "*Quién es?*" Garrett would end his book rather defensively, "The Kid's body lies undisturbed in the grave, and I speak of what I know."[15]

Four years after their Texas meeting under the cottonwoods, Siringo did see one of Billy's surviving gang again. Charlie was delivering a herd for David Beals to Caldwell, Kansas, a growing cattle town on the northern border of the Indian Territory. As he arrived, the outlaw Henry Brown was there to welcome him,

Siringo was surprised to see outlaw Henry Brown
in Caldwell, wearing a city marshal's badge.

Riata and Spurs / *Author's collection*

wearing a mustache, blue uniform, and gold star of a city marshal. "I shook hands with him," Siringo wrote, "and he begged me not to give him away, as he said he had reformed and was going to lead an upright life in the future."

Often short of law enforcement, the West was full of stories of nervy gunmen hired as peace officers who lapsed back into outlawry once badged. Henry Brown was a usefully furious lawman in a rowdy town that needed bossing; even when he later married a nice young local woman, rumors floated that he must have threatened her to gain her hand. Siringo had by now worked for an impressive collection of Texas cattlemen, and following stolen cattle for Beals had clearly honed his talent for tracking fugitives. Yet, when he met Henry Brown again in Caldwell, Siringo agreed to keep quiet about the marshal's desperado past. It was a promise he would later regret, as the marshal's leaf would not stay turned.

12

Mamie

Charlie Siringo wants every cowpuncher, "nester" and Chinaman
in the United States to know that he makes a specialty of fine cigars
and tobacco.

—*Caldwell* (Kansas) *Daily Standard*, 1884

C aldwell sat along the six-million-acre Cherokee Strip,
which ran the northern edge of the Indian Territory in
what would become Oklahoma. Originally a stop along
the Chisholm Trail, the town began to thrive by the early 1880s,
due to the arrival of the Santa Fe Railroad. After the institu-
tion of quarantine laws against Texas cattle traveling farther into
Kansas, cattlemen discovered they could skirt the law by leas-
ing land from the Cherokee and Arapaho tribes on the side of
the border just south of Caldwell, then move their livestock from
these holding ranches directly onto Kansas trains to market.

David Beals leased property from the Cherokee for his cow
ponies two miles southeast of town and hired Siringo to over-
see the operation. After the fight with the buffalo hunters in the
Dodge City Saloon, Beals had given Charlie the job that took
him down to the Panhandle. Now Beals had brought him back
to Kansas, to Caldwell, where Charlie would meet his wife. The
growing "Queen City of the Border," with its eleven saloons,
would also be the place where Charlie stopped being a cowboy
and started writing about it.

In the fall of 1882, Siringo bought his own house lot on Osage Street in Caldwell and contracted to build. Then, before starting his Kansas chapter for Beals, he took the long route home to Matagorda Bay to retrieve his mother and bring her to Caldwell. First he enjoyed a sentimental train ride to Saint Louis, reuniting with his sister, Catherine, and meeting her daughters as well as checking into the Planters House, where his scrap with another bellboy had once led to his departure. Next Charlie headed to Galveston, where he looked up his mother's brother, found some boyhood pals in what the hurricane had left of Indianola, and at last returned to Cashs Creek, where Sam Grant had shot him. His mother's only qualm about leaving was abandoning her woodpile.[1]

In Caldwell, Siringo already regretted his promise to keep quiet about city marshal Henry Brown's outlaw past with Billy the Kid. Since arriving, Brown had shot a cowboy named Boyle "in a cold-blooded murder" and killed a Pawnee named Spotted Horse, a familiar figure seen panhandling and stealing around Caldwell, who Brown claimed had reached for his pistol. These killings nevertheless impressed local businessmen, who gave the Marshal a Winchester inlaid with gold and silver and inscribed with thanks for his "services rendered." It took a gunfighter to deal with gunfighters, went the local thinking, as Henry Brown's predecessor in the marshal job had been only the latest killed in a street battle.

Siringo made a morning habit of visiting a small grocery in Caldwell, where he was allowed to stab open a fresh watermelon and eat slices off his knife as he talked with the young clerk, who especially liked to hear about the cowboy's recent adventures hunting Billy the Kid. One day Charlie was at his usual place when the daughter of another regular customer entered the store, seemingly charmed by the long-haired cowboy eating off his blade. She was Mamie Lloyd, a fifteen-year-old who had come to Caldwell with her parents from Shelbyville, Illinois. The two admired each other sufficiently that Siringo returned the next day in case she reappeared, his hair neat and wearing a bright red sash, celluloid collar, and green necktie. They did meet again, the clerk remembered, and Siringo soon made an evening visit to the grocery sporting brand-new high-heeled boots, "with the picture of a steer embroidered on the leg and two yellow silk tassels hanging from their straps." He explained that he was going to church that night and needed pointers on "prayer meeting etiquette."[2] Dressed in his cowboy church outfit, Charlie attended the ceremony with Mamie and her friend May Beals, the niece of his boss.

Siringo found himself characteristically smitten or "locoed" by the dark-eyed Mamie Lloyd. After being ordered to lead yet another drive for Beals, he was drawn up short by his sudden feelings. "I wanted her, and wanted her badly," he admitted, "therefore I went to work with a brave heart and my face lined with brass." Mamie was not just young but also her father's only daughter, so Siringo did some "considerable figuring with the old gent."[3] Within days of their meeting, they were engaged and quickly married at the Philips Hotel in the larger neighboring town of Wellington.

Strange as it might seem later, a man in his twenties marrying a teenage girl was still common enough on the frontier. People often married as soon as practical to have children and did not expect to live all that long. (This would be sadly true of Mamie.) In fact, at the time, 82 percent of Caldwell's women between twenty and thirty were married.[4] Siringo took part in a roundup and then a drive to Texas for Beals, returned to Caldwell and his new wife after guiding another herd back up the trail, then received new orders to head out yet again. Much as he respected Beals as the "best boss I ever had," he was furious, and after sending the horses "up the Territory line" and loading the wagon with chuck, he turned over the job to his friend Charlie Sprague. "I suddenly swore off cowpunching." He was no longer a cowboy except at heart.[5]

After a young manhood spent on the trail and visiting "Sunday girls" in cow towns, he was now a family man supporting his young wife and his mother. There were other reasons to quit the trail when he did: ranchers had begun protecting their investments with barbed wire, gradually closing the open range with

Siringo's store in Caldwell, the town where he first put on suspenders and secretly took up writing.
Riata and Spurs / *Author's collection*

the "devil's rope," signaling the end of the life men like Siringo had known.

He had enough to rent a vacant room on Caldwell's main strip and set up shop as a merchant "on a six-bit scale." It was a sudden if "sensible tumble" from the cowboy ranks. "Charley Siringo has quit the range," announced the *Caldwell Advance* in September 1883, "and opened up a place next door to Thrailkill's, where he will keep the best cigars, tobacco, confectionery and choice fruits. Charley is a sober, steady and industrious young man, and we hope he will prosper in his new undertaking."[6]

Siringo lost his red vaquero sash, a Texas item difficult to replace in Kansas, and was forced to wear suspenders for the first time in his life like a proper merchant.[7] When Shanghai Pierce later visited Caldwell and had dinner with the new couple, he remarked on the change, and Siringo said Mamie had confessed to burning it. Siringo was soon advertising oysters (delivered to him by train on ice three times each week) in Caldwell newspapers as well as ice cream and "a good lunch, with a hot cup of coffee—none of your weak jim-crow stuff, but genuine cowpuncher coffee that will almost stand alone—thrown in."[8]

But his biggest success was his specially designed "Oklahoma Boomer" cigar, popular with cowboys who had delivered their herds. His distinctive painted sign, showing a cowboy roping a longhorn by the heel, hung by chains from the top frame of the iron Bluff Creek bridge on the edge of town. For many riders, Siringo's sign was the first thing they saw of Caldwell, and likewise many a departing cowboy, a Boomer clutched in his teeth, would plug it on his way out.

One evening in early 1884, the parlor of Caldwell's Hotel Leland was crowded with townspeople excited to hear from the old man standing in its center, a blind phrenologist in a dark suit

Siringo's sign depicted a nostalgic Texas scene outside his Kansas town.
Riata and Spurs / *Author's collection*

who promised to reveal people's inner natures just by laying his trained hands upon their skulls.

At this time, phrenologists toured all the Kansas cow towns, drawing crowds to hotels and churches, schools and YMCAs, eager to have their lives charted or hear something intimate revealed about their neighbor. Reading dozens of heads each night, these experts could identify selfishness stored in the side head, intellectual talents in the front, or a stubborn character by a religious bump on top. "Your greatest duty to your children and yourselves is an examination of your heads," Professor J. H. Patty assured his audiences. Most on the circuit were called "professor," except for Master Walter Vrooman, the fifteen-year-old "Boy Phrenologist" of Topeka; at the other end of the spectrum was Professor O. S. Fowler, age seventy-three when his stand in Kansas City was billed as his last in the West.[9] Women were rare in the profession, though some combined phrenology with fortune-telling and its romantic applications.

For audiences in Lawrence, Kansas, a Professor Randleman (educated by Professor Carr of Illinois) explained how to spot a criminal: "There are more criminals who are short men than there are of tall men. Tall heads are not criminals' heads. A criminal head is short and round and full in the side-head, and flat on the top."[10] This belief would later aid the boyish Charlie Siringo as he nestled unsuspected among other short criminal types. He was also (through his Irish mother) descended from what phrenology disparaged as one of the "low-brow" races, as opposed to the long, smooth foreheads of the Anglos and European aristocracy.*

The most widely traveled blind phrenologist touring Kansas at this time was Professor F. L. Grover, of Topeka, a "model delineator of character," who often added a separate bonus temperance lecture for the men. Up close, the people gathered at Caldwell's Hotel Leland could see the professor's eyes were dead, yet he somehow gave a look of frightening scrutiny, intimidating at least one person in the audience in particular. Holding to the back of an empty chair, the old man said a few words about his exotic discipline, then asked for volunteers for a head reading.

The crowd called for Marshal Henry Brown, who was both respected and feared, to have his character delineated. Brown's rough past before coming to Caldwell remained a mystery to all but Siringo. Though understandably skeptical of phrenology, which held that most criminals were short and small-headed like

---

* Phrenology's racial designations of "high-brow" and "low-brow" have stubbornly survived as cultural distinctions.

himself, Siringo was intrigued by watching a blind seer and curious to learn what Marshal Brown might say under examination. "He knew better than any one else in the audience as to what was in his head," Siringo remembered, "and he didn't want to risk having his faults told."[11] As the chants continued, the Marshal grudgingly took the chair to put his secrets beneath the old man's fingers.

Though the worst details did not emerge, Siringo was impressed by the harsh reading Brown received. "Had this man not been blind, I would have attributed his knowledge to his ability to read faces," he wrote. As he left the chair, Brown was clearly angered by his treatment, which seemed unbefitting a marshal. "He heard some very uncomplimentary remarks said against himself," Siringo noted. "But I knew that the phrenologist was telling the truth."[12] The old man next questioned the bravery of a professional tracker from town, who understandably stomped out. Then he praised Siringo's charming teenage wife, Mamie, before the people finally called Charlie to the chair of honor.

The blind man found a bump on his head and explained that it revealed Siringo's mule-like stubbornness, a streak that suited him for just three professions—newspaper editor, stock rancher, or detective. That prediction would stay in his mind. In later years, explaining how he came to the detective life after growing up a cowboy, Siringo often quoted the blind old man who read his skull.

"A man who has followed the life of a desperado and robber is more than liable to wander back to his old pursuits again," the *Caldwell Journal* concluded about Henry Brown after it was too late. Months after being insulted by the phrenologist, Marshal Brown returned to his outlaw form, violently ending his pact with Siringo. Recruiting his deputy Ben Wheeler (also known as Ben Robertson) and two local cowboys as accomplices, Brown targeted the bank in Medicine Lodge, Kansas, for a robbery.

The four gunmen rode in shortly after the Medicine Valley Bank had opened on the rainy morning of April 30, 1884, tying their horses out back and leaving one of the cowboys, William Smith, to guard them. The quiet of the bank was broken by the gunmen shouting at the cashier and president to throw up their hands. (The other cowboy, John Wesley, had probably been brought to guard the bank's clerk, who was luckily away at the post office when they entered.)[13]

The bank president and his officers had planned to cooperate with any holdups, preferring to stay alive and perhaps see their money recovered. On the day of the robbery, cashier George Geppert lifted his hands as ordered while sitting at his window, then turned to see if bank president Wylie Payne was obeying. That was enough to draw four shots from Wheeler and Wesley, three hitting Geppert. At his desk, Payne had looked up when he heard "Hold up your hands!" to see Henry Brown in his rain slicker standing in the latticed doorway to his office. Payne reached for his pistol in the desk drawer, and Brown shot him once, dropping him to the floor. With the bankers' plan to surrender the money and survive now abandoned, Geppert struggled into the vault, spinning the combination dial to lock it as a final gesture before he died.

A minister across the rainy street heard the shots and alerted the town's marshal, who was fired upon by William Smith, guarding the horses, and then by Henry Brown, one marshal shooting at another, from the front of the bank. The shots continued as Brown's crew fled through the rear exit, without the money, galloping out of town through the heavy rain toward the Gypsum Hills.

A man named Barney O'Connor left his poker game when he saw the gang ride out, saddled his horse, and followed them through the downpour, sighting the thieves as they crossed the Medicine River. A brave group from town joined him, trading shots with the outlaws until the robbers made a bad turn and sought cover in a deep washout, where standing water rose around them as the rain continued, considerably weakening their resolve. Brown, the sopping, feared lawman of Caldwell, was first to surrender.

The wet prisoners were brought back to Medicine Lodge jail in the early afternoon, allowed to dry off, and posed for a sullen picture commemorating their failure. Brown stands at the center

A forlorn Henry Brown and accomplices await their fate after failing to rob the Medicine Lodge bank.

Kansas Historical Society, State Archive

of his gang before the rough wooden jail, pant legs tucked into his boots as if he is about to ride off, but is instead detained by his possemen. Outrage over the murders had already spread through town and drawn a sizable lynch mob, but a local attorney convinced the crowd to let the prisoners first tell their story to the law. Henry Brown begged on his knees for mercy, prompting one reporter to ask, "Can this be the man who has held Caldwell in terror for so long?"[14]

Brown had enough time to write his young wife, whom he had married only weeks before: "If a mob does not kill us, we will come out all right after while. Maude, I did not shoot anyone, and did not want the others to kill anyone; but they did, and that is all there is about it. Now, my darling wife, goodbye." Of course, he had, in fact, shot someone, and a large mob did return that night around nine to take control of the jail and drag the robbers out.

When they reached the jailhouse door, the doomed men tried to run. Henry Brown was killed almost immediately by a farmer's shotgun blast, while Ben Wheeler ran into the night, bullets hitting his body, shattering his arm, and severing two fingers from one hand. Wheeler "begged piteously," according to reports, and promised to give other information if his death could be just delayed. The crowd would not have it. Wheeler and the cowboy accomplices were given a chance to express their regret to the community, then fitted with ropes thrown over a strong elm branch and hoisted into the dark. Siringo later published a cinematically vivid account of this scene, in which Ben Wheeler runs into the night, flames on his coat from a close-range shot making him a bright, perfect target. But Charlie was not a witness.

He was back in Caldwell instead and could hardly be shocked by what Henry Brown had done. He finally unburdened himself to the *Caldwell Daily Standard* about the disgraced marshal, starting with the first time he met Brown, along with Billy the Kid's gang, under the cottonwoods in the fall of 1878. "From Charlie Siringo we have obtained the following particulars," announced the paper's extra edition, giving bloody revelations of not only Brown's exploits with the Kid but another suspected murder by Deputy Wheeler back in Texas.[15]

Decades later, Siringo's friend George "Pawnee Bill" Lillie remembered that, with Brown and his deputy both dead, Caldwell's mayor had offered the job of city marshal to Siringo while the town searched for another permanent lawman. Siringo accepted, according to Pawnee Bill, but refused to wear a badge while patrolling around town for some months, explaining that his Colt would be "star enough."[16] While there was a petition that spring to make him assistant marshal, there is no record he ever legally held the marshal's job. But it would have been understandable if he briefly performed its duties out of regret over keeping Henry Brown's secret from the town. A Caldwell paper later reported that Siringo won a raffle for the late marshal's inlaid bridle.

13

Dull Knife's Return

Caldwell may have been the site of Siringo's brief career as a merchant, but it was more importantly where he became the original cowboy author. It has long been assumed he began writing for the reasons he gives in the opening pages of *A Texas Cowboy; or, Fifteen Years on the Hurricane Deck of a Spanish Pony* (1885), that he was an untutored man of the range in need of money: "My excuse for writing this book is money—and lots of it." Siringo, turning thirty, understandably thought that he was a "stove up cowpuncher" whose frontier days were behind him, and that, with a family to support, he might set his adventures down in a cowboy memoir. He may have begun as soon as he put on his merchant's suspenders in 1883, having left the cattle life as the open-range days were already on the wane. Ranchers were buying up land and stringing barbed wire and trailing fewer and smaller herds. Charlie began a work of celebration and mourning for the raucous cowboy life that was ending, deploring some recent changes along the way.

But the literary market was hardly certain for such a book when he began writing it. In fact, no one had published one.

Cowboys, whose bunkhouse reading choices were often an old Sears catalog, a Bible, or rare well-thumbed *Police Gazette*, had yet to write their own literature. It was a story in the *Police Gazette* that led ultimately to Charlie's writing career: the cowboys working for David Beals on his pony ranch south of Caldwell had collected enough money in a swear jar in one day in the winter of 1882–83 to send away for a newspaper subscription. In polling the men's preferences, Siringo learned that two Texas cowboys, being illiterate, voted for the "wicked" *Gazette* because they could follow its lurid illustrations. Their choice had the majority, and Charlie soon found himself reading a continuing story in the *Police Gazette* called "Potts Turning Paris Inside Out." The story's hero, a preacher named Potts, had "made a raise of several hundred thousand dollars and was over in Paris blowing it in," Charlie explained. "I became interested in the story, and envied Mr. Potts very much. I wished for a few hundred thousand so I could do likewise; I lay awake one whole night trying to study up a plan by which I could make the desired amount."[1]

The commercial book he claimed he came up with was ghastly sounding enough to probably be the truth. In search of an "untrodden field" of literature to exploit, he decided to write a "'nigger' love story" set along the Colorado River where he once disastrously tried to peddle wares out of his schooner. The novel involved the courtship of an African American couple, until the story went off track in the first chapter, with the man going to prison for stealing a neighbor's hog while his lover elopes with a carpetbagger. It was his novel's running mercifully away from him that led Charlie to throw these execrable pages in the fire and turn to what was his natural subject as a storyteller—the "history of my own short, rugged life," which became *A Texas Cowboy*. But even as he quietly worked on his book of cowboy remembrances, he was also secretly chronicling his present life for a Kansas newspaper column. He just didn't yet dare use his real name.

The *Sumner County Standard* was published in Wellington, Kansas, the neighboring town where he had been married. Charlie wrote the column Caldwell Flashes as the paper's secret correspondent, signing with his old trail nickname Dull Knife.* The weekly column appeared through most of 1885 and can be read like an anonymous journal of Siringo's life in Kansas. As the *Standard* rightly boasted of Dull Knife, "our Caldwell correspondent gets up a newsy letter."[2]

This mysterious Dull Knife already wrote confidently. When Chicago reporters arrived in town, "having rigged themselves up as two wandering cowboys hunting a job," he noted, one of them "loomed up like a thoroughbred under a star-spangled sombrero." Another column began to tell about the town tailor's "new arrival" and then, after speculating how the baby came to be, ended: "Well, we've struck a stump, don't know how to finish that sentence, but let it go and guess at the balance."

Week to week, Dull Knife knowledgeably anticipated the great livestock "die up" that would destroy so many western ranches in the winter of 1886–87. He reported what he heard about dire conditions in the Indian Territory from visiting cattlemen, including "Wichita Charlie," who told Dull Knife of seeing dead cattle "as high as thirty in a pile," then complained at being made a "news pump." Dull Knife cheekily ran the man's full objection, "'Hey there! What are you doing with your book

---

* I discovered these columns while doing an ordinary online search of old Kansas newspapers using Siringo's name. This brought up the mention of "Charlie Siringo" in one column where its anonymous reporter was defensively denying Siringo was the author. When I saw the Caldwell Flashes columns were signed "Dull Knife," his trail nickname and an alias he later competed under in a Denver rodeo, I knew he was the writer.

out? You ain't putting down what I told you, with a view to putting it in a newspaper, are you?'"

But he was. The columns also showed the growing influence in town of boomerism for coming white settlement in the Indian Territory. Siringo had arrived in Caldwell as a hired cowboy and now as a merchant came to join the town boomer committee to make Caldwell a jumping-off point, "the place to start for Oklahoma from." Dull Knife's column of May 7, 1885, notes, "Caldwell is well fixed now [that] she has got two Oklahoma organizations." He also reports, "Mr. Mark Miller flopped over to the boomer side Wednesday night. Look out, Mark, or the cattle men will go back on you." Dull Knife's other fight was the debate over the town going dry: "Little groups of men at every corner discussing the damnable law that cut their morning drams off so short."

The columns betrayed several clues about their mysterious author: that he was a resentful Southerner when it came to the recent war (deploring the "lies" in Union memoirs being donated to the town's new war library or the fact that Black federal soldiers guarded near the town); that he often quoted visiting cowboy friends from the Panhandle; and that, perhaps most damning of all, he claimed in print not to be Charlie Siringo.

He did not exactly keep himself out of the column. In March 1885, he reported the cash drawer of "C. A. Siringo" being robbed, and on another date explained with false modesty how "Charlie Siringo by the skin of his teeth walked off with the tournament prize" at the July Fourth cowboy competition. Dull Knife related when Siringo bought out his business partner and when he took on another. But an item about Nick Kiser, "our little dude gambler," brought the identity issue to a head. "Mr. Nick Kiser don't like to be called a dude," reported the secret columnist. "He says if he could find out who Dull Knife is he would put a mules head on him, one that he would chaw hay with. Someone hissed him onto Charlie Siringo while we stood off at a distance and laughed way down in our sleeve. We feel for you, Charlie, but can't reach you."

In the fall of 1885, Dull Knife noted some landmark events for Siringo. First came the September 11 Caldwell Flashes item, "W. A. Sturm has bought Charley Siringo's confectionery store." By the September 25 column, he was finally ready to announce his book: "The Queen of the Border has just given birth to an author and in about two months the eastern 'kids' will be dreaming of the enchantment of a Texas cowboy or fifteen years on the hurricane deck of a Spanish pony. Charles A. Siringo is the author and we wish him a long and happy career in his new field of labor." His days as a merchant and secret correspondent were at an end. He was about to become an author, selling the "enchantment" of the cowboy life and the open range he missed so keenly.

Issued by Umbdenstock and Company, the book had an unmistakable authenticity and frontier language. He'd never written a book before, never yet been sued for writing anything, and published it without fear or much editorial oversight, explaining at its end, "Now, dear reader in bidding you adieu, will say: should you not be pleased with the substance of this *book*, I've got nothing to say in defense, as I gave you the best I had in my little shop."[3]

It was the freest and most natural work ever to appear on the subject, and this first small printing sold out, marketed by subscription, hawked at railroad newsstands and in smoking cars, and tirelessly hand peddled by Charlie himself. Eventually, J. Frank Dobie wrote, other editions put out by larger houses would reach a larger audience: "Many a ranch hand who had ridden a cattle train to Kansas City, Omaha, Chicago or some other

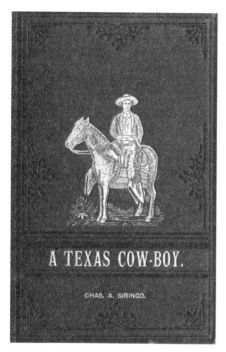

The cover of the 1886 edition of *A Texas Cowboy*.

A Texas Cowboy / *Internet Archive*

market and then came back home in a chair car bought a copy of Charlie Siringo's book from the butcher boy." It was also bought by would-be cowboys working in big cities and midwestern towns.*

Siringo left Caldwell in the spring of 1886 with his young wife and the couple's new baby daughter, Viola, for Chicago. Selling his small run of volumes had made him cocky, and in Chicago he meant to publish a larger edition of his new cowboy memoir and perhaps, despite his grade school education, become a man of Western letters.

---

* For his 1950 introduction to *A Texas Cowboy*, perhaps the finest extant piece of writing about Siringo, J. Frank Dobie proved that under the imprint of five publishers—Umbdenstock, Siringo and Dobson, Eagle Publishing, Rand McNally, J. S. Ogilvie (after the copyright expired in 1914)—it had sold in the high hundreds of thousands of copies between 1901 and the 1930s. Sales numbers from before that for the self-published book (originally "copyrighted by Chas. A. Siringo, Caldwell, Kans.") are unavailable, and the royalty arrangements unclear. But Siringo's boast that his first book had sold "a million copies" by 1919 is not impossible.

BOOK TWO
PLAYING OUTLAW

14

Human Nature

I concluded to try my hand as a detective . . . my main object being
to see the world and learn human nature.

—Siringo, *A Cowboy Detective*

Two detectives came out to Wyoming in early February 1885, seeking a boy from New York City and the $10,000 reward posted by his wealthy father. The eleven-year-old, a banker's son named Fred Shephard, had disappeared the month before but had not been abducted. An obsessive reader of Western dime novels, the young man broke open his tin bank one January night and climbed down the rainspout from his room to the Manhattan street. His latest book was left at school, his heroic intentions scrawled across the bottom of its open page, "Ime goin West to be a cowboy detective."

"It is the old story of novel reading," wrote a reporter for the *Cheyenne Leader* when the detectives arrived, their only clues being in the boy's book collection. After conducting interviews, the pair split up to search wide swaths of Texas and Arizona, but young Fred was gone, not to reappear, unprepared by tenderfoot writers for the West into which he vanished.

Months later, Charlie Siringo would enter the Chicago offices of the nation's oldest and largest detective agency, ending up with the job young Fred left home to find.

* * *

Thousands of the cattle Siringo trailed as a cowboy had ended life in the stockyards and packinghouses of Chicago, the sprawling, dirty town of nearly a million people on Lake Michigan where Siringo moved his family from Kansas in the spring of 1886. Boarding in a house on the West Side, Siringo now found the city more daunting than when he had played monte in its downtown hotels on David Beals's dime: "A few months in that great city convinced me that the proper place for me to shine was in the saddle."[1]

Siringo published a second edition of his "wild and wooly" autobiography that year (under the imprint of Siringo and Dobson, Publishers, Chicago), adding thirty-one pages of "Addenda" about the reckoning then occurring on the big ranches. It included ten pages on "The Cow-Pony and How He Is Abused on the Large Cattle Ranches." He dedicated the book (minus its spirited Addenda) not to his mother but to the memory of his adoptive parents, "Mr. and Mrs. W. R. Myers."

The city was shaken by labor battles that spring. On May 1, tens of thousands of ironworkers, furniture makers, and railroad men walked off the job in Chicago as part of a general strike demanding an eight-hour workday. Thousands of others struck in Detroit, Milwaukee, Cincinnati, and New York, where the Third Avenue Railway company had prepared for trouble by importing armed cowboys as drivers. "We have sent out West for more of these men," said the company's president, "and when the next crowd gets here we won't have any need of the police."[2] Two days later, Chicago workers stormed the McCormick Reaper works, from which they had been locked out, hurling rocks in a battle with strikebreakers and police that left several men wounded and one shot dead. A mass meeting was then scheduled for the following day, May 4, in the city's Haymarket Square, to remember the McCormick victims and continue to push for an eight-hour day. But the Haymarket gathering would be known only for its ghastly end.

Siringo and Mamie went to bed that night expecting a riot, as the newspapers had skittishly predicted. And yet the turnout was far smaller than organizers had hoped and police feared. After almost two hours of speeches, beginning with the young German-born anarchist August Spies, much of the crowd had already filed out. Perhaps a few hundred remained to hear the final speaker, a Socialist lecturer named Samuel Fielden, who was finishing his remarks atop a wagon bed when more than 180 Chicago police officers abruptly appeared. They had been waiting in the nearby Des Plaines Street station for any hint of violence, when warning came from undercover detectives that Fielden had said, "Kill it, stab it," while discussing anti-labor laws.[3] Captain William Ward now bellowed, "I command you, in the name of the people of Illinois, immediately and peaceably to disperse!" Fielden, stunned, stepped down as the police closed in; a bomb suddenly landed among them, thrown by someone (it was never confirmed whom) from someplace to the right of the speakers' wagon.

"At the discharge of the bomb," reported the *Chicago Tribune*, "the bystanders on the sidewalk fled for their lives, and numbers were trampled upon in the mad haste of the crowd to get away. . . . In two minutes the ground was strewn with wounded men."[4] The police had opened fire, managing to hit a number of their own in uniform as well as many in the retreating crowd. Fielden himself took a bullet in his knee as he ran. Six policemen died that night, a seventh succumbed later, while at least sixty were wounded; four civilians were killed and dozens injured, but the count was complicated by how many had escaped onto streetcars or into drugstores for treatment, fearing arrest in the hospitals.*

---

* According to Paul Avrich and other historians, the fact that so many wounded people avoided the hospital for fear of arrest is what makes the civilian casualty figures difficult to reckon.

Siringo wrote that he could hear the historic explosion and shooting from the couple's rooms on Harrison Avenue.* During that long fearful night, Mamie kept him from venturing out to investigate the violence, while Siringo's neighbor, unable to drag him along to the scene, borrowed Charlie's pearl-handled Colt instead. Far from offering protection, the weapon made the neighbor a target for police, who took him for an anarchist with a cowboy gun. He returned shaken and pale from the shots zipping around him.

Siringo would credit the bombing outrage in Haymarket with his decision to switch careers: "After the riot, the city was all excitement. I commenced to wish that I were a detective so as to ferret out the thrower of the bomb and his backers."[5] Although he also joined "to see the world and learn human nature," lack of money for his young family may have had something to do with it. His first book would sell many copies over time, but the writing life now seemed a streaky business. He had also used many of the adventures of his first thirty years.

It was nearly two months after the explosion, on June 29, 1886, that Charlie asked his local banker for a letter to bring to the Chicago headquarters of Pinkerton's National Detective Agency:

Gentlemen:—The bearer, Chas. A. Siringo, we know to be a person of good character, and having been a cowboy and brought up on the plains, his services and ability are commendable to you.

S. A. Kean & Co., Bankers

---

* West Harrison Street seems closer to the explosion, but Siringo remembered it as Harrison Avenue.

Carrying the letter, he entered Pinkerton's Fifth Avenue offices, where he met with Captain Mike Farley after demanding to see William Pinkerton himself. William was one of two sons of the founder, Allan Pinkerton, the Scottish immigrant and Abolitionist who had created the nation's first and largest private detective firm but died two years before Siringo's arrival. Charlie had read that William, a distinguished crimefighter himself, was called "Billy" Pinkerton by acquaintances. So he asked for "Billy," like an old friend from Pinkerton's days chasing Western train robbers. The bank recommendation was passed inside for review. A banker's word apparently went a long way with the Pinkerton family, for Siringo's letter shortly reemerged with a note:

Capt. Farley:—The party referred to in this letter is undoubtedly a good man.—Wm. L. Pinkerton

Charlie was called in at last to meet the boss, burly and mustached and sitting heavily in his chair in a dark suit. The agency's well-known logo was a large eye with the slogan "We Never Sleep," which inspired the phrase "Private Eye." Around the office, many referred to Pinkerton as the "Big Eye."

Physically the opposite of the gristly young man he proposed to hire, Pinkerton had spent a fair amount of his own career pursuing Western "bad men" while in charge of train robbery cases for the agency in the 1870s. He asked Charlie for other references, promising that if these all checked out, he could soon start learning the sleuthing business. Siringo was able to give the names of David Beals, now president of the Union National Bank of Kansas City; his LX friend Jim East, now sheriff of the county including Tascosa, Texas; and Pat Garrett, killer of Billy the Kid, embellishing his own involvement in the hunt. Pinkerton

said he would write to these
men, and with luck Siringo
could join the agency's new
office in Denver, where they
would "need a cowboy detective . . . as they figured on
getting a lot of cattle work."[6]

All seemed in order for
Charlie to become an operative and begin his indoctri-
nation into the Pinkerton
system. But one fact was
strangely overlooked in the
conversation: Siringo's bent
for autobiographical writing. His bank letter did not
mention that Siringo was the
author of a published account
of his own frontier adventures, *A Texas Cowboy*. No
matter what agreements he

William Pinkerton (with rifle and broad
mustache) in his younger days chasing
train robbers, seated between two railway
detectives, Pat Connell (left) and Sam
Finley, 1870s.
Library of Congress

might sign about disclosures, it is a mystery why this agency that
depended on secrecy for its survival would hire a young man
who seemed compelled to write about things he had seen and
especially the interesting people he had met.

Most general operatives learned how to shadow a subject on
foot, but the frontier skills Pinkerton was seeking for his new
Colorado office were rarer in Chicago. He may have looked no
further than the impressive résumé of the little Texan before
him, who had commanded men on the trail and hunted a well-
known outlaw and met Garrett, Masterson, and other serious

frontiersmen. Charlie had all the needed skills for the position Pinkerton was creating for his new Denver office, whatever his writing ambitions.

That summer and fall, eight alleged anarchist conspirators would be tried in the Haymarket case. Newspapers pictured them as a bearded gallery of mad bombers. Siringo was assigned by the agency to watch for "monkey work"—attempts at bribery, such as a passed note, a secretive conversation—while eating his meals in the same restaurant as the jurors to keep an eye out. He seems to have hated political dynamiters from the first but did not judge all the accused as guilty; one of them, Oscar Neebe, may have only helped print a political circular. His skepticism may have been based on his low estimation of some Pinkerton operatives called as witnesses, who claimed to have overheard speakers Spies and Fielden openly calling for violent revolution in the days leading up to the Haymarket affair.[7]

Throughout the proceedings Siringo also watched the rich and beautiful Nina Van Zandt, who followed the case just as intensely as he did, falling in love with the handsome August Spies in the process. Spies's final speech to the court ("If death is the penalty for proclaiming the truth, then I will proudly and defiantly pay the costly price!") would inspire many, including a young boy in Utah who had just joined the mines, Bill Haywood. When it turned out that only blood relatives were allowed to visit the prisoners, Van Zandt (simply "Nina" in the press) married Spies in jail, gaining the right to accompany his mother to his cell—and keeping his notorious name after his execution. Five of the eight defendants were sentenced to be hanged, two received life sentences, while the last, Oscar Neebe, got fifteen years. On the night before his hanging, Louis

Lingg defied his jailers by blowing his head off with a smuggled cap of dynamite.

With the dramatic trial over, Siringo did some smaller jobs, including surveilling a "red-headed, long-legged banker" suspected of stealing funds. Each night Siringo followed his man as he left work on a good-times tour through many "tough places, where he would drink wine with the female inmates." It was Charlie's duty to drink and shadow and also tabulate whether his subject was spending beyond his banker's salary.[8]

That October the Siringos finally left Chicago, in a Pullman sleeper, for Denver, climbing up into the Rockies and arriving in the city's grand new Union Station. Siringo was to work out of Pinkerton's branch office on the Opera House Block downtown. Set along the South Platte River, with its mineral wealth and mountain views, Denver was a far cry from lower-lying cow towns Charlie had known.

The Pinkerton sons had divided their father's company into eastern and western divisions, with corresponding offices as regional satellites of the main branches in Chicago and New York. The new Denver office, opened to counter a branch started by the rival Thiel Agency, seemed to confirm fears the old man had held about expansion, exhibiting many of the sins of a distant colonial outpost far from the oversight of its home office. The first superintendent in Denver was the breathtakingly corrupt Charles A. Eames,[9] who had been sent from Chicago to establish the branch, which he unfortunately made in his own image.

Bringing a questionable cast west with him, Eames favored paid-protection schemes and other shakedowns and bookkeeping tricks, while his favorite detectives stole clothing and jewelry from clients and forced their confessions to crimes the detectives themselves committed. He had stocked the office with "genuine thieving toughs," according to Charlie, who, though disgusted, was sometimes assigned to several cases at once, at least on paper, and admitted to pocketing some of the extra money from the agency's overcharging of clients.[10]

The Siringos had to live at first in Eames's own house, where Charlie discovered more about his superintendent's grafty ways. In Chicago he had learned "city work" such as basic shadowing. Now he learned a favorite job that Allan Pinkerton himself had earlier mastered as an operative, spying on a ring of train conductors suspected of double charging. In Denver his train-

Young Siringo posed in a new suit, probably early 1880s.

A Cowboy Detective / *Author's collection*

ing continued for several months, including some mountain day-trips. The experience was a trial for Charlie, though, as so many of the Denver cases involved him in Eames's petty rackets, such as peddling a Pinkerton security service to businesses that was off the books, "Pinkerton" in name only. The worst of the office seemed to be two of the operatives brought from Chicago, Doc Williams and Pat Barry. They were more bagmen than detectives and hardly cowboy material for bringing in the ranch work the agency had expected. Barry had once served time back East for safe-blowing.

Eames was temporarily free of his uncooperative new man when he sent Siringo on his first extended case, into Archuleta County, in the southernmost part of Colorado, in the spring of 1887.

15

Wayfaring Stranger

S iringo's life had so far roughly followed the route of a longhorn to market—from the Texas plains to Kansas cow towns and on to Chicago. But when he set out from Denver on his first cowboy assignment, his wayfaring undercover life began.

He traveled to Archuleta County posing as "Charlie Anderson," a scruffy Texan fleeing the law, reaching the first of many hijacked towns where, as with the later fictional detectives he would inspire, his job was to befriend criminal strangers and bring some order out of violence on behalf of the client. In this case he had been hired by a man representing a group of wealthy New Mexican sheep ranchers forced from the Colorado town of Pagosa Springs, the county seat, which they had ruled under a unique setup. The county, with about seventy-five Anglo voters, was still run by commissioners who lived outside of it in Amargo, New Mexico, including J. M. and Antonio Archuleta, for whom the county had recently been named. The commissioners defeated local Anglo candidates, who made their own best attempts at bribery. The county residents, Siringo learned, "were ruled by the Archuletas, wealthy Mexican sheepmen . . . who sent their sheep-herders into the county to vote on election day."[1]

But the commissioners were obligated to convene in town within sixty days in order to hold power, and a group of insurgents (calling themselves "revolutionaries") chased them out, hoping to force the commissioners to forfeit their positions. This caused "anarchy," according to Colorado newspapers, once their mob had "driven the county commissioners from the town, burned the house of commissioner Scase, and forced the latter to resign his office at the point of the revolver."[2] These commissioners, who held power by election fraud, now needed the Pinkerton agency's help against insurgents who had chased them out with violence, and whose own attempts at bribery had fallen short. Siringo saw the political conflict he was entering more as "anarchy against anarchy," with the Pinkertons as a deciding force. Alone among the Denver officers, Siringo spoke passable Spanish, and from following the excited coverage in the Colorado press, he already knew the names of the insurgency's principals when he set out.

Riding the train to Durango, he bought a horse and saddle before carrying on the sixty miles to Pagosa Springs, which lay along the San Juan River. He was to volunteer his services to the insurgents as a gun for hire, then secretly bring their plans across the river to the sheep ranchers before the forces clashed. No one but the man who had hired him, exiled commissioner Bendito Martinez, was to know his identity. Although Commissioner Scase had been deported and his home burned, his wife and children had been allowed to remain in another small house on his property near the river, where Charlie could leave shorthand notes about the insurgents' plans in the back of an oil painting.

On his way to town, Siringo stopped at the ranch of a man he called "Gordon G.," a ringleader with a reputation for having

escaped trouble in Texas. Calling himself Charlie Anderson, Siringo explained that he was on the run after killing three Mexicans
there. Gordon embraced him as a brother in arms and detailed
his own previous crimes (which Siringo would later report). His
credibility as a bad man established, Charlie parlayed this friendship into an introduction at the home of the rebellion's leader,
county clerk E. M. Taylor, who needed a gunman and so did
not confirm whether Anderson was featured on any of the sheriff's wanted posters. Charlie explained that he feared staying in
hotels, where he might be discovered as a wanted man, and Taylor gave him room and board. He added Anderson to the fighting
force girding for the New Mexicans' return. Siringo became such
a welcome guest that he was able to find receipts for paid votes
among Taylor's private papers.

Both sides were gathering on opposite sides of the San Juan
River bridge, with Charlie now welcomed among the group of
seventy-five insurgents at the Broward saloon, rough characters
with whom he felt at home drinking and plotting. Across the river,
roughly sixty armed riders accompanied the exiled commissioners, who stayed in a house while their guards bunked inside a
former barracks building down the bank. The "revolutionaries"
blocked the New Mexicans from crossing the bridge and, com-
municating by flags, made a plan to sneak a small force of men
across the river in the dark: at three in the morning, their sabo-
teurs would torch a haystack beside the commissioners' dwelling;
then, as the fire spread, and the officials groggily emerged, sharp-
shooters by the river would pick them off one at a time.

Several hours ahead of the attack, Charlie walked upriver
to find a place to wade across with a warning. He stripped first,
an act that would later save his life. On the other side, he told
the murder plan to Jose Martinez, brother of the man who hired
him, who agreed to wait long enough for Charlie to return to his

insurgent crowd before warning the others. But Martinez could not hold back this alarming news: the commissioners ran out carrying their valises before Anderson had returned to the Broward saloon. It was clear the plan had been given up by a traitor.

Siringo might have been killed that night, since his disappearance was suspect, except that he had returned to the group confoundingly dry. But thinking the Widow Scase had been the conduit for the traitor's message, two sentries were placed near a woodpile at her house, where Charlie was in fact hiding his notes in the back of an oil painting. The rebels held a dance that night, which Charlie briefly attended before sneaking off to return to Mrs. Scase's. He placed new messages behind the painting and had a few words with her before escaping through a hole in the wall rather than leave by the door.

But when Charlie returned to the dance, most of the men were still out looking for him at the Scase house, which he had been seen entering; the women and children and fiddlers waited until their return, when the dance crowd changed into a mob wanting to hang him. It was the first of many experiences in which Siringo would show outrage while facing execution by people he had in fact double-crossed. His rancher friend Gordon took him into a side room, calmly asked if he was a detective, and when Siringo denied the charge, demanded, "Then what were you doing at Mrs. Scase's tonight?"

He considered pulling his Colt and bowie knife to fight his way out of the hall, but decided "that would be showing bad detective ability." Instead, Charlie jumped down and "with my hand on old Colt's 45, demanded that he show me the dirty whelp that would tell such a lie on me."[3] When he was produced, Siringo was so hotly indignant that the young man backed down, declaring it might well have been Anderson he saw enter the Scase house, but it was also dark. Not everyone was swayed, but the sheriff was convinced enough by Charlie's acting to hire him as an assistant at four dollars per day, money Charlie kept as unreported "velvet."

After four days of the standoff at the bridge, a meeting was arranged to discuss a compromise. Guns were to be piled in a corner, guarded by representatives of both sides. The insurgents' secret plan, though, was to wait for the officials to assemble in the courthouse meeting room and then hijack the guns and open fire on them. According to Siringo, all the commissioners were in favor of the gathering with the rebels except for Bendito Martinez. As the others were working to convince him, he looked to Charlie, who gave a shake of his head. "That settled it. He stood pat and the plot fell through."[4] Days later, the exhausted insurgents agreed to a promise that the two sides would share power. Then the commissioners had their meeting.

On Siringo's testimony, sixteen members of the rebellion would still be indicted by a grand jury for expelling the county officials and burning their property. Two months after he first rode into town, Siringo stole away to Durango, sold his saddle and horse, and headed home by train to Denver. He didn't blame them for their uprising but remained "sore" they had tried to hang him. It would be the first of many close calls. It turned out he was not just a cowboy author but a gifted character actor with all the skills needed for his strange new job—to track, befriend, and betray.

Charlie was rarely home for long; a pattern began in which he was gone several months, then was turned right around by his boss for a new mission. It was increasingly hard on Mamie and young daughter Viola, as Siringo made little money as an operative, and the couple did not yet know many people in Denver beyond the shady characters at his office.

After a few days home from Pagosa Springs, Siringo was sent to Mexico City to follow a brakeman who had scooped up $10,000 belonging to the Wells Fargo Express Company, scattered during a crash of his own train near La Junta, Colorado. Siringo traveled by Mexican Central Railway to Mexico City and soon found his brakeman, an American who had been spending conspicuously on diamonds. But as the United States had no extradition treaty with Mexico, Siringo could do nothing but wait for him to finish his spree and return north.

Siringo's beloved first wife, Mamie, and their daughter, Viola.

A Cowboy Detective / *Author's collection*

While he waited, Charlie experienced his first earthquake, which shook his hotel from "stem to stern" and killed several hundred people, many survivors kneeling in prayer in the streets the next day. Then he saw what he considered one of the ugliest spectacles of his life, a bullfight, whose cruelty offended him to his cowboy soul. The imported Spanish bulls used in the ring were "artists when it came to butchering horses," he wrote. "One horse was sewed up six times and each time ridden back out to be gored again, until finally killed by the bull."[5]

He next made a Texan's prankish visit to General Santa Anna's grave site, where he risked prison or worse by prying loose a small souvenir of colored "broken chinaware" from the tomb of the late victor at the Alamo. Siringo was excited for one more first, when his thief booked return passage from Veracruz to New York by way of Havana. But word of a yellow-fever epidemic in Cuba canceled his voyage, so the brakeman crossed back into the United States through El Paso, Texas, Charlie shadowing him on trains all the way to his hometown of Leavenworth, Kansas, where he had him arrested.

Months after he had finally set up house with Mamie, things came to a head in the Denver branch. One afternoon he heard a beating going on in superintendent Eames's office. In the frosted glass on the door between the operatives' room and the office, a small peephole had been scratched out for spying, and through it he watched in horror as the two operatives he knew to be corrupt, Doc Williams and Pat Barry, slugged a man repeatedly to confess to a robbery that Charlie knew they had committed themselves. Grabbing his gun, he rushed in. "Throwing the cocked pistol into Pat Barry's face, I made him stand back. Then I read the riot act to Superintendent Eams."[6] After clearing the room, Eames told him he would be fired for insubordination, and in the coming months Siringo had to keep a hand to his gun whenever he entered the operatives' room, as Williams and Barry had sworn revenge.

Eames was unsuccessful in trying to fire Charlie, however, because of his growing value to William Pinkerton as a cowboy detective. Charlie soon escaped the office on a fresh assignment. While he was gone, a new man arrived from Chicago and quietly began work. Like Siringo in the field, he was not the friend he seemed but was there to observe and report back to William Pinkerton, who had heard some alarming things about his Denver branch.

16

Cheyenne

On a Saturday afternoon in October 1887, a mystery rider was introduced to the eight thousand people crowding Denver's Riverfront Park for the city's first cowboy championships. He appeared on a quick white pony following a roping exhibition by a Black cowboy named Pinto Jim. Competing under the name Dull Knife, the horseman was memorable in his embroidered sombrero, fringed chaps, and bright red kerchief, a pearl-handled Colt and knife hanging from his belt. The crowd sensed this short, sure man in a Mexican saddle was not from Denver, noted the *Rocky Mountain News*, but "such a perfect and graceful type of a Texan cowboy that the audience gave one spontaneous A-h-h-h! of admiration."[1]

Taking up his coiled lariat, he brought one bronc to the ground by twisting his rope around its legs, but he cut the horse loose when it wrapped the animal's throat. Then, after losing one steer that snapped his saddle horn, and throwing and stretching another, he was done. "They called him Dull Knife," reported the *Denver Republican*, "and he was from Meeker. That was all the information obtainable. But Dull Knife was a daisy. . . . He was all that the Eastern imagination of the typical cowboy could picture."[2]

Though forbidden to break his cover, Charlie had been unable to resist a cowboy competition, even if he had to ride as someone else. He mailed his entrance letter while on assignment in Meeker, Colorado, to establish phony residence, with permission from his superintendent to compete under an alias. Afterward, he received a fifteen-dollar award (made out to Dull Knife) for "skillfull cowboy work," and kept the uncashable check as a reminder of the cattleman he remained at heart. He was pleased when two men in a buggy later hailed him as Dull Knife on a Denver street. The real cowboy in him now had to keep undercover.

The winter of 1886–87 had been the worst seen by living Westerners, producing what cowboys would name the "Big Die Up," which ruined overstocked ranches on the northern plains and effectively ended the era of speculative ranching that had drawn eastern investors from the Vanderbilts and Theodore Roosevelt to Marshall Field and Europeans such as France's Marquis de Morès, Roosevelt's neighbor in the Dakotas.

A summer drought had suppressed the normal growth of plains grasses and weakened livestock before an epic winter struck; beginning with a widespread blizzard on November 13, 1886, the storms lasted much of a month, with temperatures often fifty degrees below zero, starving the cattle that couldn't reach what grass remained beneath the frozen snows and trapping others where they tried to hide in coulees and gullies that were filled in by drifts. In January 1887, parts of Montana reported temperatures of sixty degrees below zero. The hard snow piles stayed frozen until spring, when dead livestock by the tens of thousands lay everywhere on the landscape and in the streams, bodies bloated or gorged upon by fortunate wolves.

Alexander Swan lost his private fortune; his Scottish backers' losses were substantial, as were those of many other foreign

and eastern speculators in the beef market. The Swan Land and
Cattle Company had held six hundred thousand acres from Ogal-
lala, Nebraska, to Fort Steele, Wyoming, and from the Union
Pacific railway tracks north to the Platte River, but was forced
into receivership as the snows and cold reduced its herds from
113,000 to 57,000 head.

Months earlier, Siringo had bitterly predicted (in an adden-
dum to his 1886 edition of *A Texas Cowboy*) what would happen
to cattle left over a severe winter on ranges that were overstocked
and overgrazed:

> From where I sit while penning these lines, on this first
> day of February, 1886, I can look to the southward, into
> the Indian Territory, and see thousands of dumb brutes
> marching up and down those cursed barbed-wire fences up
> to their knees in snow, with a blanket of ice an inch thick
> on their backs, the piercing north wind blowing forty miles
> an hour, and not a sprig of grass in sight.[3]

"Just think of it, ye cattle kings," he continued, "while sitting in your city palaces roasting your shins before a blazing fire!"
He ended by warning, "From present indications and reports,
this winter will cook the goose that has heretofore laid so many
golden eggs." For many farmers, ranchers, and especially "cattle
kings," the deadly winter of 1886–87 was as ruinous as he predicted. According to the ranching scholar Christopher Knowlton, the overall count from the "Big Die Up" reached nearly a
million dead. The days of overstocking and allowing herds to
fend for themselves for the winter were done; smaller herds, winter hay, and wells were needed remedies. Ranching was no longer
to be dabbled in by remote, wealthy gentlemen; the beef boom
had collapsed. "I am bluer than indigo about the cattle," Theodore

Roosevelt wrote to his sister after riding several days searching for surviving steers on his Badlands ranch, where nearly two-thirds were lost. "It is even worse than I feared."[4]

Wyoming alone had lost several hundred thousand cattle, and in late 1887, Siringo could still see signs of the winter reckoning he had predicted as he traveled to the ranching town of Cheyenne. He was going there to meet with its district attorney, Kalter Skoll, about a murderer calling himself Bill McCoy. Known to local newspapers as "a Texas desperado of the worst kind," McCoy had broken out of Cheyenne's jail in October, assisted by two horse thieves and a burglar.

He had been scheduled to hang for killing Deputy Sheriff Charles Gunn of Lusk, Wyoming, back in January. One cold Saturday morning, McCoy had gone to the saloon of a man named Waters with whom he had argued at a dance the previous night. When Deputy Sheriff Gunn entered the bar to defend Waters, McCoy shouted, "Charley, are you heeled?" and shot Gunn in the abdomen. Then, as the lawman struggled up from the floor, he fired again beside his temple.[5] McCoy then fled Lusk but recklessly returned the next month and was captured in a restaurant by five citizens with shotguns.

After he was transported to Cheyenne, his friend Tom Hall went to work to free him. To assist with a breakout, he paid an eastern burglar named Charles Jones $500 to get himself arrested and smuggle a steel saw into McCoy's cell hidden in his shoe.[6] By August, McCoy had enlisted his other cellmates, and the four men were able to cut through the bolts of their cell doors but were caught just before they could execute their plan to rush their inattentive watchman. In early October, they tried escaping again, this time cutting a shoulder-width hole through the roof of their jail cage and slipping out the skylight at night, descending by a knotted rope. Town boys reported seeing men straddle the jail-yard fence, and a posse of fifty armed riders soon assembled.[7]

"On the night of the liberation, Tom Hall was at a designated place, with an extra horse and saddle to take McCoy,"[8] Siringo learned from DA Skoll. McCoy had likely gone to hide on the Keeline cattle range along the Laramie River, run by his proven friend Hall. The ranch was staffed by a gang of fourteen cowboys, many of them escaped Texans with warrants of their own; like Siringo, few used their given names. In the months since McCoy's disappearance, the Rocky Mountain Detective Agency had sent three men to visit the Keeline, who barely escaped with their lives. In some ways, Siringo's risky time in Wyoming would be more about Texas.

Along the snowy road from Cheyenne toward Fort Douglas, the roundup season was well finished. This was the time of year when the Round-up Number 5 saloon held on to what few paying customers strayed in. It was a low-ceilinged country bar on the Douglas road that made most of its year's money off seasonal cowboys, and so lavished attention on winter visitors like the guest who called himself Charlie Henderson. Looking disheveled but approachable, less like a killer than a common outlaw, he wore a rounded mustache slightly darker than his ruddy face, a strapped Colt bulging a little through his shirt.

His hosts were the saloon's lonely owners, an older couple named Howard. The husband had first been a policeman and saloon owner in Cheyenne, where he met his wife, who had worked as both a dance-hall girl and a professional fighter. As the Howards drank with him in their quiet bar, Charlie Henderson explained that he was a Texan driven north by mysterious troubles.

As he collected himself to go, the Howards coaxed him back inside for a last round, leading Charlie to return the favor and so on. He struggled to climb aboard his horse a second time, and asked about places to stay on his way to Fort Douglas, saying he would be all right if he could just "run across some Texas boys." Howard warned him off stopping at the Keeline Ranch several miles way, as those Texans were ex-convicts who hated visitors and might happily kill him. Siringo answered that as long as they were Texans, he would take his chances. Before mounting up, he made sure to buy a bottle of Howard's high-labeled cheap whiskey, which he slipped in his coat as a gift for the strangers. He had intended to play it a bit drunk as he rode off in search of the horse trail, but the last rounds had added to his boozy authenticity. Spurring his horse and giving a yell, he made a crashing exit through the timber toward the bridle path Howard had reluctantly described.

As his new friends watched him nervously out of their sight, he planned to fake a broken leg for his first impression on the outlaws. High in the range he was crossing, he dismounted at an inclined spot on the trail, then shoved downhill at his horse until the animal finally rolled over in a dry arroyo, leaving a dusty impression, in case his accident story was later checked. He next ripped his jean leg almost to the knee, rubbed the skin with grass and rolled up his wool drawers above the kneecap to present a scratched, swollen look, pouring on some of the Howards' cheap whiskey as a last touch. The scar from Sam Grant's long-ago shot added to the knee's injured look. After tying his loose boot to his saddle, he carried on toward the Keeline Ranch, leg hanging uselessly outside the stirrup as he emerged from a stand of cottonwoods around sunset and spotted some log buildings.

A gang of men soon appeared, led by a rangy figure who turned out to be the Keeline's foreman, Tom Hall, demanding to know "what the hell" young Henderson was doing at his ranch. When Charlie announced his leg was broken, the group carried the small stranger off his horse and into the house, where Hall inspected the knee and pronounced it merely sprained, then washed and wrapped it. A search party with lamps was dispatched to backtrail and check for signs his horse had truly rolled, as Charlie claimed, then to confirm he'd been directed to them by the saloonkeeper, Howard. Nursing his fake injury by the fireplace was the deepest any detective had penetrated the Keeline compound.

Siringo immediately recognized a "sullen, dark-complexioned man" from his boyhood days in South Texas, Jim McChesney, and worried the recognition was mutual when he asked Charlie if he was one of the scandalous "Pumphry boys" who had left town after a family killing. Siringo curtly answered, "I go by 'Henderson' now." After serving their crippled guest a late supper, Hall gave him his own room, where Charlie unwrapped and stretched his leg, sleeping with his head on his "war bag" holding his belt of cartridges. His hidden Colt and bowie knife had somehow escaped notice when the men had carried him to the house. But that night, the gang discussed hanging him to scare a confession out of him, he later learned. Hall overruled the skeptics, arguing that if he was a detective it would emerge over time anyway, and they could enjoy hanging him then. After a fitful night, Charlie rewrapped his leg and hobbled to breakfast for the gang's verdict. Hall fashioned him a wooden crutch, welcoming him for now to the desperado ranch.

Over the next weeks, Charlie stumped around with the gang, tying his crutch to his saddle when they rode as a group. His quarry, Bill McCoy, had left before Siringo even arrived, sent over the mountains on Tom Hall's roan horse and now on his way to New Orleans, where he planned to board a steamer and carry Hall's letter of introduction with him to a gang in Buenos Aires. From Jim McChesney, Charlie had learned something else about McCoy, that he was a Texas cowboy Charlie had known from the Panhandle, when he went by Bill Gatlin. Siringo's upbringing had so far kept him alive.

The gang traveled together to a sporting house a mile outside Fort Laramie. All danced and drank and shot out windows except for Charlie, who used the excuse that his crutch kept him from dancing. He sneaked into town as the party raged and checked into a hotel long enough to write home and mail reports to tell the Denver office that Bill McCoy was in New Orleans. Then, as the soberest man in the group, Siringo inherited the job of settling the men on their horses, removing the cartridges from Jim McChesney's sidearm, which Jim uselessly snapped at enemies on the weaving ride home.

The saloonkeeper Mr. Howard, who had reluctantly directed Siringo to the Keeline, appeared one night, heavy with the news that his wife was dying. Howard was a tolerant friend of the gang, so Hall assembled the men to ride together to his bar to keep a drinking vigil. Mrs. Howard demanded liquor to the end, dying around midnight, when they staged a wake for her in the saloon, shooting holes in the walls as the whiskey stocks drained. Later, during the ceremony to lower her into the hard ground, among the toasts and other songs, Charlie heard the mourners sing one that was possibly ominous:

> *Oh see the train go 'round the bend,*
> *Goodbye, my lover, goodbye;*
> *She's loaded down with Pinkerton men,*
> *Goodbye, my lover, goodbye.*

Siringo finally tossed away his crutch before the gang made its next long ride from the ranch to Fort Laramie. He staged his recovery in order to dance with a young woman whom he could later pretend to visit when he finally disappeared for the railroad station. He again slipped away from the party long enough to send more reports.

Siringo's original target had fled to South America, but he had learned enough from his weeks with the gang, including heart-to-hearts with Hall and McChesney, to send a posse back for them from Cheyenne. A little after sunrise, a group of riders appeared at the edge of the timber stand overlooking the log houses. When they rode up to arrest the sleeping gang, Tom Hall remarked, "That damned Henderson is at the bottom of this."[9] Charlie had never returned from his last visit to his girl.

Life undercover would become increasingly murky. Siringo testified against the gang to a grand jury convened in Cheyenne, but when the case fell apart before trial, he found he was strangely glad for his "friends." Having done his job well, he had nevertheless come to enjoy these Texans whose lives echoed his own. "My friends were liberated to my great joy," he wrote.[10] In one sense, the manhunt had been a failure, since the real culprit, Bill McCoy, had already killed again and joined a new group of Texas outlaws on the Argentine Pampas. Tom Hall, whom Charlie would later see in Utah running a saloon under his real name, Tom Nichols, had shown a big heart in caring for a stranger's "broken" leg and saved his life when others demanded his hanging. Charlie had returned the favor poorly.

17

The Great Detective

There's no romance in the life of a detective.

—James McParland

The train platform was covered with snow, as were the surrounding streets as four men, cuffed and shackled, were led trudging the slushy half mile from the depot to the city jail. The morning sidewalks were standing room for the curious as the scruffy prisoners passed, unwashed and unrepentant and apparently dragged from the wilderness.

Sheriff Cyrus "Doc" Shores was marching them to his small jail in Gunnison County, Colorado, in the spring of 1888. Doc Shores occasionally consulted with Eames, superintendent of the Denver office, as a Pinkerton special operative. He was investigating a robbery from the previous November of a passenger train on the Denver and Rio Grande Railroad near Grand Junction, Colorado. The robbers had disappeared into the woods for several months near Green River, Utah; two were Kansas farm brothers named Smith. Their third man was Ed Rhodes.

Enlisted to find them with Shores, Siringo had visited the Smith family's farm outside Cawker City, Kansas, as a potential buyer, flirting long enough with farmer Smith's "black-eyed daughter" to gain access to her letters from the train robbers. (In his dealings with young women related to his subjects, Siringo often reported he "had to fall in love with her" or "I made love to her," a phrase that had a broader meaning then. But he does seem to have done whatever we care to imagine for his job, with his wife's alleged permission.) After stealing their last known posting address and studying the Smith family photos, Charlie quickly "cooled" on the poor girl and lost interest in her father's farm as well.

Hearing that the three men had been flushed and trapped, Siringo switched roles, posing now as an escaped wife-killer from Wyoming taken into Doc Shore's custody somewhere along the Gunnison River. At the depot in Montrose, Colorado, Shores cuffed and shackled Siringo before they boarded the train that was already carrying the captured fugitives and supervising officers. In the smoking car, the four prisoners sullenly rode to Gunnison, where they were to be cellmates eating meals prepared upstairs by the sheriff's wife and given a few greasy quilts. In some ways, prison life was an improvement, Ed Rhodes told Doc; he hadn't "been warm or had a square meal since the robbery."[1]

The tight cell they would share had a bloody recent history, which Shores exploited to psychological advantage on his guests. He had once arrested the "Colorado Cannibal" Alferd Packer, accused of eating five of his snowbound traveling companions in the San Juan Mountains of Colorado during the hard winter of 1874. The Gunnison cell was also still spotted with blood from a recent suicide. Upon being told he would be brought back east for trial by the great Pinkerton detective James McParland, a prisoner who had escaped the Molly Maguire prosecutions (and hangings) pulled a razor from beneath his mattress, declared, "Mac will never get me alive," and cut his own throat, tossing the bloody blade to the windowsill in grisly victory.[2]

The Kansas train robbers Shores was holding got to know their cellmate, Charlie "Lawrence," the slender wife-killer awaiting escort back to Wyoming for his hanging. During their long nights locked up together, the Kansans shared many secrets with their small worldly friend, who confided in turn about breaking out of the Cheyenne jail. Having just spent months in Cheyenne and thereabouts searching for an escaped convict, Charlie spoke with authority about the details of the bust-out.

Siringo spent two weeks hamming it up with his rank cellmates, "alive with vermin" from their miserable time in the wild, one brother wearing a kerchief over a festering unhealed head wound from the other brother's mistaken shotgun blast. But they had shared many secrets by the time the prisoners parted, when the undersheriff came at last to get Charlie for his long train ride to the gallows. "I had confided in my companions," he wrote. "The prisoners really shed tears when I shook hands with them before being handcuffed to the supposed officers."[3] Then he was gone.

Outside the jail, Charlie Lawrence passed along to Doc Shores all he had learned from the Kansans about the logistics of their train heist. Feeling the sheriff now already knew too much, the men offered up the rest. Then, turning the page on his weeks of ripe camaraderie, Charlie washed up and caught the return train to Denver.

The famous detective James McParland had in fact arrived from Chicago to observe the Denver Pinkerton office when Siringo was still in Wyoming; it was an excellent time to be away, since while Charlie shared a jail cell with the Smith brothers, William Pinkerton himself had come to Denver on McParland's word. Among his other crimes, superintendent Eames had been holding out on the agency, overcharging but not putting it in the company books, and running his own patrol system of private police, "coining money on the strength of the Agency's reputation," Siringo wrote. Finally, "Mr. [W. A. Pinkerton] came out from Chicago and discharged him and all his pets." He fired everyone in the office except for McParland and Siringo, who was thought too new to be tainted by its corruption, had spent months away from its culture on assignment, and was the only employee not handpicked by Eames, whose complaint about him to Pinkerton may have counted in his favor. Being spared in the purge, he recalled, left him cocky.[4]

When James McParland arrived at the agency's Denver office, he was the best-known detective in America not named Pinkerton. A sturdily built Irishman wearing a curled mustache and round spectacles, he spoke with a brogue and often kept on his black bowler while working inside his dim-lit office. As head of Pinkerton's Western Division, he would eventually visit its new satellite offices in the northwestern cities of Spokane, Seattle, and Portland on an inspection tour every few months.

McParland's most famous case in Denver would be an investigation of the murder of the wealthy Rhode Island widow Mrs. Josephine Barnaby, poisoned by an arsenic-laced bottle of whiskey sent to her while she was staying in Denver in April 1891. Her physician back home, Thomas Thatcher Graves, had recently been granted her power of attorney as well as a stipend, and McParland settled on Dr. Graves as the likely killer, once the victim's rancher son hired Pinkerton's. McParland sent a clever telegram to the physician, inviting him to

An unusual, off-kilter portrait of young James McParland, hero of the Mollie McGuires case.
Library of Congress

travel to Denver to testify against someone else for the killing. Dr. Graves eagerly accepted the chance to help convict another man for his crime, and McParland had him arrested for murder upon his arrival in Denver, the first legal case of murder through the mails.

McParland had learned a fair amount about miners by living secretly among the activist group known as the Molly Maguires while working in a Pennsylvania coal shaft in the 1870s. The experience had nearly cost him his life but was turned into a popular book by Allan Pinkerton, *The Molly Maguires and the Detectives*, which in turn inspired a stage play, *Secret Service; or, McParlan the Detective*. McParland's investigation would also become the basis for Arthur Conan Doyle's last Sherlock Holmes novel, *The Valley of Fear*, causing a public rift with the Pinkertons when Conan Doyle neglected to acknowledge leaning heavily on Allan Pinkerton's book as his source. McParland was hailed and hated, an agent of justice or an anti-labor murderer of fellow Irishmen. (Twenty Mollies were hanged, nine executed directly on McParland's testimony.) His terrifying undercover operation with the Mollies would become a template for his dark view of trade unions generally during his career. Reporters called him simply "the Great Detective."

Born probably in 1844 in Ulster's County Armagh, James McParlan would add the *d* to his name in his forties, reflecting how many Americans heard it anyway. In Chicago, McParlan came to own a saloon and liquor store, which burned down in that city's Great Fire in the fall of 1871, leading him to join the Pinkerton agency as an operative. While working as a spotter, monitoring pilferage among Chicago streetcar conductors, he came to the attention of Allan Pinkerton, who needed a brave investigator of Irish background for his client, F. B. Gowen of the Philadelphia and Reading Railway. Gowen wanted someone to infiltrate a subset of the Ancient Order of Hibernians called the Sleepers or Molly Maguires, whose members had committed violence and murder against both coal executives and fellow miners, killing as many as a dozen victims per year at their peak. The undercover job took three years and nearly cost McParlan his life. At one point, he had lost enough hair that his superintendent bought him a wig.

Pinkerton superintendents used a standard form for evaluating their detectives, weighing strengths and "special characteristics" for future assignments but also tracking faults to cite in any possible pay discussions. The form filled out for James "McParlan" in Chicago just three years after his famed mission among the Mollies has a list of useful in-house prompts: "General deportment and appearance: 'Genteel Irishman'; Class of 'Roper,' whether makes acquaintance easily: Good"; "Class of 'Shadow': Not good." McParlan was judged "impulsive" and his chief failing, "Operating too fast." Under "Remarks," a Chicago supervisor noted he drank heavily while working in Pennsylvania but had since reformed and married. There is no mention of the deadly nature of that work or that social drinking had kept him alive, although Allan Pinkerton had already published his history of the case. McParlan's in-house form also rated his "knowledge of criminals" as "not good," yet juries in the Molly Maguire trials had believed him enough to hang nine men.[5]

McParlan's experiences in the coalfields led him to see most unions as merely conspiracies harboring terrorists. This view of the trade union as a stalking horse well served the needs of Pinkerton's growing list of corporate clients, as labor clashes grew dramatically across the West. Siringo was a tough sell at first, explaining to his new boss that he would not work against honest workingmen. It is a tribute to their relationship that Mac would even allow Siringo to question a case. But for the cowboy's first mining adventure, there would not be a conflict with his principles. It was a classic case of ore thieves; con men were the same belowground as above—only their tools changed. The anti-union work would come later.

McParland was formally given the Denver office to run in February 1888. Siringo had known bosses he somewhat admired, from Shanghai Pierce and W. B. Grimes to David Beals, and McParland would become another, even as he repeatedly sent Charlie into harm's way. The superintendent's job took McParland largely out of the field, where he had thrived as a detective, but he could send Siringo in his place.

First he would dispatch his young cowboy down into the western mines. As a superintendent, McParland might have scored his young cowboy as a good "roper" of criminals, just proved by his befriending outlaws in Wyoming and extending his acting ability while bunking with train robbers in the Gunnison County jail. Siringo had also showed what the agency called "Self-reliance and ability to originate a plan of operations beyond instructions." This ability would serve him even underground, where his cowboy skills had little application. His foreman at the Aspen Mining and Smelting Company had been instructed to be patient while he came up to speed as a common miner in the silver-mining camp and the tunnels beneath the Rocky Mountains.

18

Salting a Mine

He knows that more money is put in the ground than is taken out,
and considers it his particular mission to keep up the ratio. His wit
does the rest.

— "How They Salt a Mine," *St. Louis Post-Dispatch*, 1888

Like Leadville and Silverton, Aspen had grown quickly from a bunch of tents and mining claims to a booming Colorado silver town. The railroad that brought Siringo there had come to Aspen only the year before, in 1887.

Silver strikes were discovered through both persistence and flukish luck. What became Leadville's Little Pittsburgh strike was found in April 1878 by two German prospectors who tired on their hike up Fryer Hill and started digging beneath an evergreen near where they had rested to have a drink from their whiskey jug.[1] Many new miners came west with the same hopes young Samuel Clemens once had, expecting "masses of silver lying all around the ground . . . glittering in the sun on the mountain summits."[2] After a few discouraging months, some sold their unproven plots to more recent arrivals still full of eagerness. A hardy few stayed, doggedly working their claims, while others chose the path of feigning success.

These con men had rebelled at the dreariness of honest digging, yet could dedicate months or even years to salting a claim with imported ore, turning a hole in the ground into a "treasure cave" to fool the assayer certifying the mine's worth. "A clever man can invest $5,000 in a mine, or at least in good ore from another mine, and make it pay a big profit," one newspaper explained. "A couple of tons of rich ore judiciously distributed in a 'hole' will bear inspection and gain confidence."[3] There were both simple and sophisticated ways to fool buyers, tripped up by their willingness to believe. Some used shotguns to fire a fraudulent mixture of soft tale and silver-coin shavings point-blank into cave walls before inspection; some experts filled rock cracks with gold used for dental fillings or painted the ore bed with gold chloride or silver nitrate.[4] One group fired uncut African diamonds into the ground on a remote acre near Middle Park, Colorado, taking samples to sell in San Francisco and spread the word about their wondrous "diamond field." The most celebrated of the salters, William Lovell, or "Chicken Bill," aged bits of brass under a waterfall for a plausibly dull-gold finish.

Although he was one of the earliest residents of Leadville, Chicken Bill apparently lacked what his fellow miners called "a smell of ore" and abandoned earnest digging for making simulated riches to sell to others. But he remained best known for his defeat by a proven mining man, Horace Tabor, who at the time sold supplies and served as mayor of Leadville while holding grubstakes in several of its successful claims. Bill stole silver from a mine in which Tabor had acquired a share, the Little Pittsburgh, and loaded it at the bottom of his own dig site in Leadville to sell it to him. After discovering the relocated ore in his new property, Tabor dug past the fraud and found a rich strike that became the Chrysolite mine.[5]

Working on behalf of the Aspen Mining and Smelting Company, Charlie Siringo learned that the man he was after, Paddy McNamara, had run across Chicken Bill in his own travels but played a comparatively cruder game, stealing genuine ore on the sly rather than manufacturing phony claims. Before coming to

Aspen, "Paddy Mack" had organized successful thieving rings in the Colorado towns of Black Hawk and Central City. Paddy was "the slickest ore thief that ever did business in the West," Charlie observed, "and he bragged of how he could tell a detective by his actions."[6]

Siringo had known every kind of frontier danger, but death and injury jumped out from almost every dark corner when working down below. Carrying his candlestick while descending a mine ladder, Siringo accidentally poked himself in the cheek and missed a rung with his hand, barely keeping from plunging into the dark, "a free ride of 70 to 80 feet straight down."[7] Soon after Charlie began work, his mining tutor was using a penknife to open a new box of blasting caps, when they detonated, blowing out his eyes and sheering off his hands. He begged to be shot, Siringo remembered, but survived and was sent back east, blinded and maimed, to his mother. Charlie spent a dangerous month establishing himself as a game if subpar miner, then quit to try to join Paddy Mack's gang instead.

He learned McNamara was handling ore stolen by miners and bosses of pack trains and claimed to have already handled more than a hundred thousand dollars' worth in Aspen. After gaining Paddy's confidence as an ex-miner hungry for money, he needed legal witnesses to build a case. In those days long before surveillance cameras, Siringo had to place his mine executives in secret vantage points to watch McNamara's nighttime operation. He installed the mine's general manager and a banker-owner in empty freight cars and upper-story rooms overlooking the packing area where ore samples were loaded onto mules late at night. Charlie nearly foiled his own trap when he struck a match near Paddy's face to light him for his audience. McNamara slapped his hand away and harassed him about the hazards of being recognized.

When the clients had seen enough, Siringo was arrested along with the crew he had implicated. He remained undercover in Aspen's jail, where one of the miners confided he was planning to jump bond and offered to find Siringo other work if he wrote to him, care of "General Delivery," in Kansas City, giving Charlie the chance to betray him a second time to the law. The trial itself took too long, and many of the accused were freed, with the understanding they take their operation out of town, while the ringleader, Paddy Mack, died after his arrest.

Siringo's Pinkerton work had divided his life into two halves— the family man he was when home long enough to visit with his wife and young daughter and receive a new assignment, and the hard types he played on the road—the good and the professionally bad. Away for months at a time, Siringo missed his young family while wandering for his dangerous job.

In the late spring of 1888, he would try pulling the two sides of his strange life together, instructing Mamie to bring little Viola up to Alma, Colorado, near where he was investigating a big salting case in the Mudsill mine. As Charlie pictured it, his family would enjoy a cool summer in the mountains while he visited regularly from his job, seven miles away in Fairplay, as a kind of country husband. There he was spending nights alongside a hard-partying ore thief, hitting the town's two lively dance halls, drinking and debauching with "free and easy" ladies. Whether or not it was inevitable, his ideal self soon bumped against his worst, as the bad man he played sullied the family man he wanted to be, and Charles T. Leon met Mrs. Siringo in a hotel lounge.

By the time Mamie and Viola arrived in Alma, Siringo had already spent several months making a rowdy spectacle of himself as Charles Leon in Fairplay, spending the Pinkertons' money on every sin for sale while befriending "Jacky" (Jack Allen), a man he had come to suspect was a mine salter. He had introduced himself when he noticed that Jacky was afraid of his own mean-spirited horse, which had badly thrown him. While technically on a mining job, Siringo was happy to use two of his cowboy talents—breaking horses and hell-raising—in gaining Jacky's confidence over several weeks of moon howling, playing his favorite mysterious Texan picking up tabs.

Charlie Leon liked his fun, but offered to gentle Jacky's horse for him, riding it once each day to try to take its edge off. Though Jacky was still not easy with the bad-tempered animal, the effort impressed him. One night, after getting on a "glorious drunk" together at the dance halls, they collapsed together in Jacky's room, where he became talkative about his past, including his Leadville days, when he had known the master salter Chicken Bill himself. He showed Charlie a scar on his hip from an incident that had sent him to prison. This story, which gave away his original name, would later send him back.

Hired by the Mudsill's seller, Jacky was suspected as at least a co-conspirator in the salting of the mine, a promising property that had passed several rounds of inspection before its last ore sample failed to match the silver found in the original. In 1887, hearing about the extraordinary new millionaires picking fortunes out of the Colorado ground, the newly elected Lord Mayor of London had spent $190,000 on this silver mine he had never seen near Fairplay, a young town better known for its gold. After it cleared one engineer, the Lord Mayor sent a New York mining specialist named McDermott, who was pleased at first by what he saw, as was a later London expert.

On their collective word, the Lord Mayor had engaged a leading company that built mills to develop the ore, which presented the catch for Siringo, as McParland described the case in his office. When a subsequent sample looked suspicious to

McDermott, he cabled the Lord Mayor, who in turn empowered him to hire Pinkerton's. But one of the contractors on the milling job was Allan Pinkerton's son-in-law. To find the salting parties responsible, retrieve much of the Lord Mayor's money, and yet preserve enough of the mine's value so not to cancel the son-in-law's contract was Charlie's challenge.

On one of his early dance-hall nights in Fairplay, a drunken gang attempted to take over the bar, one member pulling a knife on a friend of Jacky's, prompting Siringo to show his loyalty by unholstering his Colt and beating the knife wielder to his knees. Charlie was then knocked down by another of the gang, who pulled his own gun, but recovered enough to jam his pistol in the assailant's face and ordered him to "put up his gun and leave the hall. This he did, and his gang soon followed."[8]

After a hero's celebration, word came from elsewhere in town that the gang was returning, with "blood in their eyes" as well as reinforcements and extra ammunition; the women with whom Jacky and Charles Leon had celebrated now pushed them together into the bar's wine closet and locked them in for safe-keeping. Drunk and with little to do but wait among the wine bottles for the gang's return, Jacky unspooled the tale of the Mudsill mine, whose tunnel had been kept locked to outsiders for three years as the salting job was perfected. When the gang reappeared at the dance hall, the women convinced them that Jacky and Charlie had gone off to bed and were unavailable for a rematch.

In the morning, emerging from the wine closet with enough information to jail Jacky and perhaps his partners, Charlie first returned to Denver to consult with the Lord Mayor's New York mining expert, who had raised the alarm after first being duped. Advised that Mudsill was a confirmed fraud, McDermott told Charlie to carry on his investigation, and so Siringo put in a bid to drill the lower section of the mine, competing with Jacky, who made his own offer. After Siringo won the rigged competition for the job, he hired Jacky as his foreman, hearing his further confessions as they camped together on the drill site. Taking his man camping, away from distractions and the suspicions of others, would become a reliable Siringo technique to elicit information, along with faking an injury for credibility or romancing a bad man's sister.

"Doc" Lockridge lived in the hotel in Alma where Mamie and Viola would be staying while Charlie was still working the Mudsill case in Fairplay. As Siringo had known Doc's late cowboy brother, he presumed to ask him the strange favor of pretending to be Mamie's uncle to "introduce" her to her own husband, who would be playing Charles Leon, in the Alma hotel. When he met her in the ladies' lounge, Siringo's wife was a widow from Kansas; his baby-cheeked girl was not to call him "Papa," since they were pretending her father was dead. Charlie stayed several nights a week with Doc at the hotel, having his fraudulent dinners with his secret family and skulking the halls late at night to visit with Mamie, the attractive widow he was seemingly courting. Being seen slipping into her room might have ended their stay in the mountains as well as compromised the Mudsill case.

Although Charles Leon was on his best behavior, guests eventually began taking Mamie aside to warn her against her new dining friend. "The landlady of the hotel and other lady guests, who had become attached to Mamie, aired my reputation as one of the worst toughs and dance-hall loafers of Fairplay and advised her not to associate with me," Charlie recounted.[9] Other men interested in the widow had seen Charlie Leon in action in Fairplay's dance halls and were eager to spread word of his exploits. He was not fit company for a nice young widow and especially for her little girl, who needed a proper father. "No doubt," he later confessed about his double life, "you think this was a rank injustice to poor, pure-hearted Mamie; and so it is, but she had confidence in me and sanctioned it, so long as it was part of my business."[10]

Seeing his family in the hotel may have lifted his heart, even if the man he had been playing was unworthy of sitting at the same table with the woman who was secretly his wife. He had loved Mamie enough to quit cowboying, his first love, within weeks of meeting her in Caldwell. But he could not, apparently, give up his adventures as a cowboy detective to come home to her for long.

The Mudsill case ended with Jacky being tricked into a visit to Denver, where McParland was waiting. He had pictures of him from prison under his previous name (which he had drunkenly told to Charlie) and threatened to make it known to Jacky's present employer that he was an escaped con unless he confessed their full mine-salting scheme. The whole Mudsill operation took Charlie eight months, and the Lord Mayor eventually got back $150,000 through the courts.

After attempting to live both his lives together, Siringo did not repeat the experiment. It is unclear exactly when in the coming months Mamie first noticed signs of the pleurisy of the lungs that would take her away from him, or how long it was before she broke the news of her symptoms to her vagabonding husband. By the time it was fully diagnosed, her father, unable to rely on his peripatetic son-in-law and not trusting frontier surgeons in Denver, would call her home.

19

"A Strange Country"

Often in his undercover travels, Siringo would run into people he had known while still a Texas cowboy, frontier characters who thought nothing of his using a different name, assuming he had done something outside the law to need an alias, not that he worked with the law himself. To guard against suspicion, Siringo sometimes traveled with phony newspaper clippings about the misdeeds of his stealth personas and would have letters mailed to him that referenced his former "crimes." Occasionally, though, he was exposed.

Tuscarora was a mining camp up in the Nevada high desert about fifty miles northwest of Elko, named after a Union sloop of war and the Tuscarora people. Since the first mining expedition there in 1867, it had seen some riches in both silver and gold, and its population included an impressive Chinatown settlement of several hundred former railroad workers. By the 1880s, the town was also a battleground in a war between labor and capital seen across the West.

On an April night in 1889, two executives from the Price and Peltier mining corporation had just retired to their separate cabins in Tuscarora when they suffered simultaneous bombings.

Long fuses were lit that touched off blasting powder beneath each of their beds, blowing the men through their own roofs. George Peltier had been tucked in his blankets before the bomb threw him into the air, landing on his mattress in the street, and was able to recover surprisingly quickly. But C. W. Price had not been as protected when the charge went off. He landed hard on the roadbed, his wounds considerable, though he would live to be an old man.[1]

According to some San Francisco detectives they hired, the clear suspect in the bombings was Clarence Buck, who had threatened to blow up his bosses several times, before witnesses. But the case broke apart, and the detectives were chased off; reports that Buck had made "a clean breast of it" and confessed to the assassination attempts were followed within weeks by his lawsuit for $15,000 in damages for "malicious prosecution." George Peltier had recovered enough from his dynamiting to travel to Denver to hire a new agency. He met with McParland, who arranged for Siringo to see Peltier secretly in the Palace Hotel in San Francisco to discuss the case's background and cast of suspects.

After developing pleurisy, Mamie had gone home to Springfield, Missouri, at the insistence of her father, for a desperate operation that he felt required the family physician. Charlie had agreed it was a better arrangement for his wife's rest and possible recovery. He began to sell their furniture and prepare for a new field assignment. Then, "seeing my wife and baby off on an Eastbound train," he wrote, "I boarded a flyer for the extreme edge of the Golden West." As arranged, he met with George Peltier in the Palace Hotel in San Francisco, on his first visit to California, marred by the knowledge that his wife would "undergo an operation without my presence to comfort her." From San Francisco the cowboy detective set out, in the fall of 1889, traveling as Charles Leon on the railroad to Elko, where he switched to the four-horse Tuscarora stage.[2]

One of his fellow stage passengers, Phil Snyder, was said to be a friend of the dynamiters. Charlie made his acquaintance by sharing the stage's front seat with Snyder and the driver and putting on a shooting demonstration—killing a coyote from the moving coach with a single shot he described as "accidental." He arrived in town already having a foot inside the dynamiters' conspiracy, presenting himself as a useful freelance gunman with a past. Another suspect, a miner named Tim Wright, brought him outside of town and asked him to confirm his marksmanship on a fence board at fifty yards. Charles Leon complied by shooting out a knot the size of a silver dollar, then smartly refused to repeat the accomplishment. He briefly took a room at a butcher's ranch, which he shared with a "Chinaman," whose exotic use of chopsticks impressed him as the two sat at the table "joking and trying to talk to each other."³ He also got more background information on the mine owners' enemies from an outlaw friend of Tim Wright's called "Wild Bill," who lived on Lone Mountain making his own twenty-dollar bills. Charlie drew out Wild Bill by commissioning him to make a steel multipurpose device that contained a foldout knife but was principally a candlestick. Over their days together, Bill assured him that the dynamiting ringleaders were "Black Jack" Griffin and Tim Wright.

Siringo had settled on Wright as the conspirator most likely to be charmed into confessing. He asked Wright if he would accept money on his behalf relayed from his rancher father (actually McParland), since his past "troubles" in Texas made it risky to publicize his new address. Wright gladly agreed to help his new friend and began collecting $150 each month from Charlie's "father," in effect proof of his cover story. Charlie moved into the boardinghouse where Wright lived, which was run by his "sweetheart," a widow whose name Siringo discreetly masked in his writings as either Mrs. Barnes or Mrs. Balcolm. He soon received a letter at the widow's from C. W. Price asking to meet him alone by gloom of night to discuss what he was finding.

For secrecy, Price chose the bottom of an abandoned mine a half mile beyond town for their rendezvous, including a diagram of the shaft. Charlie found the old entrance and climbed two hundred feet down a decaying ladder with missing rungs to the dark bottom of the shaft, where he compared notes about his new friends with his client by lamplight.

That December, Charlie also hoped to get more information by taking the teenage daughter of another conspirator for a sleigh ride, but he was a novice at this particular use of horses, and the sleigh he rented flipped over, and the team ran off; he and the girl had to walk several miles back to town, after retrieving his "old Colts 45" from the snow. "The fact that I was out riding with an 18-year-old girl while my sick wife was just recovering from a successful operation, may seem naughty to you," Siringo later acknowledged to his readers, "but you must bear in mind that there are tricks in all professions but ours, and they are all tricks."[4]

Believing a confession would emerge once Wright was "in a strange country where he could talk with no one but myself,"[5] Siringo proposed the two men go prospecting that spring in the Wichita Mountains, in the western part of the Indian Territory. After hearing tales of the gold being found there, Wright was eager. But his friends, especially Black Jack Griffin and the widow Balcolm, suspected the newcomer, who had arrived so soon after the San Francisco detective had been chased from town. The two nevertheless set off together, with the gang giving Charlie dark looks as they boarded the morning stage to Elko.

A sleeper took them from Elko to Denver, where Wright wanted to sell some of his stolen ore, but as he had not yet confessed to the dynamiting, Siringo could not throw him to

McParland while in town. Another train brought them southeast to Wichita Falls, Texas, where Siringo left Wright in the hotel while he slipped off to warn some local cowboy friends not to acknowledge him as he was traveling through as Charles Leon. He and Wright bought horses for the two-day ride across the Red River and into the mountains and the Indian Territory. Siringo had crossed the river often, but this time was escorting a criminal subject across, not some swimming steers. They headed toward the camp of the Comanche leader Quanah Parker at West Cache Creek.

Siringo had left word back in Colorado that the pair could eventually be reached in Fort Sill (near present Lawton, Oklahoma). On a visit to town to buy supplies, he retrieved a packet of mail for Tim Wright consisting of Mrs. Balcolm's pleading notes of warning against the dirty detective who had duped him; some had been sent that same day from the Fort Sill hotel. Siringo made his way out of town without the widow seeing him. Then, safely alone in the desert near Medicine Bluff, he read the widow's letters as well as the guilty notes Wright had written to her. He "shed a silent tear for her pathetic letters" before leaving the couple's would-be correspondence to die under a rock.[6]

Wright remained unshakably loyal—even gullible—about his new friend, after more than one person claimed to recognize Charlie along their journey. When a cowboy on the Cherokee Strip greeted him like an old friend, Siringo denied knowing the man. "Why, Charlie," the cowboy corrected. "You can't fool me. I would know your hide in a tan-yard."[7]

Finding his camp at the edge of the plains, Siringo introduced Wright to the tall Comanche leader Quanah Parker, who had led the attack of nearly seven hundred warriors against the buffalo hunters at Adobe Walls before finally moving onto the reservation. They were there to request Parker's permission to speculate

The Comanche warrior and leader
Quanah Parker.

Library of Congress

on his tribal lands, something
Siringo must have known the
great man would deny.* They
went ahead anyway—being
chased by tribal police and deputy marshals alerted by Parker
would only strengthen the
friendship Charlie needed for
Wright to confess his part in the
dynamiting ring.

Camping on hilltops, the
pair lived off wild turkeys and
deer and found just enough
traces of gold to keep excitedly going. Then Siringo made
the most extravagant gesture in
the courtship: naming a pair of
mountains after them. He stuck
some found elkhorns into the
tops of two peaks, each wrapped
in part of a Tuscarora newspaper,
with attached notes containing their own names and those of
the mountains they were claiming, one for Wright and the other
named for his own alias, Mount Leon. "I often wonder," Charlie
wrote later, "if these antlers have been found since the opening of
these mountains to white settlers."[8]

While the men were staying at a cattle ranch on the Cherokee
Strip, another guest, known as "Six-Shooter Bill" and wearing

---

* Parker's famous Star House was built by 1890, the year of this visit, but Siringo does not mention it, only saying he saw him in his "camp," perhaps still a
tepee. He also colorfully describes Parker's mustache, which does not appear in
any photos of Parker I have seen.

two guns, recognized the cowboy detective among the group eating breakfast. Charlie had noticed him staring as they ate. When he left Wright unattended after the meal to go get their packhorse reshod, Six-Shooter Bill approached Wright and asked if he was wanted for any serious crime. If so, he cautioned, he should "shake that detective you are traveling with." Though unnerved, even surly after the stranger's advice, Wright refused to fully believe it and continued riding in silence with his alleged friend.

It was also too late now, unless he killed Siringo: while they were still in the mountains, Charlie had "secured a complete confession . . . as to how he and his gang had blown up Price and Peltier," cutting the fuses the same length and lighting them simultaneously, "so that the mine owners would sprout angel wings together."[9] Wright had told him he lit the fuse that launched C. W. Price.

They somehow carried on the six hundred miles back to Denver, saving Charlie the legal trouble of extricating Wright across state lines. Wright was then arrested and brought to the Pinkerton offices to see C. W. Price, with a notary ready to make Wright's confession official. He would agree to testify in return for not serving time himself. Charlie had spent nine months on the Tuscarora case.

Mamie's operation had proved unsuccessful, and she returned with Viola to Denver in the late summer of 1890. Charlie found new quarters for the family, now joined by Mamie's aunt, Mrs. Emma Read, but his wife's condition only worsened. "H. C. Floyd has received news that his daughter, Mrs. Mamie Siringo, who spent last winter in Springfield, is dangerously ill at her home in Denver," warned the *Springfield* (Missouri) *Daily Leader* in early August.[10] Siringo asked McParland to assign him mostly city work so he might stay nearby his dying wife.[11]

Mamie seemed to be in her final days when Siringo went downtown one Saturday night to collect his paycheck, not long after completing the Nevada job. Walking on Laramie Street, he was on his way to get his favorite "old Colts 45" back from the Rocky Mountain pawnshop where he had left it, needing money. He was still carrying the inferior gun he'd borrowed from a fellow operative while his Colt was in hock when he came upon a sudden crowd. A chemical factory had blown up, and people were gathered out of curiosity to see a rumored body brought out.

After climbing on an iron fence for a better view, Siringo was hauled down by a big policeman guarding the crime site and a ground-floor shop window with diamonds shining in it. He tore Charlie's coat in the process. Already on edge about Mamie's condition, Siringo broke his favorite umbrella over the cop's head. Each aimed his weapon at the other, and Charlie pressed the trigger. The lives of both men were arguably then saved as a second policeman seized Charlie from behind, and "his right hand grabbed the pistol, and the hammer came down on his thumb instead of the cartridge."[12]

Siringo was hustled away into the police wagon and to the Denver city jail. Word quickly got to McParland about what had happened to his troubled star detective. He paid a quiet visit to the jail that night, followed by the chief of police, who was grudgingly convinced to free the man who clubbed and nearly shot his officer. As fond as Mac might be of his cowboy sleuth, a favor was now owed.

Late that August, Mamie died at home, struggling to breathe as Charlie held her by the open window. "Her suffering had been something awful," he wrote, "and our physician . . . shed tears when the end came. This was a surprise to me for I did not think a doctor could shed tears, as they became so accustomed to great suffering."[13] Siringo felt he was unable to raise his five-year-old girl by himself, and so he let Mamie's aunt, Emma Read, "one of God's great and noblest women," take Viola when she returned to Anna, Illinois, "as she had no children of her own and begged so hard for the child to raise, as I had no way of caring for her."[14] He saw the pair off at the station and made sure the sad news of his wife's passing reached the place where Mamie had seemed happiest, informing the *Caldwell Advance* that "consumption" had taken her.

Whether or not McParland thought the change would benefit his grieving detective, Charlie was still the only operative in the Denver office who spoke even rudimentary Spanish, so he was "sent off to Santa Fe, New Mexico,"[15] on the investigation of a political shooting. His time there would almost kill him but lead to a new home in the high desert.

20

White Caps

Thomas B. Catron had moved from Missouri to the New Mexico Territory after the Civil War, a Confederate veteran who joined the Republican Party and studied both Spanish and the law. By the night of the shooting, February 5, 1891, he had become a power broker in the territory, leading the legislative council's judiciary committee in its evening planning sessions. Several council members were gathered in a ground-floor office of Santa Fe's Griffin block, fronting the plaza at the corner of Washington and Palace Avenues. Behind the room's glass double doors, some stood and others sat around a flat desk near the front, including the young senator from Silver City, J. A. Ancheta, author of a bill to establish public schools in the territory. He had just taken the place nearest the street left by a senator who was fetching a book of statutes from a shelf. Catron sat opposite Ancheta behind a pile of books.

At about 7:15 p.m., a council page noticed an armed man try the outside door and peer through the glass, partly hidden by a lattice. "What is it, *amigo*?" the page recalled saying, spooking the lurker. Less than an hour later, with the senators still seated, there was the sound of horses in the street.[1]

A man named Barney Spiers, who had left work at the Broad Gauge Saloon, on the east side of the plaza, saw two men riding in a nervous hurry. They had dark mustaches and black slouch hats, slowing their horses before the office doors long enough to fire and gallop off. A shotgun blast smashed the pane of glass and struck Senator Ancheta in the neck and ear, and a rifle shot passed in between Catron and former governor Stover, lodging in an adobe wall. The riders nearly collided with Barney Spiers as they escaped up Palace Avenue. The other senators hurried to mop up Ancheta's blood, using handkerchiefs and the legal documents at hand.[2]

Ancheta survived the shooting, but the conclusion the next day was that the real target had been Thomas Catron, whose office it was. He had been sitting facing the street, shielded by the pile of law books before him. A $20,000 reward was created by the legislature to find the assassins. It was put in the charge of the territorial governor, L. Bradford Prince; the solicitor general, Edward L. Bartlett; and Catron, the assumed target but also Prince's rival in the New Mexico Republican Party. A posse followed the shooters by lamplight several miles to the junction splitting toward the New Mexico settlements of Las Vegas or Ojo de Vaca (Cow Springs) but lost the trail.

These were thought to be the facts when the governor hired the Pinkerton agency: that "a brace of horsemen" had tried to assassinate Thomas Catron. Governor Prince asked for a detective who knew Spanish; Siringo was still the best speaker in the Denver office. Calling him in, McParland explained that a New Mexico vigilante group calling itself Las Gorras Blancas (The White Caps) was probably responsible and naturally compared them to his own Molly Maguires. Siringo would have to befriend these men and learn for himself when he reached New Mexico later that February, traveling as "C. Leon Allison." After buying many rounds, he had learned at first only one clue about the mounted shooters: "One of the horses had a crooked hind foot, only half the hoof making an impression in the snow." But it was a case that would bring him back to a part of the country he had admired during his first youthful bit of detecting, searching for Panhandle cattle rustled by Billy the Kid. This time, with no remaining family in Denver, he would try to stay longer.[3]

The White Caps had originated in reaction to Anglo cattle ranchers moving into northeastern New Mexico and squatting and fencing off plains and streams in what had been a land grant of thousands of acres used for common sheep grazing. Wearing white on their heads and mounts, the vigilantes rode at night, cutting barbed wire, scattering cattle, burning railroad ties, and sometimes killing ranchers. They also influenced ballots. "During the last election, the 'White Caps' had carried the county of San Miguel, Las Vegas being the county seat, and elected to the legislature one of its leaders," Siringo wrote. Pablo Herrera was not only a founder (with his brothers) of Las Gorras Blancas but had emerged from a stretch in the territorial prison to get elected senator, infuriating Governor Prince. Siringo recalled, "My mind was soon made up to win the friendship of this ex-convict member of the legislature, and through him to join the 'White Caps.'"[4]

A sheriff who was also a member made the introductions one rowdy night at a Santa Fe saloon, and Charlie, "by spending money in the tough dance halls . . . soon won the friendship of Pablo Herrera."[5] When the legislative session ended, Siringo was invited aboard the train with Herrera to ride the eighty miles back to Las Vegas, where he bought a horse and lived for a time on brother Nicanor Herrera's ranch outside town. When he learned of a big upcoming meeting of White Caps in the village of Tecolote, he "laid plans."

Siringo was suspected many times while playing outlaw around the West. But the night he accompanied Pablo Herrera to his first White Caps meeting, seeking membership on little but his own affability and passable Spanish, was a standout: after drinking all day with him, he offered to ride with Herrera the eight miles to the meeting place, a large adobe hall with heavily curtained windows near Tecolote, hoping privately to be invited in by his drunken friend. At the door, Herrera gave the secret knock, but his "gringo" sidekick was

Pablo Herrera (standing), with his brothers, introduced Siringo into their vigilante society, Las Gorras Blancas, an assignment that showed him the pleasures of New Mexico.

A Cowboy Detective / *Author's collection*

understandably barred, and the pair nearly caused a riot as they pushed through among a couple of hundred "Mexicans and half-breed Indians in the hall," including "one negro who had married a Mexican woman." Herrera seized the room's attention and made an intoxicated appeal on Charlie's behalf, declaring he would never bring a treacherous snake among his brothers. With a leader so passionately vouching for him, Siringo was accepted, and later in the evening joined other new members in a ceremony that he claimed resembled that of the Knights of Labor.[6] Now he was a White Cap.

Charlie liked almost anyone he met who didn't mistreat a horse, and his membership allowed him to travel the region chatting up new friends, staying with families, and becoming trusted enough to attend their funerals. Having gained acceptance, Siringo was gradually convinced that the White Caps were not behind the shooting he had been sent to solve and that Catron had not even been the intended target. Senator Ancheta, actually wounded that night, was the sponsor of a public-schools bill controversial enough among those who wanted the Catholic Church to control education in the territory. Shooting him no longer seemed a mistake to Charlie.

The governor objected throughout Siringo's employment to the lavish sums spent on Pablo Herrera and his cohort week after week, especially the rich nights entertaining at the Montezuma Hotel outside Las Vegas. He also complained to McParland about being billed for the three weeks Siringo was down with the smallpox, which had actually almost killed him. (Siringo was asked to write a last testament by a Santa Fe doctor and claimed his nighttime nurse was instructed to give him regular doses of a medicine to gradually put him out of his suffering—but the nurse had been drawn outside by a celebration in the plaza, his dereliction allowing for Siringo's revival.)

Once he was recovered, it was Santa Fe's city marshal, John Gray, who led him to Ojo de Vaca, where he found the shooters' horse with the broken hoof and secured an unsatisfying confession that told him who (Victoriano and Felipe Garcia) but not exactly why. He was "never able to satisfy myself positively, as to the motive," beyond a desire "to kill Ancheta and [former] Governor Stover for their part in helping to pass a public free school law," challenging church control.[7]

To this point, the story had followed the script of Siringo's other investigations of Western gangs—finding the roughest possible drinking partners and running a dance-hall gauntlet to prove himself. It was the Molly Maguire approach designed by McParland for Allan Pinkerton. But here Charlie was going against McParland's theory of the case, which had echoed Governor Prince's private political wish. The result made Prince unhappy, as it did not blame the White Caps and perhaps would air an intra-Republican feud. He declined to go forward with prosecution. Three years after Charlie's induction to the White Caps, Pablo Herrera was accused of murder and killed by a deputy sheriff charged with bringing him into a Las Vegas court.

The New Mexico case wound up after eight months, but Siringo found himself reluctant to leave the territory. For one thing, he had no home to speak of in Denver. He had also fallen in love with Santa Fe, its landscape, and a climate he considered "the finest that I had ever been in." He filed a homestead claim for 160 acres on public lands outside the city, then added another 65 desert acres, and a third claim in his mother's name for 140 acres.[8] These 365 acres would eventually make up his Sunny Slope ranch. But first he was called north.

21

"Oh, Mr. Allison, Run for Your Life"

Such damnable outrages as have gone on here could not happen in
any country but my own.

—Siringo operative's report, Gem, Idaho, 1891

L oose gold had been found in 1883 in Idaho's panhandle by two men working the North Fork of the Coeur
d'Alene River. There followed a bitterly short-lived rush
to find fortunes, leaving most prospectors disappointed, but a few
kept hunting, wandering far enough to find not gold but deposits
of silver and lead in creeks emptying into the South Fork. The
bigger deposits were deep down, and claims were soon filed for
mines requiring eastern capital and industrial machinery, as well
as hard-rock laborers for the risky, low-paying work below.*

By 1891, the small town of Gem, in the Coeur d'Alenes, had
emerged in a valley between two steep, timbered mountainsides.
Half its roughly one thousand inhabitants were miners, served
by a half dozen saloons and gambling halls and several stores.
The Union Pacific Railroad ran straight through the town, where
the major nearby mines were the Gem, Helen-Frisco, and Bear.

---

* "If refugees from the 'dark satanic mills' of Europe and the eastern seaboard
had hoped to slip the bonds of nineteenth-century industrialism in the West's
wide spaces," J. Anthony Lukas wrote, "western mining replicated the very
worst of the industrial system beneath the Rockies' sparkling spine" (Lukas,
*Big Trouble: A Murder in a Small Western Town Sets Off a Struggle for the Soul
of America* [Touchstone/Simon & Schuster, 1997], 875).

(The district's most productive mine was the Bunker Hill and Sullivan, near the town of Wardner.) The area miners formed a union, one mine at a time, starting in 1887 and merging in 1891; this was countered weeks later by the formation of the Mine Owners Protective Association of the Coeur d'Alenes. With the two sides poised for some kind of showdown, the mine owners hired the Thiel and Pinkerton detective agencies.[1]

Siringo claimed he turned down the Coeur d'Alenes job at first when McParland described it to him in the summer of 1891. Catching ore thieves and mine salters and dynamiters was one thing, but this seemed a different animal: forced to join the growing conflict between labor and capital in the West, Charlie told his boss he identified with the working miners in the Coeur d'Alenes. But after another operative was smelled out by the miners, McParland made the offer again. Siringo qualified his answer, "As my sympathies were with the men I accepted only on condition that I was at liberty to throw it up if I decided that the miners were in the right."[2]

He was thirty-six when he finally agreed to head for the Idaho panhandle at the beginning of September. He would later tell a grand jury: "My object and purpose in going there was to look over the ground and see where was the best place for me to locate; that is, where the worst element of the miners' union would be congregated."[3] He looked at Gem, then Burke, before returning to Gem, said to be the "toughest" of the surrounding mining camps and so the likeliest for trouble. He began as a "mucker" in the Gem mine, doing less skilled shovel work, first on days and then the night shift, far from the plains saddle life.

When Siringo arrived, remembered John Hays Hammond, an owner of the Bunker Hill mine, "he was a slender, wiry man, dark-eyed, dark-mustached, modest. Lately recovered of smallpox, he was noticeably pitted. This would be an undistinguishable identification in a tight place, but he did not seem to mind."[4] After two weeks, Charlie had learned enough to agree to see the assignment through, concluding that the union leaders were "anarchists" who had "duped the hard-working miners" into demands that would never be accepted. After dark, Siringo walked some four miles to the next town, Wallace, to mail each day's report, suspecting the postmaster in Gem was too loyal to union leadership. Each report went to Pinkerton's Saint Paul branch for transcribing before distribution to the mine owners. In one he wrote, delighting his client: "I find leaders of the Coeur d'Alene unions to be, as a rule, a vicious, heartless gang of anarchists. Many of them were rocked in the cradle of anarchy at Butte City, Montana, while others are escaped outlaws and toughs from other states." His nighttime strolls out of town for posting would soon mark him as suspicious.[5]

About September 19, one of the leaders requested Siringo come see him. George A. Pettibone, the union's financial secretary, explained that it was time for the new mucker to join. Siringo was happy to sign up, and Pettibone seems to have taken a liking to the genial Texas liar, as everyone did, soon confiding darker union business to "Mr. Allison." Siringo's affability and writing skills got him elected recording secretary of the Gem lodge, taking notes in its strategy meetings, learning about plans to flood mines and drown "scab" workers and to drag uncooperative miners from their cabins and drive them off at night. He talked the lodge president, Mr. Hughes, into letting him take the recording book home to complete his entries, which of course he copied and mailed to Saint Paul. To see the long investigation through, however, he would have to get out of the mines, getting himself fired from mucking but claiming he needed to devote all his time to his other union work, using his regular line about living off funds from an imaginary Texas

father (a figure who saw Charlie through much of his undercover career).

As part of his duties, Siringo not only was party to resist-
ing efforts to bring in nonunion workers but also saw the expul-
sion that winter of so-called loyalists already working, miners
friendly to the owners' offer, for which they were paraded and
spat on before being marched out of town. He wrote: "Often
many as half a dozen scabs would be taken from their homes,
sometimes with weeping wives and children begging for mercy,
and with tin pans and the music of bells, they would be marched
up and down the streets to be spit upon and branded as scabs
before the public eye. Then, half clothed and without food, the
poor devils would be marched up the canyon," pistols fired over
their heads to send them through the deep mountain snows.[6]

When, late in the year, the railway raised the price of transporting ore to the smelters in Omaha and Nebraska, the Mine
Owners Protective Association in turn lowered miners' wages,
starting with the less skilled muckers, bringing on a strike. In
January 1892, the mine owners saw a chance to break the union
by closing the mines, although the Bunker Hill's John Hays
Hammond would recall it the other way around: "The unions of
the district declared war on the mine owners . . . and we closed
the mines down."[7]

In the spring, Charlie bought a twelve-room frame boardinghouse on Main Street in Gem with what must have been most
of his savings, $3,000, hoping to hang on to the place and let
rooms after the strike. He shared it with a woman named Kate
Shipley and her five-year-old boy. Mrs. Shipley, whose husband
was farming elsewhere, would run the house as well as a store
she opened on its first floor, while Siringo lived upstairs, com-
manding a good view of Gem's one street to watch for trouble,
especially outside the saloons. He laid in ammunition for his

Winchester in his room, and in the backyard he had a sixteen-foot fence built with a loose board on the bottom for escaping if he was discovered.

The mine owners brought in unsuspecting immigrant workers on trains; the striking miners had sympathizers among the "railroad boys," who would tip off the leaders when a "scab train" was due, Charlie learned at the meetings. The union men gathered to meet one of these trains with violence on the platform at Wallace. The union-loyal sheriff was there to arrest the arrivals, backed by several dozen union men with clubs; the train approached, then sped through the stop. As the sheriff pursued on horseback, it skipped the next town as well, finally stopping at Burke to unload its imported workers close to the mine. It was not hard to guess that someone had alerted the mine owners to the union's plans to meet the train.

Around the first of July, Siringo was talking to a member of the Burke miners' union about preparations for coming violence. The man, John Doran, was summarizing private talks he had with his lodge brothers, Charlie later testified, who had "assured him that the trouble was coming and that it would be a bad one when it did come, and that they had canvassed the different unions to find out how many men they could rely on to do the fighting; that they found 200 in Burke; that in Gem they could only get a few because they were afraid of a traitor that was there and that they had not found out positively who it was."[8] Charlie thanked him.

In July 1892, a man calling himself Tim O'Leary was sent from the sponsor union in Butte, Montana, out to the Coeur d'Alenes to identify a snitch. Siringo remembered this man as a one-eyed "Irish hyena" whose real name was Gabe Dallas. His union had been disturbed to read its secrets in a Wardner newspaper friendly to the mine owners, the *Barbarian*. The information disclosed in the paper about their strike plans was not only embarrassing but dangerously accurate. Someone was leaking secrets from the union meetings to the owners.[9] Discussions about murdering the *Barbarian*'s editor had been taken up at several lodge gatherings that spring, Charlie later testified, with a hypothetical plan that "if they could get him close to a train they would tie a rope around his neck and tie the other end to the train when it was going to drag him to death."[10]

It didn't take O'Leary long to suspect the small and personable new recording secretary with a Texas accent, C. Leon Allison. He set a trap for Charlie and called a large meeting of miners. After opening in the usual way, with Siringo reading minutes from the last meeting, O'Leary seized the moment with a stem-winder about union brotherhood and treachery, warming the men's desire for vengeance. "Brothers of the Gem Miners' Union," he continued, "you have allowed a traitor to enter your ranks. He now sits within reach of my hand. If you do your duty, he will never leave this hall alive." Charlie clapped along with the others until it became clear who was the suspect among them.[11] The disclosures in the *Barbarian* could only have come from the man in charge of the Gem union's record book, O'Leary went on. Siringo was asked to hand over his book to be inspected during a ten-minute recess.

Siringo feared he was discovered when O'Leary announced the meetings' logbook was missing a page. Charlie could see that the several hundred miners filling the room suddenly wanted him dead. The page in question had been a list of plans for flooding the mines and drowning scabs, which he had been ordered to remove and burn so it would not fall into the hands of the mine owners' association. (He had instead sent the incriminating page straight to the owners.) "Why is this page torn out?" O'Leary demanded. Siringo gripped his pistol, holstered under his arm, and answered, "Ask the President. He ordered me to cut it out." After calling this explanation a lie, Hughes at last remembered asking him to remove the page, and the meeting quieted somewhat. It was finally adjourned with only a temporary reprieve for Charlie, with "the president informing the members that though there was obviously a traitor somewhere the evidence was not sufficient yet to point him out."[12] Clearly they would try again.

He barely escaped the union hall with his life, and weeks later he would tell mining executive William Stoll, who later quoted it in his book *Silver Strike: The True Story of Silver Mining in the Coeur D'Alenes*, "That was the most exciting moment I've had in years; I had an idea the game was up."[13] But he was still marked as suspicious. Mrs. Shipley called his attention to a man she said had been watching the boardinghouse. Sitting in front of the post office, Siringo recognized Black Jack Griffin, an escaped conspirator from the dynamiting case in Tuscarora, who knew Charlie's real name was no more "Allison" in Gem than it had been "Leon" in Nevada.[14]

While Charlie was shunned by many members, a union friend warned him he would certainly be killed at the next meeting, on July 9. Instead of entering the union hall, he handed over his logbook to the guard at the door, as well as an outraged resignation letter written in character:*

---

* In each of his accounts, except for *A Lone Star Cowboy* (in which the Coeur d'Alenes story does not appear), Charlie says this union rep called himself O'Leary but was really named Dallas. Strange, then, that he would refer to him in his resignation letter as Dallas. But the letter appears this way in William T. Stoll's *Silver Strike*, which also quotes a number of Siringo's reports sent to the mine owners. The letter, therefore, may have been in Stoll's possession, as it is only paraphrased in Siringo's *Cowboy Detective, Two Evil Isms*, and *Riata and Spurs*.

Dallas and the others have knifed me in the back under the impression I am a Pinkerton detective, the lowest and most degraded calling any man can follow. To be accused of a crime so black by my best friends is more than I can bear. For this reason I will never set foot in the union hall again. I remain

Yours to the end,

C. Leon Allison[15]

While trying to warn two nonunion men that they were going to be killed in Dutch Henry's saloon in Gem, he faced down a hostile group with his pistol. He escaped and then sneaked to the Gem mill to get help for the pair, but they had meanwhile been beaten, and one thrown half dead into the river. Charlie walked to the next town, Wallace, for a doctor, then risked returning by train, meeting his former financial secretary George Pettibone as he exited. Pettibone now saw Siringo as an enemy and warned him against bringing the rifle he was carrying back to the boardinghouse. "You just watch me and see!" Siringo replied and made his way up the street to his room to dig in for an attack.

War in the valley may have been inevitable, but a disastrous Pinkerton operation in Homestead, Pennsylvania, on July 6 certainly brought violence closer in the Coeur d'Alenes. The Carnegie Steel Company, following a lockout of union workers, hired some three hundred Pinkerton detectives (many for the day) to attempt to hold the Homestead works to enable nonunion men to enter and replace its striking workforce. As the Pinkertons approached on towed barges along the Monongahela River, steel workers fired at them from the banks and nearby hillside; the Pinkertons, charged with opening and guarding the plant (which had been surrounded with barbed wire) shot back with Winchesters. A dozen people had been killed by evening, when the strikers accepted the Pinkertons' white flag but continued to beat them, joined by members of their gathered families. The Homestead riot would rile the public and Congress against the agency.

But even before Homestead, Siringo had warned his clients that full warfare was coming to the mines in July. Close to six o'clock on the morning of July 11, union men joined a full shooting war when one of them was fired upon outside the Frisco mine. Then they came for the traitor Allison, pushing through the front doors of his rooming house, where Mrs. Shipley kept her store. Siringo's rear escape route had been watched for several days by armed sentries hoping to pick him off, so he cut a hole in the floorboards of a front room. Trading his cowboy hat and raincoat for an old leather jacket and dark slouch hat, he climbed down into the foundation to hide, bringing a sandwich and coffee Mrs. Shipley had made him. She covered the hole with a rug and large trunk, and as the union men approached the building, she gave him the news through the floorboards. "Oh, Mr. Allison, run for your life," she said, telling him what she'd heard about the Frisco mill being blown up and the scabs killed and wounded. "Now they are coming to get you and burn you at the stake as a traitor." Then she bravely faced his mob for him.[16]

Led by George Pettibone, the men had blown up the Frisco mill with a Union Pacific car filled with 750 pounds of explosives. From an injured survivor of the explosion, Charlie would learn that Pettibone had lit the fuse himself, rolling the car down toward the mine and destroying the mill. The miners threatened to blow up the Gem mill in the same way, unless given custody of a band of scabs taking refuge there.

O'Leary (Gabe Dallas) led the lynchers that came for Siringo, demanding, "Where's that infernal detective Allison?" and explaining their grisly plans for him. Kate Shipley claimed to have no knowledge of the whereabouts of Mr. Allison, while

Siringo crawled from his dark hiding place through the wall and toward the street, inching along on his stomach and dragging his rifle beneath the wooden boardwalk where the armed group was waiting. Through a gap he could see his enemy Dallas now lurking above him, "leaning on a double-barreled shot-gun."[17] He considered taking an easy, suicidal shot, but that would have given away his location, which offered no quick escape. Instead, he bellied his way the length of three buildings down the street and emerged under a saloon, next door to the miners' union hall. Beneath the saloon he could stand, as it was stilted over a "brush-wood swamp," but discovered his watch and its gold chain had been hung up on some of the brush. He decided against going back to find the timepiece, even though a gold charm on its chain was engraved with his alias initials, C.L.A.

He recalled being too scared to spit, which he had never before experienced. He now faced a high railway embankment and beyond it the Gem mill. He could not climb it without attracting some Swedish riflemen watching for him. A single bullet flew past him as he climbed into a boxed water culvert to the left and struggled through its current, holding to the beams with one hand and keeping his Winchester dry with the other. Climbing out from beneath the raised house of a Swedish woman who knew him from the union, he risked being shot by both sides but dropped his gun in front of an armed guard at the mill, who asked if he was the detective and then let him join the men sheltering within.

Under threat of bombing, the Gem's superintendent first sent a group (including Charlie) to block the tramway against a wagon of explosives possibly rolling into it. Despite Siringo's advice, the mine owners then ordered the superintendent to surrender his nonunion men in order to protect the Gem from further violence. Charlie thought he would never survive if caught

Gem, Idaho. This photograph shows the labeled route of Charlie's escape when a mob came to kill him. He wrote: "A. The author's building, where [Siringo] sawed a hole in the floor. B. Jenny Nelson's hotel, where the author escaped through a window. C. Saloon building, where the author crawled from under the sidewalk. D. Miners' Union hall. E. Where the author entered the culvert. F. House where the author emerged from the culvert. G. Daxon's saloon. H. Company store."
Riata and Spurs / *Author's collection*

by the union and so escaped with a mine guard into the mountain woods. But despite their battle victories, the union's triumph was short-lived after martial law was declared. From the hills above Wallace, Siringo and the guard he had been camping with, Stark, saw federal troops and state militia arrive on July 14 to round up union officials. Being rescued by the federal government had a strange effect on the Texan: "When the large American flag was planted near the Carter hotel my heart broke loose from its mooring, where it had been hitched under the Confederate flag of my babyhood. Stark and I gave three cheers for the

Star Spangled Banner of our united country, and deep down in my heart I made a vow to die and bleed, if necessary, to uphold the honor of this flag."[18]

More than a year after he first arrived, Charlie testified at the trials in Coeur d'Alene and Boise. The man the community had known as Allison reappeared as a cowboy in a suit, reciting what he had seen in shocking detail. When he was done, noted a reporter, "The evidence so stunned the defense that [lawyer] Reddy did not cross examine him."[19] In all, eighteen union leaders were convicted, including George A. Pettibone, but their verdicts were later reversed by the US Supreme Court, and they spent less than a year in prison. After their experiences in the Coeur d'Alenes in the 1890s, Pettibone and other mining leaders would help form the radical Western Federation of Miners and would meet McParland and the Pinkertons again in a national trial with Clarence Darrow. Despite his feelings about their leadership, Siringo later regretted his work against "miners in their fight for justice" as a "blot on my conscience."[20]

An elegant Siringo as he looked when he returned to testify in the Coeur D'Alene trial, 1892.

Haley Memorial Library and History Center

What was left to show from Siringo's fourteen months on the mining case was his boardinghouse, which he had kept to offer to his late wife's aunt Emma Read and husband to run. But that was soon lost too. Mrs. Shipley's share was sold to the couple, who moved out to Gem, bringing Charlie's daughter, Viola, and opening a barbershop next door. Charlie had returned to Denver and begun receiving monthly income from his boarders when the building was burned to the ground in January 1893. According to Charlie, he lost most of his original $3,000 investment in the fire. The family briefly joined him in Colorado before eventually resettling in Silver City, New Mexico. "It pained me to know that the hole sawed in the floor went up in smoke," he wrote. "It would have been a satisfaction could it have been bottled up and handed down to my grandchildren as a relic of the time their grandsire had climbed into a hole in time of danger!"[21]

In Denver, Siringo took a brief assignment posing as a mining executive, a personality he could well imagine after his employment in Idaho, but a case made slightly chancy by working undercover in a town where he was already known. In the summer of 1893 in Denver, he met Lillie Thomas, "a pretty, blue-eyed girl" who would become his second wife. It is not clear if he was still in character as the successful mining executive Charles LeRoy or presented himself simply as a Pinkerton cowboy detective between missions.

Lillie was twenty-one and Charlie thirty-eight on the day they married in the fall of 1893. She came with him on assignment to Cheyenne, where he was working on a railroad case. Lillie's parents were both English immigrants, and she had been born and raised in Michigan before coming to Denver. The detective's life was an awful one for a wife, he would later write, as explanation for the couple's troubles. "We lived together long enough to have one son," whom they named William Lee Roy Siringo, calling him Lee Roy, echoing Charlie's frequent alias.[22]

In the family portrait they had taken in 1897, she is a beautiful young woman in a shirtwaist dress and exuberantly flowered hat, her dark eyes and faintest of smiles reflecting pride in her new family; on the other side of their bonneted baby wrapped in a white gown sits her detective husband in a three-piece Sunday suit, hair receding slightly along the rim where his dark hat normally sits, which he holds on his knee. Around this time, the couple was arguing about moving to Los Angeles, where her parents were, or staying on in Denver for his work, or possibly building his ranch on the land he had near Santa Fe. But Siringo would soon be gone again, and the argument postponed.

22

For the Taking

The first peacetime train robberies roughly coincided with the original Texas cattle drives after the Civil War, made possible by the arrival of the same railroads; they seemed a holdover from wartime, guerrilla sabotage carried out by men who may not all have known or accepted that the war had ended. When railroads began to cross the country, creating an eastern cattle market and a network of railroad towns, they had offered banks and express companies a quicker alternative to the vulnerable stagecoaches for transporting bullion and currency. But wealth traveling long lonely tracts soon became its own temptation.

Only weeks after the April 1865 signing at Appomattox, a train was "thrown" from its tracks near North Bend, Indiana, and an employee of the Adams Express Company was threatened at gunpoint. One of the robbers, a Kentuckian calling himself George Sturgeon, was caught and turned over to Indiana military authorities, but derailing the train before using his gun in the robbery seemed to keep this theft from being memorialized as a classic holdup.[1]

The biggest early rail theft was carried out in the Northeast, on the night of January 6, 1866, when a group organized by a bored Union veteran and railroad brakeman pilfered an Adams Express car carrying nearly a half million dollars on the New York–Boston line. The ringleader, John Grady, had noticed on his runs to Boston that the Adams clerk was prone to regular naps, and so Grady's fellow conspirators had little trouble riffling through the car's packages and strongboxes, dropping much of their haul from the railroad bridge at Cos Cob, Connecticut, intending to return to the leafy hamlet along the Mianus River. They attempted to retrieve it the next day by renting a horse and wagon from a Norwalk stableman, who grew suspicious enough to have his son follow the strangers, then tipped off the nearest sheriff, who alerted the Pinkertons.[2]

Since the Adams Express theft did not take place out West, and no one was held up at gunpoint by bandits boarding the train, a heist from later that year is widely considered the first classic train robbery. In October 1866, brothers John and Simeon Reno stopped a moving train on the Ohio and Mississippi Railway line in a remote section of Jackson County, Indiana. They received $13,000 for their risk. After further robberies by the Reno family, three of the brothers were lynched in 1868 in a jail corridor in New Albany, Indiana, by a "vigilance committee" that had come by railroad just to hang them.[3]

The railroads were already business clients of the growing detective agencies, which investigated their staffs for varying offenses from pilferage to unionizing. Then the temptation of bullion and banknotes traveling new rural rail lines led to an age of celebrated train heists from the James and Younger gangs in Missouri to the Sontag brothers in the Pacific Northwest and down to the last and greatest of the robber gangs, outlaws Siringo would spend four years chasing.

At the close of the nineteenth century and the end of the Wild West period, a train-robbing group emerged from the collection of criminals loosely known as the Wild Bunch.* They worked largely out of Brown's Park, near the Utah-Colorado border, and the natural fortress-like Hole-in-the-Wall, southwest of Kaycee, Wyoming. Known for rustling and well-planned stage and bank robberies, some members of the gang had robbed a Southern Pacific passenger train at Humboldt, Nevada, in July 1898. But early on the morning of June 2, 1899, the Bunch would draw national attention when a westbound passenger train traveling through a rainstorm, the *Overland Flyer*, was stopped at 2:18 a.m. outside Wilcox, Wyoming, where it was already overdue.

The rain and dark obscured the hatted figure holding a red signal lantern beside the track; whether friend or highwayman, the engineer, W. R. Jones, could not tell without stopping the train. After leaning out of his cab to learn the reason for the red lamp, a second man, who Jones later identified only as "the leader," climbed down from the coal tender behind him holding a pistol.

As events progressed, all the men Jones and his fireman would meet—from the lamp bearer to the coal-dusted leader and several others who emerged from the dark—wore long masks and were armed with Colts and Winchesters. The engineer had stopped in case the lamp meant the bridge ahead was washed out, but instead the men wanted him to uncouple the train and pull one half across the bridge.

---

* An original Wild Bunch, also called the Doolin-Dalton gang, roamed Oklahoma territory in the 1890s.

The gang's leader that day is sometimes assumed to have been Butch Cassidy (Robert LeRoy Parker), the Mormon-raised ranch hand, rustler, and bank robber who designed many of the gang's exploits. A broad-shouldered outlaw with a soft face, light brown hair, and what his wanted poster described as "a remarkably square jaw," he was the third-generation son of his namesake, an English-born Mormon rancher who had made the trek to Utah. There Butch would later be introduced to the frontier network of criminal hideouts by a ranch hand and rustler named Mike Cassidy, who mentored him sufficiently before his own departure that Butch honored him by using his last name. Called "Bob," except by his parents, who favored LeRoy, he possibly picked up "Butch" during a short-lived job as a butcher's assistant in Rock Springs, Wyoming.

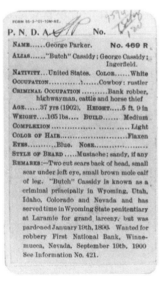

Pinkerton mug card of Butch Cassidy (with description), carried by detectives in the field.
Buffalo Bill Center of the West, Cody, WY, McCracken Research Library

But the train crew's accounts of the leader as "a small man, almost under size" suggested it was not Butch (who was about five feet ten) but possibly his harder colleague Harvey Logan, also known as Kid Curry, the most vicious and deadly of the group, short and dark-complected, with a black, brushy mustache and a deep killer's stare.[4] For a time, law enforcement (including Siringo) considered Curry the gang's leader. His partner at the front of the train was most likely Harry Longabaugh (the Sundance Kid), but the masks of the outlaws and the jangled nerves of their victims made it difficult to untangle their identities. If Cassidy was not along that day, he surely planned the robbery and met up with the gang afterward for the split.[5]

When hit with a pistol butt and asked to name the mail clerk, the engineer made one up, "Sherman," which the robbers called out while trying to get inside the mail car. "I told them Sherman was not there," recalled the actual mail clerk, W. G. Bruce. "They told me to open the door and come out anyway." He and his colleague inside declined and put out the lights in hopes of confusing their attackers, but "the bandits then fired several shots through the mail car, sending the bullets crosswise, lengthwise and cornerwise."[6] When the clerks still refused, the robbers blew the door off its hinges with powder, fired another shot inside, and announced they were going to place dynamite beneath the mail car, at which point the clerks finally emerged. A search of the mail sacks proved disappointing, and the robbers moved on to the express car.

The express messenger, Charles E. Woodcock, went even beyond his brave colleagues and famously refused to open the door. The train had already been uncoupled, and the mail and express cars pulled away to prepare for dynamiting the safe, which Woodcock still guarded. Like the mail clerks, Woodcock would not show himself and instead put out the lights of the car.

The gang fired a shot through his window, then blew the door, the explosion taking off much of the side of the car and shredding its roof. A slightly concussed Woodcock then stumbled or was dragged out to take his place alongside the other clerks as the gang exploded the iron safe.[7] The messenger's standoff with the outlaws would be depicted seventy years later by screenwriter William Goldman in *Butch Cassidy and the Sundance Kid.**

The robbers made off with between $30,000 and $50,000 in unsigned banknotes; the figure is unclear partly due to how much money they had blown to confetti but also because the railroad companies understandably downplayed the full amounts of their losses (in this case listing the theft of "$40,000 incomplete currency"). A shipment of packed raspberries had exploded along with the safe, staining the ground near the ruined railcar a violent red. The fact that the notes were unsigned would make the job easier for the detectives following the gang's frayed currency passed around the West.

Rested horses were waiting for the group, which probably included Harvey "Kid Curry" Logan and his brother Lonnie Logan, George "Flatnose" Currie, Ben "the Tall Texan" Kilpatrick, Will "News" Carver (so called because he liked reading news reports of his exploits), and Harry Longabaugh, as it traveled north. Having sets of relay mounts stashed along their routes was a hallmark of the Wild Bunch robberies, as fresh horses would always outrun the weary rides of local possemen. The gang of six train robbers then split into two groups of three, one heading farther

---

* In addition to express messengers like Charles Woodcock, many bank tellers heroically risked their lives in holdups. Both the James-Younger gang and the Daltons were overcome by townspeople because a brave teller stalled them by claiming he could not yet open the vault. This delay gave locals time to arm and organize in Northfield, Minnesota, in 1876, destroying the James-Younger gang, and in Coffeyville, Kansas, finishing the Daltons in 1892.

north and another to the south, but they would soon meet their match in a professional force that traveled by both horse and train.

In Casper, Wyoming, men guarded the bridge in the rain while trains carrying detectives departed from Cheyenne and Laramie. The posse that assembled at Casper included two sheriffs and a Union Pacific detective and picked up the trail six miles from town, where a rancher had seen three of the gang camping on Casper Creek before they raised a rifle and warned him, "Hit the road and hit it quick." They would turn out to be Harvey Logan, Flatnose Currie, and Cassidy's best friend, Ellsworth "Elza" Lay. Near the cabin where they had stayed, the lawmen followed the trio's tracks west until a point where they had dismounted and walked their horses. The posse followed this trail right into a surprise firefight, in which Sheriff Oscar Hiestand's horse was spooked and run off, and bullets struck the mount of posseman Tom MacDonald.

Now horseless, Sheriff Hiestand walked fifteen miles back to Casper for help while the posse's leader, Sheriff Joe Hazen of Converse County, pressed on. After chasing the outlaws the rest of that day and night, Hazen rediscovered their tracks in a draw between rocky hillsides. The gang, lying in wait, then made another stand, one shooter (probably the proven killer Harvey Logan)* firing from behind a boulder and hitting Hazen in the stomach; Dr. J. F. Leeper jumped down from his horse to help but had to hide until a break in the shooting allowed him to tend Hazen's grievous wound. The sheriff would be laid aboard a train and would die on the way home to Douglas, Wyoming. The three outlaws would run off their own horses to confuse their

---

* He was known to the law variously as Harvey Curry, Kid Curry, and finally by his birth name, Harvey Logan. Calling him by each of his names as the Pinkertons learned them would take a longer book. At this point, McParland still thought they were after Harvey Curry until Pinkerton operative Billy Sayles learned otherwise.

Della Moore and Kid Curry.
A Cowboy Detective / *Author's collection*

remaining pursuers and clamber their way along a ridge, bearing heavy sacks of gold around their necks, guns in their free hands.

After the death of Sheriff Hazen, up to two hundred lawmen and a half dozen bloodhounds came after the gang; the railroad companies combined forces to pledge $3,000 per outlaw head. The race was on to catch them before they escaped through the famous Hole-in-the-Wall, a gorge reported to be "so narrow that two horses can not walk abreast."[8] Once behind the thousand-foot red granite wall, they would be hidden among armed friends in an enclosed barracks for rustlers, road agents, and wayward cowboys with its own stores of food, natural tunnels, and streams. The interior, once a prehistoric lake, had natural springs and meadows, where residents did minimal farming as well as kept horses, cattle, and sheep.

The Hole-in-the-Wall had long been a favorite place to keep stolen livestock, and the James gang had sheltered there in the 1870s, as had the Northern Cheyenne chief Dull Knife, eluding government forces in 1876. "Indians and outcasts have used the Hole-in-the-wall as a place of refuge for two generations," reported the *Anaconda Standard*, a Montana newspaper, that summer of 1899.[9] It had filled with unemployed cowboys after the "Big Die Up" of 1886–87. The cast of visitors behind the wall varied wildly over the years, the *Standard* explained: "It is estimated that as many as 100 outlaws are living there—all in harmony, for they dare not quarrel."[10] Well into June, printed reports speculated that the Union Pacific train heist was the work of "Laughing Sam" Carey's gang, known to hide in the Hole-in-the-Wall basin, while others nominated the feared Roberts brothers.

Railroad detective Fred Hans had survived multiple missions behind the Wall on manhunts, following his first bandit inside in 1879, a stage robber inexplicably called "Shack Nasty Jim." Hans had made a number of subsequent visits as a lawman and warned that with the right shooters guarding the entrance, it was a natural breastwork: "If I were in the Hole-in-the-Wall with sufficient ammunition and a Howitzer, I would defy the world to dislodge me."[11]

Even if the train robbers were to slip behind the wall, claimed a dispatch out of Casper in mid-June 1899, righteous forces were on the way: "The 'Hole in the Wall,' for years a refuge for outlaws, promises to be cleansed of its desperate inhabitants."[12] But while the killing of Sheriff Hazen had brought the large posse together, its riders did not risk a battle inside the walls with an unknown number of gunmen.

As it turned out, much of the train gang was traveling south by then; riding so quickly over the desert on their relay horses as to almost provide their own alibi, wrote one historian. News of the hunt went national late that June as the *New York Herald* ran a prison photo of a man identified as "Buck" Cassidy in a story about the Hole-in-the-Wall gang.

Through much of this period, robberies had appeared as flags pinned to the worn map of the West behind the desk in James McParland's Western Division office in Denver; red flags marked lingering robberies that had not been resolved, white stood for cases closed through detective work or violence or both. As the century closed out, the pattern of robberies still flagged in red on his map troubled him enough to summon the best detectives he knew to Denver for a conference. William Pinkerton wrote him about what he would fancily name "The Train Robber's Syndicate": It is "composed of outlaws and thieves headed by George LeRoy Parker, alias Butch Cassidy, a cowboy gambler and rustler, and is composed of members of the Curry and Logan gangs. From reliable information we have received, they intend to make railroads and express companies their victims."[13]

McParland thought he knew just the men he needed. One was recently returned from an ore-theft assignment in South Africa; the other had just worked a murder case in Cripple Creek, Colorado, before briefly bodyguarding that state's governor.

On July 8, 1899, William Pinkerton wired McParland from Chicago:

SAYLES LEAVING HERE TODAY. CONSIGN SIRINGO AND ASSIGN THEM TO THE WILCOX ROBBERY FOLLOWING YOUR SUGGESTION.

Many of the gang's tracks were now weeks old, but its members would be spending the distinctive money from the robbery. A "remarkable stranger" would soon ride out, bragged the Pinkerton agency's internal report, to ingratiate himself into the outlaw ranks.

BOOK THREE
Last of the Wild

23

To the End

[Siringo] is as tough as a pine knot and I never knew of a man of his
size who can endure as much hardship as he does.

—William Pinkerton to James McParland, December 22, 1899

Out of the desert, the two riders appeared like sun-dark-
ened brothers, slight, sinewy men in shirtsleeves and
mustaches and wide-brim hats, each trailing a packhorse coated in dust. They had traveled southeast over the arid
country of the Utes and Mormons to reach the town of Price, in
Utah's Carbon County. There they checked in as prospectors,
although they seemed powerfully armed for the mining life and
showed more interest in human events than geology, browsing
the exchange papers at the offices of the Price *News-Advocate*.

Men with a half-civilized look had been nervously expected
in Carbon County since the Union Pacific passenger train was
held up that spring near Wilcox, Wyoming. Thieves regularly
crossed the county from a rocky hideout known as Robbers'
Roost, fifty miles east of Hanksville, Utah. But Price's sheriff, C. W. Allred, had been readying for a fight with the robber
gang even before the recent heist, in which the express car was
dynamited open. Only the year before, the Sheriff had joined in
a morning raid that breached Robbers' Roost, the posse carrying two dead outlaws back to Price, including one the lawmen
hoped was Butch Cassidy, worth a $1,000 bounty.[1] Shown to

men who'd known him, though, the corpse lacked any of Butch's remembered scars; this was not what reporters called the "King of Outlaws" but a ripening dead cattle thief.[2]

Sheriff Allred had more recently made notable purchases of rifles and ammunition in Salt Lake City and was armed for war when the strangers caught his eye riding into Price.[3] One of the pair taking a room at the hotel seemed to bear a skinny resemblance to a small, mustached, dark-complected man from the train-robbing crew known to some as Kid Curry. But before the Sheriff could visit with them, they had checked out of the hotel next day, riding off into a full-blown rainstorm in a mysterious hurry toward the Henry Mountains. The Sheriff, a brave, large man with a surprisingly high voice, was preparing to set out after them when they reappeared in Price instead that evening, with a story they had spent much of the day blocked by an impassable creek ahead of them and another flooded at their back, waiting for the water to subside before retreating to town.

The wet prospectors returned to their hotel, where they were soon followed upstairs by a man who knocked at their door and cheerfully introduced himself as the editor of the *News-Advocate*, whose offices they had enjoyed. Since their first arrival, he explained, there had been a suspicion they were the robbers of the Union Pacific, and if they looked out the windows, they would now see Sheriff Allred and a posse of men pointing Winchesters up toward them. The editor had been sent to announce the news of their arrest and claim the scoop.

The visitors insisted they were not outlaws but prospectors who had outfitted in Salt Lake and were headed for the mountains; that their packs carried gold pans, pickaxes, maps, and shovels as well as their weapons. After talking with the pair, the newsman made up his mind the men were probably not thieves or killers and carried his message downstairs to the Sheriff, who agreed to let them leave his town a second time, whatever they were. The strangers stayed the night, promising to ride out in the morning.

As they saddled their horses again next day, a photographer appeared and asked to take their portrait, for newsworthiness or identification. They gave him matching looks of squinty purpose, each standing with a hand grasping the reins, guns tucked calmly into their belts and pant legs stuffed in their boots. They rode out of Price as neither outlaws nor prospectors but Pinkertons on a "still hunt," seeking the very men they had been taken for.

W. O. "Billy" Sayles had returned from South Africa in time to ride again that summer of 1899 with his fellow cowboy detective Siringo. Since the robbery, "any one who looked suspicious of ever having robbed a train, was to be 'spotted,'" they had

Siringo and Sayles on the morning after a sheriff took one of them for Kid Curry, 1899.
A Cowboy Detective / *Author's collection*

learned in Price.⁴ They had come there after outfitting in Denver, buying blankets and camp supplies and one .30-40 smokeless-powder Winchester apiece, instructed to take the train to Salt Lake City to buy their horses and saddles and extra cartridges, then ride over the Colorado border to Brown's Park, a sometime haunt of the Wild Bunch in the Uinta Mountains.

But in Salt Lake, they learned from their friend Cyrus "Doc" Rivers that two of the train robbers had been seen driving a group of thirteen horses south from Brown's Park several hundred miles toward Robbers' Roost, on a plateau bounded on one side by the Green River. One of the outlaws was reported riding a cream-colored mount, while the other man sat on a dappled iron gray. By the time their superintendent allowed them to change course, Sayles and Siringo had wasted five hundred miles on horseback. From Price, they made a wet, mud-trudging ride south for several days before crossing red desert country to reach Dirty Devil River, which they followed to where the bandits and their horses had last been noticed, Hanksville, Utah.

Some of the unsigned bills taken in the train job at Wilcox turned up here and there, like unintended bread crumbs marking the robbers' trail. At the hotel in Hanksville, the agents learned that a third man trailing five horses had come through a week after the pair they were following. He had broken one of the gang's twenty-dollar bills while there, then crossed the Colorado River at Dandy Crossing; from the description by the man who'd helped him get his horses across, he sounded like the genuine Kid Curry, planning to camp where "the grass was good" and wait to hear from his friends.

They decided to leave the hunt for their original pair of outlaws and follow this figure on his slightly fresher trail. It led them to a place called White Canyon, where, after a steep climb up a rocky bluff, the trail ran out atop a mesa, tracks lightening to nothing as the sun began to set. But back down in the deep bottom of the canyon they rediscovered the trail of their original quarry, the men with the thirteen horses, riding their iron gray and cream-colored mounts that people so easily remembered. The canyon hoofprints were still readable weeks later because the trail was so seldom traveled.

Along a desolate ride of 120 miles to a Mormon settlement called Bluff City, one of the Pinkertons' packhorses was killed by a rattlesnake; they had to sort and purge supplies before carrying on. Once arrived, they learned their outlaws had been in Bluff City before them and that they were now competing with a second pair of operatives. Sayles and Siringo outraced them to chase down another sighting near Lumberton, New Mexico. Then they decided to split up, going after separate clues.

It was clear why McParland had put Sayles and Siringo together, as the pair complemented each other as skilled trackers and inexhaustible riders. They were gristly men of the range who could keep a secret and to whom nothing inessential clung. Sayles had been a cowboy in Montana before detecting, and by the end of his career, his Pinkerton bosses would claim, he had made at least one arrest in every state in the Union. Despite their fraternal appearance, Sayles was the laconic opposite of Siringo in one sense, not feeling compelled to leave behind thousands of words about his adventures.

The two men had last worked together on a comparatively exotic mission, going after $10,000 in gold stolen from a refining mill near Juneau, Alaska, in 1895. The agency's new Portland, Oregon, office had already failed on the case when Siringo sailed north in March, seeing his first whales on the boat to Juneau, "a swift little city built on stilts." He took a job as a machine oiler in the Treadwell gold mill on Douglas Island—learning that two men had left it after the theft and bought their own schooner. Once Sayles joined him, Charlie borrowed a page from his Cheyenne case, where he had reached the outlaws' Keeline Ranch with a seemingly broken leg, and decided to leave the gold mill without suspicion by staging his own injury down the basement stairs. For his part, Sayles spotted the two suspects, Hubbard and Schell, and their schooner, "lying on the waterfront among the other boats in Juneau." They would need their own craft to give chase.[5]

The pair bought a large canoe, which they filled with twenty-five gallons of Canadian rye whiskey, posing as liquor salesmen. "We had both trailed horses, cattle, and men, but never a schooner on water," Siringo admitted.[6] The liquor helped them make quick friends while paddling in unfamiliar country, as Native people they met remembered the white men who had passed in their schooner. Eventually they found the vessel moored in a place called Chieke Bay, the thieves living as guests of a white Southerner who'd married into a Native village, their stolen gold buried in the nearby woods.

By then, Charlie had had quite a lot of practice passing himself off as an experienced miner, and the two detectives announced they were after "Lost Rocker," a fabled gold mine supposed to be near a local waterfall. They busied themselves making tests of rocks in the camp and generally talking like miners, until they piqued the interest of the thieves, anxious to learn how to melt their stolen gold into bricks. At one point, Hubbard suspected Sayles of being "a fly cop, a detective," because he had referenced his wide travels, but Siringo talked him out of his suspicion.

While allegedly going to Juneau for supplies to do a proper job of melting the gold, Siringo alerted a deputy US marshal to the camp on the far side of the island, who waited to be summoned. One morning, after the thieves had uncovered their entire stash, Siringo beat his way along bear trails to rouse the sleeping marshal, who returned with him to the camp to make the arrest. Hubbard was outraged at the betrayal by his miner friends. "'How in hell can you face the public again after the way you have treated me?'" he demanded of Siringo, who answered, "My conscience wouldn't bother me on that score."[7]

Whenever Siringo lost the trail chasing the Union Pacific train robbers, he would wire his contacts around the West for possible sightings. In Lumberton, New Mexico, J. M. Archuleta, from Siringo's first extended detective assignment, reported seeing the two men and their memorable horses. Hearing the pair were traveling toward Bland, New Mexico, he followed that lead while Billy Sayles returned to Colorado for any sign of the stolen money. Charlie thought at first he was trailing members of the "Curry gang," and he got information of greater and lesser usefulness on what became a very long wander, making detours to see old friends while waiting to learn the next clues by wire.

Outside Fort Smith, Arkansas, his investigation overlapped with that of another Pinkerton, known as Darkbird, who next summoned Charlie to Nashville, where it turned out he had been trailing the wrong set of desperadoes. Then, suffering from malaria he had picked up in the swamps, Darkbird was ordered back to Denver. Deep in rural Arkansas, Siringo got a tip from a moonshiner steering him back toward the true outlaws' trail, but he was still weeks behind his robbers when called back to Denver to learn that Sayles had had a bit of luck.

While Charlie thought he was pursuing Kid Curry, that outlaw was by now in New Mexico Territory. More likely,

Charlie had been following Flatnose Currie, unrelated to the Kid, although they sometimes rode together. At this point, Siringo was also unaware of the participation of the man he would later call "the shrewdest and most daring outlaw of the present age"—Butch Cassidy, who lived a second, nearly respectable life in New Mexico.[8]

24

Alma

Members of the Wild Bunch with cowboying skills had gone south after the Wilcox train robbery, taking ranch jobs under other names near what Siringo called "the outlaws' Paradise near the border," Alma, New Mexico. Some were returning to positions they had held the previous year. The biggest ranch around Alma was the WS, which needed men like them not just for wrangling but to clean up the petty thieving among its existing staff. For legitimate work breaking horses, Elza Lay adopted "Bill McGinnis," the name of a boyhood friend, while Harvey Logan (Kid Curry) became the cowhand "Tom Capehart."

They arrived with "Jim Lowe." The WS's manager, an Irish immigrant and ex-soldier known as Captain William French, had admired Lowe's previous work and the easy command he had with the men he brought on. Lowe, the ranchman later wrote, "was a stocky man of medium build" with "a habit of grinning and showing a row of small, even teeth when he talked."[1] Captain French would soon learn what else his capable ranch hand had been doing.

After only several weeks, two of the gang (Logan and Lay), along with a man called Red Weaver, left their ranch jobs to rob another train, the Colorado and Southern, at Folsom, New Mexico, that July of 1899.* They also invited a member of the Ketchum gang they had met, Sam Ketchum, as he was better acquainted with the territory. Although Butch Cassidy was not present, the robbery showed his influence, with the uncoupling of the train and dynamiting of its express car, but the railroad safe proved a bust, having been emptied at the previous stop. Instead of fleeing with their expected loot, the robbers returned to where they had camped beforehand, a place called Turkey Canyon. It was soon the site of a furious shootout.

A posse tracked the thieves there days after the luckless robbery, coming upon their camp in the late afternoon. Elza Lay was either shot by surprise as he went to fill his canteen or hit in an exchange of fire. Less likely was his claim that his hands had been innocently raised. However it began, the gun battle raged for much of an hour. Shots struck Sheriff Edward Farr first on his wrist and later pierced his eyes; a deputized cowboy named H. N. Love was killed, while Lay and Sam Ketchum were each badly wounded. Harvey Logan carried much of the shooting on the outlaw side and yet stood unharmed at the end. The blinded sheriff later died.[2]

Lay was helped onto a horse by Logan, who judged Sam Ketchum too weak to ride and left him among some rocks before escaping himself. Riding woozily through the hills, Lay collapsed outside the house of a rancher, who brought the bloodied

---

* The cast of characters on this job varies source to source; sometimes Will "News" Carver or Red Weaver, or another character, "Deaf Charley" Hanks, rounds out the crew. I go with Charles Kelly, *The Outlaw Trail* (Devin-Adair, 1959), and period newspapers on this. I also bow to Kelly (and Pinkerton letters) on the question of "Elza" versus "Elzy" Lay.

stranger inside, where he was ultimately arrested (and tried) under his adopted name, McGinnis. After having his arm amputated, Ketchum would die in prison of blood poisoning from his wounds. Butch Cassidy may be paired in popular history with the Sundance Kid, the man with whom he likely died a few years later. But to this point Butch's best friend since they met in 1889 had been Elza Lay, now a prisoner under another friend's name, which he would keep, after having his sentence commuted, to the peaceable end of his life, in 1934. (Answering a written Pinkerton query in 1900, the New Mexico Penitentiary's superintendent assured, "McGinnis and Elza Lay are not the same.")[3]

Weeks after Sam Ketchum's death in prison, his more infamous brother Tom "Black Jack" Ketchum, who had not joined the fruitless robbery at Folsom, attempted to hold up a train on his own near the same spot. A wary conductor was waiting, on edge against any bandit business, and blasted Ketchum with buckshot, wounding him in the shoulder. Black Jack fired back, using his other arm, hitting the conductor and the express agent, and briefly escaped, only to be caught, weakened, the following day. Tom Ketchum nearly died of blood poisoning in prison as his brother Sam had. His arm was also amputated, but he survived to be sentenced to hang in Clayton, New Mexico. In a news photo, he stares evenly toward the camera as the noose is laid around his collar before the drop. His inexperienced executioner used a long rope that afternoon, and Ketchum was decapitated. Blood "spattered on some of the guards' shoes," wrote a reporter. "Strong men looked away."[4]

In August, a Pinkerton from the Denver office named Frank Murray came to Alma, New Mexico. He was following unsigned currency from the Wilcox robbery that had been spotted by a local bank clerk after being passed in a town saloon. Once in Alma, the detective chatted about the Wild Bunch with a square-jawed bartender, Jim Lowe, who cheerfully bought him several drinks, then encouraged him to sneak out of town that night, probably saving his life. (Lowe's face matched up pretty well, it would turn out too late, with the wanted cards for "George Cassidy" that operatives carried in their pockets.)

According to rancher French's memoir, when Butch was told a detective had visited the WS, he was not surprised, recalling the evening at the bar, "We all knew who he was and what he wanted, but he didn't offer to start anything so we let him go." The man who had named the town of Alma, M. E. Coates, was also a witness, drinking with the credulous Pinkerton man that night.[5] Whether he was ignorant or simply lacked the extra force to take Butch back with him, Murray returned to Denver and did not mention that an outlaw had bought his drinks and spared his life.

Called back from his long journey trailing Flatnose Currie, Siringo was ordered to meet Billy Sayles in Helena, Montana. Sayles had learned the whereabouts, in Harlin, Montana, of a Curry Brothers saloon run by Lonnie Curry, who fled before he arrived. He had also learned that Harvey and Lonnie Curry were really named Logan and hailed from Missouri. Sayles suggested Siringo go to Landusky, in Montana's Powder River territory, where Harvey Logan owned an interest in a horse ranch for his rustling and was accused of killing the town's eponymous founder, the prospector "Pike" Landusky. Siringo was instructed to buy a horse and saddle and then "ride into the Little Rockies and get in with the friends of the Logan brothers."[6] Sayles thought Charlie might also use his charm to draw out Lonnie Logan's common-law wife, Ellie Landusky, who went by Ellie Curry. (Her house, it would turn out, was full of letters from the father of her four-year-old son, the brother of the man who had killed her father.) Sayles would meantime continue following Lonnie's trail.

Siringo set out in February 1900, riding the train to Great Falls, Montana, where he bought an excitable saddle mare and then traveled east until he was knocked off course by a blizzard. He watched the storm blow from a hotel in Lewistown for two days, then headed back into the squall to finish his ride over the Little Rockies, until he was detoured once more, arriving well after dark at a mining camp, frozen and snow-crusted in his woolen mask, where some hot whiskies and a porterhouse steak began his revival. When he set out again, he used a helpful drawing to reach the Red Barn Ranch, whose cowboys told him a chinook wind would be along to melt the snow enough to navigate. They also said that other men had stopped at the ranch both before and after robbing the Union Pacific in Wyoming.

A warm wind did arrive, transforming the snowy waste into mud he had to knife from his boots to get in the stirrups. A piece of glass he found from an old telegraph pole told him this sticky stretch of badland had once been a roadway, and he soon reached the Missouri River crossing at Rocky Point, where an old man and his son ran a trading post and ferry.

When he rode into Landusky, a crowd of miners and cowboys was gathered in front of the saloon. His mare slowed, then bucked when he spurred her forward, causing his Colt 45 to spill from its holster to the muddy street. He looked small but knotty when he swung down and introduced himself as "Charles L. Carter" (or perhaps "Lee Roy Davis"—accounts differ), but his name would change again.

A man he called "Thompson" retrieved Carter's gun where it fell. He was the business partner of the man who had killed

Pike Landusky, in the saloon of "Jew Jake" Harris, who was missing part of his leg from yet another gunfight and used a rifle as a crutch around his bar.

Charlie was here not so much about the Landusky killing but the Wilcox train robbery. Harvey Logan was wanted for both crimes, and Siringo worked to get in with the "worst element," playing a wanted character hailing from "Old Mexico." He had deep cowboy skills of course and over the weeks made himself increasingly useful in his new town, roping and branding when it was roundup time, breaking broncos with the younger men, charming Lonnie Logan's longtime girlfriend Ellie into sharing her "secrets" from Lonnie's letters.

One June day the team of horses Siringo was driving for Thompson ran away, and the buckboard flipped, knocking him out and injuring his back. Waking after lying some hours in the hot roadbed, Charlie crawled and stumbled back several miles toward Thompson's house, where he was laid up long enough to deepen their rapport and draw his host out some about his friends in the Wild Bunch. So often people were more trusting of an injured man, and Thompson told Charlie that Kid Curry would soon take his revenge on the Union Pacific Railroad for the recent killing of his brother Lonnie by hired detectives, who had come for him at his boyhood home.

After a long chase, Lonnie had finally sold his horse and saddle and ridden freight cars the final leg of his escape to the run-down farmhouse of his Aunt Lee in Dodson, Missouri. Then he made the mistake of cashing one of his stolen Adams Express notes in town. That brought four buggies filled with detectives out from Kansas City on February 28, 1900. They divided to cover the front and back yards, and as Lonnie sat with his aunt in the kitchen of his youth, he saw lawmen stalk across the snowy ground. One of them was Siringo's partner, Billy Sayles, summoned by McParland's telegram from Hardin, Montana, where he had lost Lonnie's trail, to Missouri, where the serial number had turned up.[7]

Lonnie Logan spotted the approaching lawmen and bolted from the kitchen door, firing at them from behind a snowy mound. Sayles later recalled one of the outlaw's bullets jerking his sleeve as it passed through at the elbow. The answering shots killed Logan and bloodied the surrounding snow. That same month Flatnose Currie too was shot dead, by a posse trying to take him in a basin outside Thompson Springs, Utah. His body was taken to town to be propped up and cataloged by a photographer. The massive manhunt was cutting down the gang.

25

The Phantom Limb

As predicted, Harvey Logan took his revenge for his brother's shooting by detectives when he and Butch and Sundance robbed the Union Pacific line again, on August 29, 1900, this time at Tipton, Wyoming. As later memorialized by the movie, the same express clerk who had survived the dynamiting in the Wilcox job the year before, Charles Woodcock, was unluckily guarding the safe on this train as well. This time, though, he was convinced by his conductor to surrender his car to the robbers before they could blow the door. They then dynamited the safe, gaining an unknown amount of usable dollars (from the possible $50,000 on board) while blasting the rest to the winds. The gang eluded two separate posses, one led by the great deputy US marshal Joe LaFors, whose group followed a set of hoofprints almost to the Colorado border, where they moved in to surround a restive group camouflaged in a stand of willows. It turned out to be some Wild Bunch relay horses.[1]

Siringo rejoined the hunt and followed two of the train robbers into the Blue Mountains of southern Utah. He was riding as his gregarious desperado self when he fell in with a group that included a ranch manager with a criminal past, who each autumn

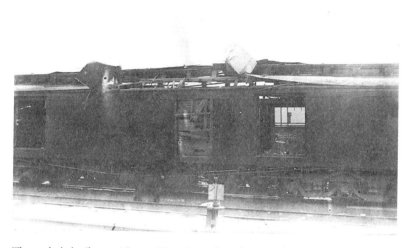

The exploded rail car at Tipton, Wyoming, where this time the brave express
messenger Charles Woodcock opted to come out ahead of the blast, August 29, 1900.
Pinkerton Archive, Library of Congress

put out a hidden haystack for his passing outlaw friends. Siringo
enjoyed a night in the haystack that had recently been shared by
someone who roughly sounded like Kid Curry, riding with a
taller man and a third bandit the robbers had picked up named
Lafe Young. They had no money from their last robbery, they
groused, and the ranch manager had to sneak them food. (When
the writer Charles Kelly met this same generous rancher in 1937,
the old fellow still fondly remembered the visitors to his haystack, both the hungry outlaws and their talkative little pursuer.)

Next Siringo rode over to Indian Creek and met a rough but
trusting character known as "Peg Leg," who offered to show him
where his bad men had camped next, in Monticello, Utah, but
stopped to rest as they made their way atop a mountain ridge.

From there Charlie could see at least a hundred clear miles, the landmarks of what would be his longest case spread before him like an outlaw's map: north toward the Wild Bunch stations at Brown's Park and Rock Springs; west to the Colorado River, lined with cliffs the gang traveled; and beyond the difficult plateau of Robbers' Roost, the uninviting desert and the Henry Mountains into which the gang often scattered.* He and Peg Leg entered Monticello after dark in case there were any outside law officers in town who might arrest him; the town sheriff carried a warrant for him but was friendly to the outlaws.

Having learned more about the gang from Peg Leg, Siringo drifted to Bluff, Utah, on the San Juan River, and then returned to Hanksville, which he had last visited two years before while searching with Sayles. There, a saloonkeeper named Charlie Gibbons told him how he had once held for safekeeping Cassidy's collection of gold pieces from the robbery of the Bank of Montpelier, Idaho. Siringo soon received orders to ride to Cassidy's family home in the "straggling" village of Circleville, Utah, and learn what background he could about the outlaw.

While visiting the farmhouse, he flirted with Butch's younger sister, who was deputy postmistress in the little town, while keeping from "falling in love with her." Butch had worked to protect his Mormon family from his later colorful life, and Siringo did not learn much of current use about the Wild Bunch during his week there, although he did ride Butch's mule Ikey and learned his boyhood nickname had been "Sallie," which was surely "enough to drive a sensitive boy to the bad."[2]

---

* Charles Kelly learned every trail and hideout and met quite a few surviving cowboys who remembered the Wild Bunch while researching his Cassidy history *The Outlaw Trail*, published first privately, in the 1930s, and then in an expanded edition in 1959. Kelly pronounced Hole-in-the-Wall "second in importance" for the gang but a place that, "because of its name, has received an unmerited amount of attention from fiction writers."

From the Parker family farm, Siringo started a thousand-mile ride toward Alma, New Mexico, where he still hoped to find Cassidy and other players from the Tipton robbery. On his way, he spent two weeks with an eye out for Wild Bunch figures hidden across the Navajo and Moqui reservations, then crossed the Atlantic and Pacific Railroad at Gallup, New Mexico, and traveled south "through the Zuni Indian country to a salt lake a few miles east of the Arizona line," finding "a great curiosity in the form of a bottomless lake on the top of a round mountain." To swim in it, he had to follow a trail around the mountain to its top, where another trail brought him down to the warm salt water for a memorable float.[3]

Finally he reached the small but rowdy town of Alma, which loudly supported "one store and one saloon." Once there, he met a friend of Jim Lowe's named Jesse Black and learned that Lowe and Red Weaver were now hiding in a mining camp near the Arizona border, and that Lowe and Butch Cassidy were one and the same. The friend also recalled that Frank Murray, whom Siringo knew as a manager in the Denver Pinkerton office, had been nearly killed when he visited Alma, after boasting to Lowe in his saloon that he was hot on the trail of the Wilcox train robbers. Murray had found no local officers to assist him, Siringo concluded, and so made the mistake of confiding his mission to Alma's "two leading business men," one of them his bartender. Siringo now wired Murray (in cipher code) that Lowe was Butch Cassidy and seemingly for the taking in a mining camp outside the town of Frisco, New Mexico.

Murray answered by ordering Siringo to sell his horses and return to Denver, as he himself had met Lowe in Alma and could not believe him to be Cassidy. However mistaken and infuriating this order seemed, Siringo came to feel it might have saved his life, keeping him from raiding the camp by himself, undermanned and outgunned. Still, the national manhunt would be tightened considerably after the gang made a mistake of its own.

After selling his horses and checking in at the branch office, he was sent to Grand Junction, Colorado, with a new lead, to find another friend of the Wild Bunch in western Colorado he called "Jim Foss." Traveling as "Lee Roy Davis," Charlie came especially well documented for making his latest outlaw acquaintance, carrying fictional clippings of Davis's recent "shooting scrapes in southern New Mexico."[4] Foss lived up the mountain, twenty miles outside Grand Junction, and was reluctant to go into town, where he was wanted as a cattle rustler. Instead, he had his new friend Davis pick up his mail. Charlie retrieved a letter warning that a Union Pacific Railroad detective was on the hunt for Foss. The two then traveled, visiting Foss's other friends for much of August and were going to go together to meet others in Rawlins, Wyoming, when a merchant warned Foss to avoid the Union Pacific, as he would be arrested by detectives working for the railroad. Fearful, Foss sold his packhorse and outfit to Lee Roy Davis, sent him off with the Wild Bunch gang's cipher codes, and picked a new name for him, contained in a letter of introduction: "This is Harry Blevins. He is righter than Hell."

Trailing a new packhorse to the "sheepy" town of Rawlins, Harry Blevins was beautifully received by Foss's saloonkeeper friend, who had profited from Wild Bunch members spending stolen gold coins at his bar. Siringo made more friends at the bar, including another associate of the Bunch he called "Bert C." From him Siringo learned about the gang's system of "blind post-offices," which allowed members to find or leave messages (sometimes deposit slips or news clippings) from Hole-in-the-Wall all the way down to Alma.

Next he headed toward the New Mexico territorial prison, where Jim Foss wanted him to deliver a reassuring message to inmate Bill McGinnis (Elza Lay). Although the warden would not entertain the idea that his model prisoner McGinnis was actually the infamous Lay, lawmen were happy to have the gang's codes in hand. Charlie had a brief meeting with McGinnis, who was understandably suspicious but listened. When about this time the Wild Bunch robbed some $30,000 from the First National Bank in Winnemucca, Nevada, Siringo suspected "some of this money would be used to free McGinnis from prison."[5]

After the visit to the territorial prison, Siringo returned with his Wild Bunch friend Bert C. to Rawlins. The town's sheriff sent off a letter to Denver reporting a dangerous outlaw calling himself Harry Blevins. But another man was unconvinced, Siringo would later learn. One evening in a Rawlins saloon, Kid Curry looked out from his backroom hiding place to notice a stranger at the bar who seemed suspiciously alert, a friend later told Siringo, too "bright and wide awake" to be a "common rounder." It was the closest the two ever came to meeting, and Siringo considered it "quite a compliment to be called bright by such a wide-awake judge."[6]

In all of Texas at this time there were only two towns with their own rogues' galleries of photographic portraits of known or wanted criminals. One was Dallas, the other Fort Worth, where it was managed by a dedicated city detective named Charley Scott, whose mind buzzed with the likenesses of pickpockets and sneak thieves and holdup men gathered in his gallery. To make his own mug shots to grow the collection, Scott had to bring his subjects in custody over to the nearby John Swartz photo studio.

A peculiar group portrait hung in its waiting room in early 1901. The photograph showed the murderer and train robber Harvey Logan with several of his criminal friends, including Butch Cassidy, whose idea the fancy portrait may have been, in

The "Fort Worth Five" portrait that launched a thousand wanted posters: Wild Bunch members pose in John Swartz's photo studio: (L to R) the Sundance Kid, Will "News" Carver, Ben "the Tall Texan" Kilpatrick, Harvey Logan, and Butch Cassidy, 1900.
Buffalo Bill Center of the West, Cody, WY, McCracken Research Library

November 1900, weeks after the Winnemucca robbery. They had brought their holdings on the train to Fort Worth, staying at a rooming house called Maddox Flats and ready to spend their loot in the town's red-light district, "Hell's Half Acre."

A dozen copies of the portrait were printed originally, perhaps to honor the engagement of Will "News" Carver to a woman he met in a San Antonio brothel, Callie May Hunt, or also as a kind of team photo commemorating the gang's recent success. Detective Scott regularly visited Swartz's second-floor studio, where one day he recognized "a group photograph of [Harvey] Logan and three pals, dudish looking guys," noted the *Fort Worth Telegram*. In fact, the five men, wearing suits and bowlers and pocket watches, were the Sundance Kid, Butch Cassidy, Ben Kilpatrick, News Carver, and Harvey Logan. Robbing a railroad company that employed the Pinkerton agency was a miscalculation, unleashing detecting forces more powerful than the small-town posses Cassidy usually encountered after bank jobs. But if the "Fort Worth Five" portrait was Butch's idea, it certainly compounded the mistake, aiding the creation of more accurate, even stylish Pinkerton posters when so much identification was still done by line drawings and description.

For decades, Wild Bunch historians repeated the account that a Pinkerton or Wells Fargo detective spotted the fatal picture. That was, after all, how the Pinkertons told it. But Detective Charley Scott had borrowed the photograph and sent a copy to Pinkerton's Denver office, where it was broken out into individual portraits for posters.[7] Months later, when Harvey Logan was arrested in a Knoxville, Tennessee, pool hall, a Pinkerton arrived from Chicago armed with Logan's Fort Worth likeness to confirm the prisoner was Kid Curry. The days of identifying outlaws from sketches and scars were dwindling.*

The gang had divided over escape plans, with Butch Cassidy and Harry Longabaugh wanting to start over as homesteaders in Patagonia (reserving the option of banditry), and Harvey Logan favoring going north for at least one more robbery. Instead, the

---

* To Ben Kilpatrick's "bertillon measurements," a Pinkerton manager in the Chicago office added, in 1905: "Color of eye a very pale yellow with violet blue. The yellow is as pale as can be and there is not much of it, but it is enough to notice" (Pinkerton box 88, folder 7, LOC).

mysterious Ethel or Etta Place, Longabaugh's lover and companion, joined Butch and Sundance for their final adventure.

Recalled as lovely and nervy, able to ride and shoot well yet with an air of eastern education, Etta Place had worked either in a schoolhouse or bordello or both, historians have long assumed. Longabaugh may have met her in Fannie Porter's sporting house in San Antonio, but that is less certain than that he traveled with her to New York in early February 1901, a visit documented by another well-known photograph, taken in a studio near Union Square.* As "Place" was the maiden name of Longabaugh's mother, and he sometimes registered at hotels as "Mr. Harry Place," it is doubtful this was the actual name of the poised young woman with high-rolled dark hair and an adventuring look in the New York portrait.[8] Cassidy joined the couple in Manhattan, taking his own quarters at their hotel, spending their heist money together, attending Lillian Russell's show on Broadway, and shopping at Tiffany's.

On February 20, 1901, the trio sailed from Manhattan's Pier 32 on the freighter SS *Herminius* for Buenos Aires, establishing a homestead for several years in Patagonia before moving on to Bolivia and returning to robbing banks as well as mine-company payrolls. In 1903, another brave, diminutive operative, named Frank DiMaio, was on assignment in São Paulo, Brazil, when he was ordered to Buenos Aires to locate the trio of the Sundance Kid, Etta Place, and "George Parker" (Butch Cassidy). The men were now going by Harry Place and James Ryan.

---

* "After more than a decade of searching into the lives of the Wild Bunch and the enchanting Etta Place," confesses James D. Horan in his own footnote to *Desperate Men* (Bison, 1997, 338), "I must reluctantly accept the fact that she was one of Fanny Porter's girls and not a starry-eyed school teacher who fell in love with the Sundance Kid and followed him—not caring where he went."

Harry Longabaugh (Sundance Kid) and Etta Place in their romantic New York portrait, 1901.

Library of Congress

DiMaio, who had almost died in a New Orleans jail during a long undercover assignment on a Mafia case, met with the head of the American legation, who put him in touch with Buenos Aires's "leading dentist," a Dr. Newberry, who recognized the photographs DiMaio showed him. The dentist said the Americans were living "on a sheep ranch at Cholilo Province of Chubut, District 16th de October." Dr. Newberry had the neighboring ranch. But the May rainy season was about to begin, making any excursion to arrest them impossible, unless DiMaio took a boat 250 miles south and then a horse ride fifteen days into the jungle with a willing guide.

Instead, DiMaio toured the biggest banks in Buenos Aires, sharing his pictures and biographies of the three resettled outlaws, who might be their customers. One manager recognized Mr. Harry A. Place, who had recently opened an account with $12,000 in gold notes. "A circular was gotten up and I personally delivered one to each steamship office and ship broker's office," DiMaio recalled. He next watched all passenger and freight steamers departing Buenos Aires for signs of his criminals attempting to leave the country.[9] Then he returned to New York.

Etta Place managed to come north again, vanishing into the American landscape before the men famously died in an adobe hut under a barrage of Bolivian soldiers' bullets, in November 1908. Charlie Siringo had no trouble imagining what had happened at the end. "It took about 100 South American soldiers to finish them," he assured a reporter. "Cassidy killed himself with his last cartridge."

But Siringo refused to believe the reported end of Kid Curry, in 1904. Harvey Logan had been convicted of passing stolen money, despite being wanted for killing two Knoxville policemen who answered the call when Logan attacked some pool "sharks" he felt had cheated him. (None of the murder witnesses dared testify.) He later escaped from Knoxville County prison in spectacular fashion, tying his guard to the cell bars with wire extracted from a broom, according to investigators, then riding off on the sheriff's own horse and disappearing for a year. He

Siringo loaded for "war" while hunting the Wild Bunch.
Haley Memorial Library and History Center

worked as an intense and capable stock hand named Tad Duncan until the day he reemerged with two others to rob the Denver and Rio Grande Railroad, in June 1904.

The last job was a bust: the safes they blew open were nearly empty, and a posse soon found the thieves near Parachute, Colorado. "The train robbers hid in some thick underbrush and a gun battle ensued," Pinkerton Lowell Spence, who identified Kid Curry, recalled in 1939. "The posse withdrew at dark, but returned to the scene of the battle the following morning where they found the body of a man who had been shot through the chest and finding himself badly wounded, had evidently shot himself through the head with his own gun. I went to Glenwood Springs, Colo. to view the body." It had been buried in a box "without any preparation about the spot where they found it. It was exhumed and I recognized the body as that of Harvey Logan." Much of the public refused to accept the death of the murderer, Spence would learn. "I have been joked about this identification by those who have shown me articles about Logan being seen in South America and elsewhere, but I know my identification was correct."[10]

One of the chief skeptics would be Siringo, citing a scar on the Kid's wrist supposedly missing from the corpse. "Harvey Logan is still alive," he insisted to the end. "He went to South America, but I think he's in this country now."[11] After Charlie's hard years spent chasing him, the outlaw lingered like a phantom limb.

26

The Fiery Pools

The Wild Bunch case had been Siringo's longest, a four-year pursuit by horseback, railroad, foot, and stagecoach over some twenty-five thousand miles. But in 1903 he accepted the most "interesting" investigation of his career, seven uncomfortable months on a kidnapping case among the moonshiners of Kentucky and Virginia, where his cowboying prowess could not help him. He would be searching for a wealthy young man named Edward Wentz, who had disappeared in the Cumberland Mountains that fall of 1903 and was presumed dead. Wentz was the son of Philadelphia's Dr. John S. Wentz, whose vast estate in southwest Virginia included the Virginia Coal and Iron Company, which Edward had been sent to manage, along with his older brother, D. B. Wentz. In his riding suit and Woodrow Wilson spectacles, young Wentz cut a lordly figure on the day he disappeared on his way to see one of his managers. Local boys recognized his riderless horse that evening in the woods near the village of Kelleyview and returned it to his worried brother at the family mansion.[1]

McParland told Siringo all Pinkerton offices had been "scoured" for an agent brave and savvy enough for this dangerous mission being run out of Philadelphia. Charlie came east and also visited New York, where he was surprised after all the battles he had survived to hear Robert Pinkerton warn that he might not return from the assignment—even asking for his dental records and descriptions of his watch, scars, and pocket-knife to help identify his poor body if found. It was reportedly murderous country where he was going. But should he survive, Pinkerton asked whether he would consider becoming an assistant superintendent in a branch office; his old partner Billy Sayles had taken a desk job and recommended Charlie be brought off the trail as well. Siringo said he would rather stay in the field, however dangerous.

He traveled to Jackson, Kentucky, and bought a mule and a light wagon. As "Charles Lloyd," he would try his default pose of a mysterious Texan on the run, but it seemed he had entered a country beyond his cowboy comprehension, whose violence impressed him, as that of few other regions he had visited: "At least twenty murders were committed in these mountains during my short stay."[2]* Every visiting stranger was suspect, either as a Pinkerton on the Wentz killing or a revenue agent going after stills.

Even starting out, he seemed a little spooked:

> The next day after my arrival in Jackson, I saw something which convinced me that the human race is slightly mixed with the pig family of animals. An old man on a mule started out of town with two jugs of whisky tied across the back part of his saddle: he hadn't gone but half a block when the string broke and the jugs fell to the ground and broke.

---

* In *Riata and Spurs* (Houghton Mifflin, 1927) he upped the count from twenty to "about thirty" murders.

The street was quite muddy and the whisky lay in pools on the ground. The old man got down on his knees and hands and began to drink from the fiery pools. Soon others came and followed suit. They put me in mind of a drove of animal swine.[3]

After waiting two days for a blacksmith sober enough to shod his mule, he trekked inland by cart, arousing suspicion as he went. Siringo's life would be threatened many times in these mountains, sometimes by "feudists" drunkenly waving pistols or shooting at him down a road, and he went around much of the time with his shirt loosely buttoned, ready to reach for the Colt strapped under his arm. But the case would call on his darkest skills; at one low point even keeping himself alive by playing teenage girls off each other, a middle-aged stranger participating in a backwoods kissing contest. One moonshiner threatened to shoot him for not admiring his sister-in-law.

He eventually reached Donkey, Virginia, "given to me as the toughest little spot on earth, and a likely place to get some information about young Wentz." He pretended to "fall in love with" a young local woman there named Emma, "even though I was old enough to be her father, to have an excuse for visiting Donkey."[4] Emma's actual father, "Doc," canvassed for an insurance company. After much drinking of moonshine, Siringo was pressured to buy an accident policy with a $1,000 payout. When he explained that as a fugitive he did not want any of his Texas relatives named as beneficiaries, Emma interrupted, asking him to make her the beneficiary. It spooked him to know he was now worth more dead here than alive. At another house, he survived being poisoned, barely escaping with his life and his money roll.

Eventually, a woman he called Lottie H. repeated an account of the abduction of Edward Wentz. Lottie had come to trust Siringo (or Charles Lloyd), who confessed to some alleged crimes of his own back in Texas and let her read their descriptions in his carefully prepared letters from home. "While I had hoped that she would let the secret out about my being an outlaw, she didn't do it. She was just as true as steel to me, and kept her promise not to give me away."[5] In return, Lottie confided that Wentz was taken because of his opposition to two local saloons near his coalfields. The buildings had been built to cleverly straddle the state line so that their liquor holdings and works could be moved from one end to the other to elude state inspectors. Wentz's opposition led to his end.

In May, his body turned up in the woods not far from where he disappeared, near Big Stone Gap, an area that had been searched that fall by detectives and hundreds of Wentz miners under orders. He had been dead from early in the investigation, and when the body reappeared it was staged like a lonely suicide, with a single hole in his chest from a nearby .32 pistol alleged to be his. One of his hands had been removed but never sent to the Wentz family by his kidnappers. It was reported that two men were held after Wentz's bloody riding suit was "found in their quarters in the mountains."[6] But when a coroner's grand jury convened on the crime site, the members were surrounded by at least two hundred people, "coming as it seemed, from every rock and crevice in the mountainside," according to the Associated Press.[7] The grand jury ruled it had not been a murder or even suicide (the popular belief among local people, claimed a Norfolk reporter) but "death by the accidental discharge of his own pistol" into his chest. A train finally brought his remains home to Philadelphia, and the grieving father accused the jurors of shielding his son's murderers. Siringo noted that a fair trial was impossible in the region.

Of the many times Siringo had tried to fit in playing outlaw, his months with the moonshiners left him uncharacteristically shaken: aging and out of place, surviving by his romantic wits "among a strange class of people who think nothing of taking human life."[8]

27

"Dean of Black Sleuthdom"

When a detective dies, he goes so low that he has to climb a ladder to get into Hell—and he is not a welcome guest there.

—Bill Haywood

On the snowy evening of December 30, 1905, in Caldwell, Idaho, the state's former governor Frank Steunenberg, a large, hearty man of forty-five, returned from his business in town and approached the gate to his home around a quarter to seven. His children watched for his appearance from the front window as usual, but this evening when he opened the swinging gate, he was blown ten feet into the yard by a bomb that shredded his clothes, tore his right side, and made pulp of his legs. He deafly shouted commands at his horrified family, who gathered round him and wrapped his ruined body in a blanket before dragging him inside the house, where he still complained of the cold. While one of his brothers held him, he blurted, "Someone has shot me. Lord help us," before he died.

A man calling himself Harry Orchard (born Albert Edward Horsley), under James McParland's strong guidance, would gradually confess to having rigged the bomb, which he had kept in his hotel room in Caldwell until he attached it with fishing line to the gate, moments before the ex-governor returned home, the tugged line spilling sulfuric acid onto blasting caps and dynamite. Orchard was no stranger to the western mining wars in which Steunenberg once figured and was linked to other acts of paid murder, including the bombing of the Independence Depot in Cripple Creek, Colorado, where he had nimbly also been a paid informant for the District Mine Owners' Association. He and George Pettibone had made a similar but failed attempt on the life of Colorado's Governor James H. Peabody; a moving coal wagon had smothered the bomb's trigger wire, while Orchard held the other end a block away. Orchard was described as a mercenary without scruple or regret.*

Although years out of the field, McParland was still called "the Great Detective" by newspapers and traveled from the Denver Pinkerton office to Idaho, where Orchard had been transferred from a city jail to state prison. There he could have exclusive access to the prisoner away from the influence of rival detective agencies. McParland immediately saw a chance to please his agency's anti-union clients by linking the killing to the leadership of the feared Western Federation of Miners (WFM) in a larger scheme. This he shaped during his sessions with Orchard into an evolving confession that strayed very little from his initial take that an "inner circle" of union leadership—Bill Haywood, George Pettibone, Charles Moyer—had directed the heinous act.

Since they had not committed a crime in person in Idaho, McParland could not pursue legal extradition against the three WFM leaders, and so he had them arrested in Denver for conspiracy, then transferred—kidnapped with the cooperation of legal authorities in both Colorado and Idaho—by a special Union Pacific train to the Ada County jail in Boise to await trial. Mac had the raid start at 12:01 on a Sunday morning so as to be on a legal holiday; Moyer was arrested on a train, while Pettibone and

---

* Siringo had been serving as Peabody's bodyguard during this time and surmises he would have blown sky-high with the governor if not for the coal wagon.

Haywood were nabbed in their beds. "The kidnapping," Siringo came to believe, "was a boomerang which flew back and hit the prosecution in a tender spot."[1]

Governor Steunenberg had been no friend to the miners. After the labor wars Siringo had witnessed in 1892–93, the miners had struck again in Coeur d'Alene seven years later, when Steunenberg declared martial law and called for federal troops as his predecessor had done; a railroad train seized by miners had rolled through a series of mining towns picking up comrades and gaining strength before the men took control of the Bunker Hill mine and dynamited it. Governor Steunenberg then had hundreds of miners arrested and held in "bull pens," crippling their union (whose leaders would afterward help form the Industrial Workers of the World, whose members were known as "Wobblies"). Steunenberg's private businesses received funding from the grateful mine owners.[2]

As payback, McParland argued, these leaders of the weakened WFM had contracted the bomber Orchard for revenge on the former governor. Pettibone was the same man who had brought Siringo into the miners' union in the Coeur d'Alenes, and against whom Charlie later testified. The first of the trials in Boise would be that of the WFM secretary-treasurer, Big Bill Haywood, who was born in Salt Lake City before leaving at fifteen to work in the Nevada mines with his stepfather. Having lost the use of his right eye in a boyhood accident while constructing a slingshot, throughout his career battling for the miners he insisted on being photographed on his left side. If Big Bill was convicted, his fellow WFM officers Pettibone and Moyer had real cause to fear.

To make Orchard a more palatable witness, McParland attempted to give him the appearance of a soul, creating a fiction of the assassin's religious awakening in prison under his own pious tutelage. He could not promise actual salvation, but did say Orchard might escape execution if he repeated the account they worked up together. Using an example from his work dismantling the Molly Maguires in the 1870s, McParland cited the case of one of the Molly killers, Kelly the Bum, who had been spared for his cooperation. Orchard knew the Kelly case already and got the message. By the end, Siringo asserted, "There was not a shadow of doubt, in my mind, about the truthfulness of Harry Orchard's testimony."[3]

The trial promised to be a national fight. Correspondents, photographers, and sketchmen began arriving in Boise that May from wire services as well as newspapers in Chicago, Denver, New York, Montana, and Boston, all staying together in the big, handsome Idanha Hotel, which became its own city. There they could drink alongside detectives and lawyers for both sides, including William Borah, James Hawley, and the charismatic Chicago defense attorney Clarence Darrow, who formerly had worked for the railroads but would undergo his own radicalization during the Haywood trial. Even the director of the Harvard Psychology Laboratory, Hugo Münsterberg, was sent by *McClure's Magazine* to plumb the ugly depths of Harry Orchard's psyche.[4]

McParland, who was losing his eyesight and getting death threats, brought out Siringo to serve as his bodyguard as well as guard Orchard. He also kept a few Winchesters beneath his hotel mattress, which he proudly showed to the young Broadway actress Ethel Barrymore when she arrived in town for a performance of the play she was touring in, *Captain Jinks*. Undercover for so much of his career, Siringo took his new public role seriously, drinking with famous journalists, his likeness in newspapers nationwide, strolling the town in his dark cape, planting himself on a sword cane, his Colt as handy as ever.

During the Haywood trial, the bodyguards of bomber Harry Orchard (center, in Derby) posed often. Siringo stands on the right, sporting his walking stick that held a ten-inch blade, 1907.

Idaho State Archives, Idaho State Historical Society

Deputy Sheriff Bob Meldrum was in the Idanha one day that spring when he saw an aging outlaw he recognized in the lobby, a small, leathery gentleman in a suit he remembered once firing at and missing while chasing a gang of horse thieves Meldrum believed was possibly led by Kid Curry. Meldrum was a grizzled lawman known for gunfights and sometimes questionable killings—dispatching a miner in an argument over a dice game in Telluride, or shooting an escaped Texas prisoner in Dixon, Wyoming—when this survivor in a hotel chair caught his attention, then quickly jumped up and held out his hand. "Hello, Bob," grinned Charlie Siringo. "It's all right. I call it all off." According to Meldrum, he had not realized until that moment that the outlaw he had shot at had been a secret operative. "I've felt worst about not getting you than any man I ever missed," he confessed.[5]

When Ethel Barrymore asked to meet with the infamous Orchard, keenly interested as an actress to study a killer up close, she was at first turned down by the prison authorities, to her great disappointment. But Siringo was delighted to take her to see the assassin. (He would also take the Harvard psychologist Münsterberg, who claimed to "examine" Orchard for eight hours.) Siringo was also charmed by her performance later that night before most of the town and its out-of-town guests. As Barrymore prepared to leave Boise late that night for her next performance, in Walla Walla, she sent a message that Siringo might come see her off at the depot. He was of course easily persuaded and appeared around midnight, bouquet in hand. She would remember the charming "little Pinkerton man" who showed her a live killer and sent her off with flowers.[6]

Now fifty-two, Charlie was happy with his public role in Boise, guarding his boss and the infamous killer Orchard. He had begun his Pinkerton career in another courtroom in 1886, watching the Haymarket bombing trial in Chicago. He would end it listening to the catalog of crimes his agency was accused of during this latest bombing case over the spring and summer of 1907. The crimes alleged by Clarence Darrow were not all news to Charlie.

"This is not a war against organized labor," McParland insisted, "but it is a war against organized anarchy and dynamite." Darrow disagreed, and for the defense put the agency's and McParland's reputations on trial as professional enemies of working people. Haywood's would be the first of the three trials, its verdict an indication of how those of Moyer and Pettibone might go.

On the eve of the Haywood trial, a former Pinkerton ste-
nographer from the Denver office, Morris Friedman, published
The Pinkerton Labor Spy, a muckraking account of the agency
and its methods for a left-wing publisher, even printing the names
of a number of its successful undercover operatives. He memora-
bly called James McParland the "Dean of Black Sleuthdom." His
job had allowed him considerable access to agency records, many
of which he stole and brought with him to the Boise courthouse,
where Darrow put him on the stand. (From his Brooklyn brown-
stone, Robert Pinkerton told the *New York Times* that if Friedman had been their employee, he was a minor one and would not
have had access to the papers he somehow had.)[7]

To Darrow's delight, Friedman named Pinkerton secret
operatives who had undermined unions and strikes around the
West. But if *The Pinkerton Labor Spy* somehow did not expose
Charlie Siringo, the very public trial was doing that. A testifying
miner identified Siringo in the courtroom as the man who had
become a secretary in his union, but the anecdote was stricken
since it predated the formation of the WFM. The worse effect
of Friedman's book for Charlie would come afterward, when he
attempted to publish his own Pinkerton memoir.

Harry Orchard's account had first been backed by a supposed accomplice named Steve Adams, who recanted before trial
after his uncle had a mysteriously powerful meeting with Darrow. This, despite McParland's best efforts at shaping the killer's
narrative, left Orchard an even less believable witness when he
finally took the stand that summer. The defense openly mocked
his religious awakening:

Q: *And McParland told you about King David, who was a murderer, had repented and become a man after God's own heart?*
A: *He told me about King David, yes.*

The proceedings became a national reckoning for the Pinkertons and their lucrative work for mining corporations in the Western labor wars. This line of argument impressed the jurors as much as it inflamed the national press for the nearly three-month length of the trial. Darrow made his theme capital versus labor. The agency had contrived the case, he argued, in order to punish Haywood and the other union leadership for defending the workingman. That was certainly true, even if years later historian J. Anthony Lukas would come to believe the WFM leaders in fact had foreknowledge of the bombing. Charlie Siringo certainly had no trouble imagining George Pettibone, who he knew had overseen the dynamiting of the Frisco mill in Gem, directing another bombing in revenge.

"The life of a detective is a living lie, that is his business," Darrow would say at trial, and Charlie, sitting in the courtroom, could hardly deny it: "he lives one from the time he gets up in the morning until he goes to bed; he is deceiving people, and tricking people and lying to people and imposing on people: it is his trade."

Unknown to Darrow or Morris Friedman, another Pinkerton, Operative 21, had done secret work for the defense team using the nondescript name of "C. A. Johnson"; he had worked undercover as a miner before making enough of a radical nuisance of himself to get thrown out of one of Caldwell, Idaho's less desirable hotels, strengthening his credentials as an agitator and gaining him work canvassing potential jurors for the Haywood defense team.

Bill Haywood had gotten everything in life through fighting and working hard, and so did not easily take the advice offered by Clarence Darrow about how to properly carry himself during the national trial. But he would never forget what Darrow did for him at the end:

When Darrow rose to address the jury he stood big and broad-shouldered, dressed in a slouchy gray suit, a wisp of hair down his forehead, his glasses in his hand, clasped by the nose piece. . . . He told of the Coeur D'Alene strike of 1892 and the strike of 1899 which had been called an insurrection. . . . He told again of the illegal arrest, the special train and military guard, showed that the prosecution would have shrunk from nothing in order to implicate me in this murder.[8]

In his eleven-hour closing argument, Darrow gave a public haranguing to the Pinkerton agency and McParland in particular. The prosecution's case, he maintained, was "a lie out of whole cloth, manufactured by the chief perjury manufacturer in this case . . . in his perjury office down in Denver."[9] His stirring closing oration was printed up for newsstand sale:

I want to say to you gentlemen, Bill Haywood can't die unless you kill him. You must tie the rope. You twelve men of Idaho, the burden will be on you. If at the behest of this mob you should kill Bill Haywood, he is mortal, he will die, but I want to say that a million men will grab up the banner of labor at the open grave where Haywood lays it down, and in spite of prisons or scaffolds or fire, in spite of prosecution or jury, or courts, these men of willing hands will carry it on to victory in the end.[10]

The trial ended in a dramatic acquittal and a threat of violence. "Haywood owes his liberty to the masterful plea to the jury by Clarence Darrow," Siringo admitted.[11] Although disappointed to lose, when Charlie got wind an outraged mob was on its way to Boise by train to lynch Darrow and his clients, he warned McParland, who was able to tell the governor of Idaho, staying in the same hotel for the trial, who in turn met the train of would-be vigilantes and talked them down. Siringo had survived more than a few such crowds himself and "didn't have the heart to see Clarence Darrow hanged by an angry mob just because he is always for the 'under dog.'"

After returning to Denver, Siringo resigned his position and turned down an offer from McParland to become superintendent of one of the other western branches, feeling "there was not kick enough in office work."[12] He also felt he would be exposed to the unseemly part of the business that he largely avoided while wandering as a lone cowboy detective. Instead, he hoped at last to move to his Sunny Slope ranch outside Santa Fe. Run by a series of cowboy caretakers he hired, it had long been a place where he dreamed of retiring, and often visited, if not for long enough. Now he hoped to finally have time enough to stay, ride his horses, help milk the blooded Jersey cows he had added or tend to his White Leghorn chickens and homing pigeons. He might also write a second book with all he had learned about "human nature" as a detective. For years he had described his Sunny Slope as less a working ranch than a "hobby horse" for his retirement years. Instead of merely visiting, he might live full-time in the small adobe house he had built on a hillside overlooking the Sangre de Cristos.

First, he had to travel to Oregon to collect his new (and third) young wife, Grace (he never wrote her last name), whom he had met on undercover assignment in horse country there in 1905, and who had recently accepted his proposal after a passionate correspondence. Grace Siringo had never been away from home before August 1907, when Siringo's ranch foreman met the new married couple at the Santa Fe depot in his buckboard. But she would soon find herself alone.

28

Ghosts

Bringing Grace to the ranch, Charlie began to spend time with his pet horses and wolfhounds, and planned to write down the twenty years of sleuthing adventures he had collected. What he pictured his new bride might do at home was vague as ever. "My taste of real heaven on the ranch lasted only a month," he wrote, "as I got an urgent letter from Mr. James McParland, asking me to hurry to Denver and undertake a complicated cattle operation in South Dakota."[1] Taking the job as a freelance, he spent several months drifting the snowy cattle ranges and Pine Ridge and Rosebud Indian reservations, playing the bad man "Charles Lloyd" and learning that the missing cattle had been slaughtered by hungry railroad crews. He briefly returned to his ranch before he was off again on an investigation of Nevada miners who were "high-grading" gold, this time working for the William J. Burns agency.

A friend and writer of Westerns, Henry Herbert Knibbs would later call him a wandering "Ulysses of the Wild West," but that didn't mean his wives were required to play Penelope, waiting at home for their hero's return. After months alone, Grace went back to be with her family in Oregon. When it became clear she never meant to return to the isolation of the Sunny Slope, despite her husband's continued letters, Charlie moved to dissolve their marriage in April 1909.

He was looking for a purpose, and one case caught his attention the following year: the robbery of the Gila Valley Bank in the small mining town of Morenci, Arizona, in September 1910. When he learned about it, Siringo felt in his bones the robber could only be Kid Curry, and he eagerly accepted the chance to hunt him for the Burns agency.

A single masked bandit had entered the bank late one morning and ordered that the available "change" lying on its marble counters be put into a double canvas bag. He then lugged his sack of silver dollars toward his horse, laid it over the pommel, and swung up, trading fire as he rode off.

The bandit had chosen his ride well, since even with the extra weight of the coins the horse could leap a high ridge while pursued by two town deputy sheriffs, whose own mounts balked at following. "On reaching the top of a ridge the bandit left the road and turned down a gulch," Siringo reported. "When the officers came in sight the robber was several hundred yards down a gulch. Soon he disappeared. He had jumped his mount over a ridge twelve feet high into a sandy *arroyo*."[2]

Newspaper reports of the Morenci robbery did not mention the leap but one did say, "It was rumored that the man wanted was sighted in the canyon and escaped amid a volley of shots from the posse."[3] There had been speculation in other newspapers that the infamous Kid was still loose—in Argentina with his bandit brothers ("Curry Was Not Shot Here: Famous Outlaw Supposed to Have Been Killed Near Tucson in 1906 Is Now Terrorizing South America," declared the *Arizona Daily Star*)[4] or escaping jail in Montana under another name on the eve of his trial for train robbery in 1908 ("It is believed that MacDonald is none other than Harvey Logan").[5]

Siringo rode from Santa Fe to Morenci, in Greenlee County.* He interviewed witnesses to the crime and examined the narrow exit the robber had taken out of the valley past the few dozen workers at the town's machine shop. He marveled at the leap the laden horse had made and was even more certain that only a particular "daredevil" bad man would have pulled off the robbery. He spent several weeks on the Kid Curry search, filing a report after giving up the trail but not his belief in who had boldly robbed the Gila Valley Bank. Feeling the living Kid had eluded him, he later sold an account of Curry's career to the *Wide World Magazine*, implying that much of the Wild Bunch gang was alive and scheming as late as 1910.

Not long after resigning, Charlie had contracted with the W. B. Conkey printing company in Hammond, Indiana, to publish *A Pinkerton's Cowboy Detective: A True Story of Twenty-Two Years with Pinkerton's National Detective Agency*. He had financed his first book with money from his Caldwell store. But his friend Alois Renehan, whom he had known in Santa Fe since 1894, agreed to pay for printing costs of his second book and keep one-third of the profits. Renehan, an attorney, financed an edition of two thousand hardcover copies of *A Pinkerton's Cowboy Detective*, but once the agency learned of the project he would find himself a long-suffering partner in legal battles to come.

No one wrote about the company but the Pinkertons themselves. Even McParland hadn't written his own story about his near-death ordeal among the Molly Maguires in the 1870s; that was left for Allan Pinkerton (and a ghostwriter) to tell in a

---

* Siringo places the robbery in "Morencia," Arizona, but "Morenci" is on the map, and the Gila Valley Bank there was robbed by a lone masked bandit in September 1910.

best-selling book. The negative attention generated by the Haywood trial and Morris Friedman's labor-spy book had also left them in no mood for outside publicity, even if largely positive. And by the time Siringo's detecting memoir was ready, sometime in early 1910, they certainly did not want their clients named in print.

While typesetting the book, the Conkey publishing company had begun placing promotional posters at railroad-station newsstands, which was how Siringo's detecting memoir came to the agency's attention, recalled the man Pinkerton hired to represent it in its suit, John A. Brown of the Chicago firm Kern and Brown. Handbills for the book at a railroad newsstand were spotted by a Pinkerton man buying his newspaper on his way home. Told that the book was not yet available, he took a few of the notices with him, and the agency eventually secured a galley proof, which proved to contain many clients' and agents' names as well as other matters of "a confidential character."* After reading the galley, Brown examined Siringo's original contract with the agency, finding that its rules about confidential disclosures had no time limit.[6]

A box at the Library of Congress holds a bound galley for what was originally *A Pinkerton's Cowboy Detective: A True Story of Twenty-Two Years with Pinkerton's National Detective Agency.* It is marked up with blue pencil, but the pencil marks are not questions of grammar and usage; they underline the many

---

* John A. Brown had spent more than fifty years representing Pinkerton's National Detective Agency when he appeared at Chicago's Normandy House in January 1960. The organizers had added extra seating for that day's event, sponsored by the Westerners Club, whose audience was there to hear the old lawyer speak about his long legal campaign waged against the cowboy author they admired. The notes of his talk appeared in the organization's *Westerners Brand Book* 16, no. 12.

passages found objectionable by the agency in seeking an injunction against its author and publisher.

The Pinkerton lawyers were charmed by Siringo when they met him in Santa Fe for his deposition, but Brown still filed a legal injunction to quash the story he had "turned over to the Conkey Company for publication."[7] For a revised version, significant names would have to be altered; James McParland became "McCartney," while Tom Horn, a fellow cowboy detective who later performed paid shootings for Wyoming ranchers and was convicted of murdering a teenage boy, became "Tim Corn," and Pinkerton was changed to the fictional "Dickenson Agency," even substituting it in the satirical song: "Oh see the train go 'round the bend / Goodbye, my lover, goodbye; / She's loaded down with Dickenson men, / Goodbye, my lover, goodbye."

Fond as he claimed to be of his tough little cowboy detective, William Pinkerton, when he read the revised edition and found that it still retained "real names and confidential information," ordered a new legal action, suppressing the already sanitized book by making the temporary injunction permanent against use of the Pinkerton name and others. "They kept me tied up in [Chicago] Superior Court for two long years, at great expense," Siringo wrote. "Finally my lawyer . . . advised me to make the changes."[8] Even if he had prevailed, he was told, the case might have lasted five years, at great expense.

Published at last in 1912, *A Cowboy Detective* was still a rowdy and entertaining read, even if its fictionalized names would weaken many Western histories whose authors repeated them. But despite its compromises, the book charmed new readers almost as much as his original cowboy memoir had. Even if the first print run did not sell through, the book would last to inspire writers of detective fiction. Siringo dedicated his litigated book to his attorney and friend Alois Renehan, who had funded and then defended the book, and warned the reader at the front: "The author is not a literary man, but has written as he speaks, and it is thought that the simplicity thus resulting will not detract from the substantial merit of the tales, which are recitals of fact and not fiction."[9] To his last days, Siringo would make emendations in copies he signed of *A Cowboy Detective*, stubbornly changing "McCartney" back to "McParland," "Tim Corn" to "Tom Horn," "Dickenson" to "Pinkerton."

29

Last Chances

Well into the twentieth century, a favorite subject of Western newspaper editors was when had the last buffalo died, in Montana or Kansas or Nevada or Texas, and who had put it down. These stories often sparked nostalgic counterclaims on the letters page: the hunter who dropped a bison in Furnas County, Nebraska, in 1875 corrected by the killer of a "straggler" six years later on Nebraska's Birdwood Creek; the memorable noontime appearance of a shaggy bull who wandered a town's Main Street to his end; or the winter night a lone beast stood steaming breath in a moonlit clearing before someone's uncle brought his rifle from the hearth.

In Utah, the last surviving buffalo made its way to settle on Antelope Island, in the Great Salt Lake, while a reporter visiting Montana, tired of being told repeatedly, "I got the last one," concluded: "It is quite difficult to find the man in Montana who didn't kill the last buffalo."[1] Retired cavalrymen published melancholic narratives of final tribal hunting parties they had escorted for the government: a solemn 1873 expedition of Pawnee or a party of Cheyenne and Arapaho hunters traveling out on their last sanctioned hunt in September 1878.

Near Amarillo Lake in 1877, Siringo claimed he once saw the landscape darkened with a million bison. The true number is incalculable, but it would leave an impression over time as the slaughter continued. In 1883, suspecting that buffalo hunters camped on the Panhandle were also taking LX cattle, Charlie followed the railroad to Sand Hill Station and then went in search of buffalo hunters' camps: "Knowing that buffalo were getting scarce, and having heard of a great many hunters being in the vicinity of Ceader Lake, I thought it a good idea to go out there and see what kind of game they were killing. Being nearly south of the Canadian River, I thought maybe they were killing cattle which had drifted down in there during the winters. But I was mistaken. I found their camps black with genuine buffalo hides."[2]

Three years later, crowds would gather to see what locals called the "last buffalo" on the Texas plains packed off for rail shipment as a novelty to an Illinois ranch. "The grand old fellow was driven in from Mr. Rush's ranch in Martin County where he had contented himself for some time," lamented a witness. "He has gradually become tame and was making himself friendly with the other stock. He became a pet to all. No one who had been familiar with them could take a last look without going back to that time when they in their wild condition by the hundreds played and fed undisturbed on the staked plains. The buffalo has passed away."[3] After a final glance at a Texas sky, the bull was fondly pushed onto the train car.

By December 1910, there were perhaps two thousand buffalo living in the United States and Canada, when Colonel Buffalo Bill Cody, now seventy-four years old, who had killed roughly twice that number, shot what he promised would be the last buffalo of his long career, staged on the ranch of his great friend Pawnee Bill Lillie near Guthrie, Oklahoma. Surviving bison now lived "in small herds in parks or upon fenced ranches or in menageries," grumbled a reporter covering Cody's gloomy stunt, with only 1,999 of them remaining "since his unerring rifle . . . brought the two thousandth one low."[4]

Some buffalo stampedes had once been big and furious enough to knock a frontier train off its tracks when the beasts were angered by its shrieking whistle. But the buffalo had become a rumor in much of the country, the Chisholm Trail a fenced and plowed-over memory, when Charlie Siringo decided to see what was left of the trail and perhaps get a book out of it.

After Christmas dinner in 1912, he sent his pet saddle horses, Rowdy and Pat, and his Russian wolfhound, Eat 'Em Up Jake, from his Santa Fe ranch on a railroad horse car, taking a separate passenger train himself the next day and meeting them at Amarillo, in the plains landscape he had long ago seen covered by bison. He also brought along copies of his new book, *A Cowboy Detective*, to sell, lowering the price by fifty cents to a dollar per copy during the trip and remarking on the difference it made. He stopped in Amarillo long enough to be honored with a cut from a dressed buffalo bull in the window of a friend's butcher shop. The bull had come special from the JA Ranch of Charles Goodnight, and buffalo meat was now scarce enough that the excited conductor on Siringo's train telegraphed ahead to the hotel manager at the Harvey House in Sweetwater to prepare to host a midnight supper with their iced hump loin. Who knew when they ever might taste it again.[5]

On the train, Charlie also invited an aged brakeman named Dumek, with whom he spoke about old days on the plains. The brakeman told him he had once been a buffalo hunter in the early 1870s. How many buffalo had he seen at one time in his hunting days? Charlie asked, one veteran plainsman to another. Ten million, the brakeman answered, like a bluffing gambler. "Even though Mr. Dumek stretched the truth by nine million," Siringo concluded, "that would leave a good-sized herd."⁶

Whatever the truth, Charlie knew those woolly beasts, shoulder to shoulder under a plains sky, had been something to behold before the hunter sighted his heavy rifle. The buffalo herds once reported at five miles across, rumbling past witnesses for days at a time, were long gone. Now Charlie and the trainmen were hurrying a single hump loin down the line, where they would séance around it at his late-night table, savoring a final taste.

As nostalgic as he was restless, Siringo traveled on to Matagorda County for some "harking back" with old friends before starting the rest of the Chisholm trip in the spring. He had accepted the invitation of his old employer at Rancho Grande, Jonathan Pierce, to stay in his new hotel in the town of Blessing. Pierce then took him out to Hawley Cemetery near the old ranch headquarters to see the looming statue his brother, Shanghai Pierce, had built for himself before his death in 1900. Charlie thought the huge likeness—a six-feet, five-inch marble man standing on a high granite pilaster—was about right, suggesting the great rancher's outsize presence and volume.

Then, at fifty-eight, Charlie met a charming widow of a cowboy friend he had known at Rancho Grande. Ellen Partain was a mature woman almost his age who also owned her own ranch, although hers was a little grander. The Chisholm research trip that spring of 1913 would have to wait. He sent his horses home in order to linger and propose, and was able to coax her away from Bay City and back with him to New Mexico to become his fourth wife. They married at the Majestic Hotel in Hot Springs, Arkansas, where the couple posed for an odd photo, looking like a wealthy, tolerant aunt traveling with her roguish cowboy nephew, and left the impression with a local reporter they were "childhood sweethearts" reunited after forty years.

It may not have been a coincidence that he married a wealthy widow during the time of his deepening money troubles, but it did not solve them; their marriage would be as short-lived as his previous one to Grace. Unlike his younger brides, the widow from the coastal plain was used to more than a dark two-room house in the high desert and did not feel she should have to remain there constantly.[7] After several months and a few sustaining trips back to her own ranch, she stayed in Texas, and the marriage ended. The divorce was final by October 1913.*

After his latest divorce and his ugly legal experience with *A Cowboy Detective*, Siringo decided to publish a cheaper paperback version of the book. Since Renehan still held the remaining hardcovers and had not earned back his investment, Siringo took out a mortgage on his ranch in order to pay $625 to the Hill Binding Company in Chicago, which printed five thousand copies, keeping three thousand and delivering two thousand to Siringo to send to various news distributors on consignment. Although the text remained the same, he restored the book's original subtitle, which had been squelched in court: *Twenty-Two Years with Pinkerton's National Detective Agency*. Even after the paperbacks went on sale, it did not provoke a new challenge from Pinkerton.

Sadly, Siringo's "tiger blood" was still up. Still feeling his life should be his own to write about, he next lashed out with a bitter revenge tract of 109 pages, *Two Evil Isms: Pinkertonism and Anarchism* (1915), detailing the agency's corruption in the muckraking spirit of Morris Friedman's tell-all, *The Pinkerton Labor Spy*. He sent a copy of the brief manuscript to Alois Renehan, who was alarmed and advised against publishing it. Charlie

---

* In his 1919 account of the homecoming to Matagorda County, Siringo does not mention meeting his fourth wife, but claims he came home rather than continue on in March with his Chisholm Trail researches because mosquitoes and horseflies were making his horses miserable.

hand-delivered it to Clarence Darrow in Chicago, who was no doubt pleased to see him admitting much that had been alleged in the Haywood trial. Darrow offered his opinion that Siringo might risk a year in jail and a $500 fine for libel, a risk Charlie claimed "wouldn't kill" him. Unsurprisingly, William J. Burns encouraged publishing the attack on his rival, assuring Siringo his book would sell a million copies.[8] To get it printed, Siringo had to take out a third mortgage on his ranch, this time borrowing from his married daughter, Viola.

Perhaps he did not intend to publish the little book but hoped only to be paid to withdraw it. If so, the threat certainly backfired. Siringo sent a letter to the agency warning of his impending work, copies of which he threatened to sell at an upcoming trial: "I dislike to act as a witness against your agency, but I need the money."[9] John A. Brown was again dispatched, methodically untying the protective layers Siringo had used to obscure where he had gotten it secretly printed and warehoused: "This book was printed by one company, bound by another, and distributed by a third, so that there was some difficulty in tracing it."[10] The Pinkerton lawyer was able to seize the book publisher's plates but not its author, who, after selling some copies to stores around Chicago, escaped back to Santa Fe once it had received a review that alerted the Pinkertons. The ex-detective alleged the agency "employs murderers and puts over frame-ups," reported the Chicago journal *Day Book*, which announced the book with a full review of Siringo's "big squeal" in March 1915.

Not amused, Brown wrote to Siringo that his manuscript was "false, scandalous, malicious, and libelous."[11] A Chicago police sergeant named Donnelly was sent to chase Siringo to New Mexico with orders to cuff and retrieve him for a northern trial for criminal libel. Alois Renehan met with Governor W. C. McDonald and Attorney General Frank Clancy of New Mexico.

"You can't have Siringo," the governor, a friend of Charlie's from his old LX days, was quoted saying in the *Day Book*. "I shall write Gov. Dunne of Illinois my reasons for refusal to honor this writ."[12] Although protected within New Mexico's boundaries, Siringo was also confined there for the time being. However satisfying it was to defy the agency, the book's plates had still been seized, and his debts had only grown.

By early 1915, Charlie decided it was safe to make a new attempt at raising money for his plan to trace the remains of the Chisholm Trail from Abilene to central Texas, proposing to mark it with bronze (later aluminum) steer horns and write a new book telling its story. He told a Santa Fe paper in March that "the various towns along the way would pay for the markers and I think it is up to me to write a history of the trail itself."[13] He then alerted newspapers up and down the old trail as well as the Citizens' Frontier Committee of Cheyenne's Frontier Days, which he told that summer of his future hope to enter its steer-roping contest despite his age.

Siringo planned to mark the old trail as he had known it, announced a Wichita paper, to "identify its location in connection with the landmarks of civilization" and settle the debate over its origins and namesake.[14] He traveled parts of the old route and interviewed old-timers about the trail's history. But America's entry into the Great War in April 1917 would make metals like bronze and aluminum too scarce to use for the longhorn markers he had imagined, and the project was suspended. If he roped any steers at Cheyenne, it was not reported, even by him. Luckily, in 1916, Governor McDonald had offered him steady if dangerous work as a Mounted Ranger for the Cattle Sanitary Board of New Mexico. The job provided him a steady income as well as some last adventures as a lawman against rustlers, though not undercover, before the board lost its funds for paying officers in 1918.

Returned fully to his money problems, Siringo was forced
to sell the adjoining property he had bought for his mother, who
had recently died, at eighty-six, in the Sisters' Sanitarium in Santa
Fe. "With almost her last breath she begged me to make my peace
with God, while the making was good. I have been too busy to
heed her last advice."[15]

When the copyright expired on his popular first book, *A
Texas Cowboy*, Charlie seized the chance to expand it, producing *A Lone Star Cowboy* (1919) as well as a short collection of
favorite cowboy ballads, *The Song Companion of a Lone Star
Cowboy: Old Favorite Cow-Camp Songs*. The following year
he published another work he hoped would sell—a short life of
his outlaw acquaintance, *History of "Billy the Kid"*—recounting
events (and much lore) that safely preceded his Pinkerton career.
During this same creative flurry, he also wrote a historical novel
with a female Western hero, "Prairie Flower, or Bronco Chiq-
uita," which he was unable to publish (and whose manuscript was
later burned up by his son's ignorant tenants). Sales of the three
new published books did not make "so much as a dent in Siringo's indebtedness."[16]

In May 1919, Charlie's old boss and sometime friend James
McParland passed on, following a decline that included a foot
amputation for gangrene after surgery and then a stroke. Most
newspapers looked past McParland's final defeats in the cases
against Haywood, Pettibone, and Moyer in favor of recalling his
undercover triumphs among the Molly Maguires. "Really, the
dead detective ought to be called the best actor that modern times
have produced," summed up the *New York Herald*. "He lived
'under the skin' of an imaginary man so perfectly that he was
accepted for what he pretended to be by men unused to trust to
appearances. . . . James McParland was an actor so supreme that

the stage has never produced his like."[17] Living "'under the skin' of an imaginary man" was what he had taught Siringo to do.

While hunting in the Jemez Mountains in the fall of 1921, Siringo developed bronchitis that would linger the rest of his life; he was sickly and alone by the time he put down his last saddle horse, Patsy, closed up the Sunny Slope, and boarded a train for his daughter's house in California in December 1922. When he decided to tell his story a final time, John A. Brown would be ready.

30

Hollywood

The bigness of the West makes men quiet.

—William S. Hart

In January 1922, a Wyoming cowboy calling himself "Prairie Jack" Edwards set out from a ranch in Casper, Wyoming, on a hazardous winter mission. Having heard that the Western film star William S. Hart, at age fifty-seven, was retiring from making frontier pictures, he rode off through the snows, swearing to collect ten thousand signatures to deliver to Hart's door in Hollywood and compel "Big Bill" to saddle up again.

The story that Hart was quitting had come from a regretful note the actor sent his friend Boyd Townsend of the Wyoming Frontier Association, along with a print of his forthcoming film, *Travelin' On*. Townsend arranged for a private screening for his fellow Wyoming cattlemen, where he repeated the sad news, alarming Prairie Jack enough that he proposed riding to the coast gathering names. With the backing of the others, he set out. "Bill Hart typifies the West as the Westerner hopes to have it remembered," he explained, the real cowboy coming to rescue the screen hero.

Traveling through ten-foot snows in Wyoming, Prairie Jack broke down one mount after several hundred miles. Changing horses in Morgan, Utah, he carried on through more drifts and by March had reached Salt Lake City, where he stayed overnight with the owner of the Paramount-Empress Theatre. He now had three thousand names and hoped to add a few hundred more before leaving Salt Lake, where he was solemnly quoted: "Moving pictures will better preserve to the minds of future generations the hardness of this great country when it was in the making than the most vivid story, and Hart comes nearer to visualizing the true west than any other actor."[1] Prairie Jack vowed to reach Hollywood before May, his petition growing as he rode.

Whether or not it was due to the cowboy's campaign, Bill Hart had a new picture in production by April. To Hart, who (with Thomas Ince) had pioneered the romantic Western drama, his intrepid fan riding through the western snows advertised the frontier scholarship behind what he called his "horse operas." Charlie Siringo left his New Mexico ranch months later in 1922 and, after recovering at his daughter's home in San Diego, came to Hollywood in the spring of 1923.[2]

Siringo's timing seemed fortunate. By the early 1920s, the movie Western was being elevated from gunfighting serials and plains melodramas to big-budget historical epics of high seriousness. Although it was also the modern era of flappers and bootleggers, there was a sentimental longing for the frontier and the ranching life being left behind—the struggles of many moviegoers' parents and grandparents.

The cowboy life Charlie had written about was getting its full treatment in movies and books when he arrived in Los Angeles, a place that had been largely farmland the last time he saw it, in the 1890s, with Hollywood then an unincorporated village in the foothills skirting what was the city's northwestern edge. Returning in 1923, he could see national epics like James Cruze's *The Covered Wagon*, dramatizing an 1848 trek by pioneers from

Kansas to Oregon. Its producers had advertised to find families that still owned their ancestral wagons, and the prairie schooners were used to reenact the journey for the cameras, down to the lashing of flour barrels to the sides to float the wagons in a simulated crossing of the Platte River. Colonel Tim McCoy had recruited five hundred extras from the Arapaho, Yakima, and other tribes, who came by railroad to join the film and stage clashes with the wagon trains. It had its historical flaws, but the film gained such an aura of truthfulness with the public that the daughter of the explorer Jim Bridger sued Paramount over its depiction of her father as a drunkard with two Native wives. (Investigation found that, drinking aside, he had in fact married two Native women, if one at a time.)³

The young director John Ford answered *The Covered Wagon* with his own ambitious spectacle, *The Iron Horse* (1924), about the "Great Transcontinental Railroad." Born in Maine, John Martin Feeney had found his way to California with his brother Francis and, using "John Ford" as his professional name, worked various film jobs on the Universal lots. An uncle had often told him stories from his days laboring on the great railroad, and Ford also consulted a number of retired Chinese railroad cooks, while carrying his own small prairie town and two hundred crew on a circus train.

Nonfiction films such as *Sundown* (1924) would mark the passing of many western ranches that had sent so many cowboys seeking work in Los Angeles, while a less successful epic, *The Last Frontier* (1926), captured the last of the great longhorn drives as well as a large buffalo stampede engineered for the cameras by Cree hunters in Calgary, Alberta. Only a decade before Siringo's arrival, Western stories were still being simulated on painted film stages in New Jersey. Now even cowboy satires had to be filmed in California sunlight.

Whatever Siringo had started with his wry, self-published books, the field had grown beyond him now. Interest in the West was keen and serious enough that Philip Ashton Rollins's exhaustive nonfiction work, *The Cowboy: An Unconventional History of Civilization on the Old-Time Cattle Range*, sold out six printings in its first year, 1922. Rollins was a New England–born Western scholar troubled by the "picturesqueness" and caricature of the cowboy he saw depicted in movies and literature. His four-hundred-page study of ranch life—from the cowboy's basic "uncomplainingness" to diversions such as "Tarantula duels"— became a sociological background to the movies the public continued to love. It was a long way from the bunkhouse swear jar that led to Siringo's first cowboy book.

The interest in Westerns had attracted so many cowboys to Hollywood that a vivid little Cowboy Row had grown in the area around Siringo's favored bar, the Water Hole, on Cahuenga between Sunset and Hollywood Boulevards. This had become "the assembly place of the cowboys who work in the movies," wrote a reporter, "two blocks of saddle shops, tight little eating places with wooden counters and tin cutlery, two-story rooming houses, tobacco shops, where chewin' he-men still find solace, and little stores where $7 plaid wool shirts and $30 high-heeled boots still find a want." It was understandable that Cowboy Row also had the only pawnshop then in Hollywood, where "losers in crap games, or the boys 'in between pictures' heap its window with fancy carved saddles, six shooters and trinkets in the lean spells between paydays."[4] A man might do a Hoot Gibson picture, then put his saddle in hock while waiting for the next job, rescuing it again with his pay from Tom Mix.

Sometimes their small Western colony took on the drama of the violent frontier. One of the men lingering around Cowboy Row needing a payday was James Anson, first recruited off the

Yakima reservation in Washington State as an extra for Cruze's *Covered Wagon.* By 1925 he was a forty-two-year-old Hollywood stuntman known as "Yakima Jim" and had just returned from working on Cruze's new film, *The Pony Express.* He found himself low on cash and tapped his cowboy friend Tom Bay for a loan of twenty-five dollars. Bay told Yak he had to call his wife over such a large amount, and when he reported back that she had refused permission for the loan, Yak referred to his friend's wife by an ugly name. When they had each done some more drinking, the men met again in Yak's hotel room, where Bay shot Yak in the chest with a borrowed pistol before escaping through a second-floor window, losing a roll of bills where he landed. The killing was the talk of the Water Hole and the newspapers, who loved when movie cowboys reverted to the rough frontier types they played.

Short and red-headed, Al Jennings signed photos of himself around Hollywood as "Al Jennings. The Outlaw!" and would tell lunch partners how he went from Oklahoma lawyer to vengeful long rider after holding his murdered brother in his arms.[5] Of the many frontier characters drawn to Los Angeles to make William S. Hart's acquaintance, at least Jennings could claim to have met him before. Hart had been a stage actor performing in Muskogee and Jennings a fugitive when they met briefly in the Oklahoma woods. The lanky young actor, out for a horse ride, had blundered into the midst of some desperate-looking strangers. He eagerly gave free theater passes to the Jennings brothers, who turned out to be wanted for bank and train robberies.

After serving five years in the same Ohio prison as his friend William Sydney Porter (who later became O. Henry, inspiring Jennings's 1921 book *Through the Shadows with O. Henry*), Jennings was pardoned by President Theodore Roosevelt and then found his way into film. He staged convincingly bleak portraits of bank robbers and small-town holdup men, after returning the long-ago favor to Bill Hart: "Dear Bill—You will find enclosed a pass to my first picture. It may remind you of the passes that you gave men many years ago, in the wooded mountains of Oklahoma."[6] The message of Jennings's films and lectures was that crime did not pay; it certainly had not for him until he came to Hollywood and started exaggerating his exploits.

Emmett Dalton came to Hollywood in 1919 as a Lazarus man who had almost died with his brothers at nineteen in the infamous Coffeyville raid. When the Dalton gang rode into Coffeyville, Kansas, on October 5, 1892, it had been a fatal act of outlaw hubris: they planned robbing two banks at once, something Jesse James himself had never done, in the town where they had lived as boys. Instead of accomplishing a double heist, though, they were famously shot down by townspeople, almost none of

The survivor: a wistful Emmett Dalton during his Hollywood years.
Woodbutcher.net

whom (not even the sheriff) had been armed when the gang rode into town that morning, uselessly disguised with false whiskers. The locals may have been unarmed, but knew how to use the guns they found on the racks at the town's two hardware stores, taking aim from the upstairs windows of one, Isham's, with a good view of the Condon bank. The shooting took roughly twelve minutes.

Youngest of the gang at nineteen, Emmett had been shot off his horse as he tried to carry a sack of money in one broken arm and reach the other down for the hand of his dying brother Bob. Four townspeople and four robbers died in the battle, which young Emmett somehow survived, despite over twenty wounds, and being listed with the dead in the evening editions.[7] As he lay apparently dying, the corpses of his brothers had been lugged to his room for his tearful identification.

Dalton lived to become a model young prisoner and would write his own confessions twice, in two different moods about his past. The first, *Beyond the Law*, in 1918, showed the proper contrition of a former prisoner, especially about the events at Coffeyville. He took the book to Hollywood the next year and managed to play himself as a younger man, a portly figure who could still ride like a border outlaw. But while continuing to submit screenplays, he soon found that the Daltons' story belonged to everyone, appearing in Westerns regardless of the truth or his permission. By 1925, he was forced to sue the publisher of *True Confessions* magazine for $1 million over its first-person accounts of the gang's robberies by a man writing as Emmett Dalton.

Before the 1920s, former outlaws like Jennings or Emmett Dalton could star in their own screen lives—what many deplored as instructional films for bank robbing—as long as the ex-convict toured with his picture, lecturing about the lessons to be derived from his young misadventures. But virtue was not what filled the seats; it was realism, and Congress eventually barred the importation of such films by ex-outlaws across state lines. (The man who had stopped the Jennings gang, deputy US marshal Bill Tilghman, later collaborated with Al on *The Bank Robbery* before forming his own film company. Tilghman would also befriend Bill Hart.)[8]

An element of realism almost entirely missing from the new Westerns was the experience of Black cowboys, who were common on the cattle trails and ranches. Bill Pickett, the famous Texas bulldogger, had thrilled audiences the world over by leaping from his pony and wrestling running steers by the horns, biting their underlip, and rolling them to the ground. Performing with the 101 Ranch Wild West, he had toured with both Will Rogers and Tom Mix. In 1908 in Mexico City, his boss publicly wagered five thousand pesos plus the gate receipts that Picket could survive five minutes against the fiercest Mexican bull the authorities could produce. Feeling that bullfighting was being mocked, the Mexican public turned out to see the Yankee die. The bull gored Bill's favorite horse, then, without cape or sword, Pickett leapt on the animal's head and horns, holding on despite being shaken and thrown against the walls. As the minutes passed, the crowd bitterly hurled things at Bill, breaking his ribs with a beer bottle and bloodying his face with a stone. When he finally slumped to the ground, Pickett had lasted seven and a half minutes, leading to a riot that had to be contained by soldiers.

In 1921, Pickett finally got his well-earned chance in movies. Billed as "The Colored Hero of the Mexican Bull Ring," he made the first of his two films, *The Bull-Dogger*, whose ads for movie-house proprietors read, "Give Your Colored Patrons a Treat. Book a picture that's different." Pickett had thrilled rodeo audiences around the world, but Hollywood afterward opted to screen a whiter West.

When not at his bar or writing in his cottage on Eleanor Avenue, Siringo was taken along to parties around Los Angeles, sometimes bringing storytelling props or a satchel full of his self-published books into the hills. He ate much better at these affairs than at his cabin and shared stories with Western connoisseurs for whom he was an original source. Through the writer and cowboy poet Henry Knibbs, he entertained the group of Westerners that gathered at the University Club, which included the painter Charlie Russell and Western novelists Will Irwin and W. C. Tuttle and the cowboy humorist Will Rogers, recently thrown his own party at Charlie Chaplin's.

Siringo did disappointingly little paid advising on films, considering the cowboy craze in Hollywood, perhaps because he gave away so many stories, a desired guest and unpaid font of authenticity. Despite Charlie's growing circle of friends, his economic situation had changed little. He asked his lawyer and friend in New Mexico, Alois Renehan, for more copies of his books to sell, still his main income since arriving in Hollywood, and then sold Renehan the deed for a remaining parcel of his indebted ranch. Too old for stunt jobs, Siringo did find brief work as an extra in a 1924 serial called *Ten Scars Make a Man* and may have also advised on the full series.[9] Although he was an adviser to Hart, he also gave free counsel to all manner of professional Westerners then in Hollywood at the evenings he attended. In February 1924, he was invited to dinner at the home of Will Rogers, a man he admired as "the only cowboy able to throw a loop large enough to encircle the globe."[10] But it is perhaps a sign of his deteriorating health that he had to decline the dinner.

Charlie saw himself as a writer, putting "wrtr" in his 1924 voter registration. He was still struggling with his expenses, trying to sell his frontier stories and mingling with more successful cowboy exiles, when the February 1925 issue of *Scribner's Magazine* pronounced him dead. John Hays Hammond, who had long ago employed him during the labor wars in the Coeur d'Alenes, honored him in a reminiscence of "Strong Men of the Wild West," along with two actually dead figures, George Armstrong Custer and Wild Bill Hickok, lamenting, "Siringo, brave man, is in his grave."[11]

The cowboys Siringo saw at the Water Hole knew better, as did his new writer friends. But being declared dead turned out to be a lucky break. The *Los Angeles Times* sent its own reporter out to profile him in his cottage, finding a "frail little gentleman" at his desk in shirtsleeves and dark vest, his table strewn with pages from "carefully writing with his worn fountain pen an account of the stirring and legendary events of the West that he witnessed in his youth." He noted Siringo's South Texas drawl and apparent poverty, his kind brown eyes, white mustache, and cowboy stance as well as the rain puddles he tolerated on his cabin floor from leaks in his roof. His Sunday dinner simmered on the stove.

Siringo assured his visitor the room's fresh air soothed his raw throat and launched into a short history of his remarkable life and of hazards far greater than a porous roof or long case of bronchitis. ("Doesn't mind a leaky roof," read one of the subheads). He was also reluctant to call attention to the shabbiness of the quarters his friend Jack Cole had found for him. With little urging from his guest, Siringo spun his 1880 Colt Frontier on his bony finger.

Only weeks after his death in *Scribner's*, Siringo was pronounced alive in Hollywood. The *Times* article, running on Easter Sunday, led to his rediscovery and even published his city address. The portrait of an impoverished old cowboy drew many responses, including from lost friends who were delighted to find him still among the living. Dr. A. M. Pelton invited him out to his Hollywood home, where they remembered the night he had cut Sam Grant's pistol ball out of Charlie's kneecap in Texas fifty years before. The article also brought one hostile guest to his door, who bitterly recalled Siringo's labor spy work in the mines. Then, on a rainy day that same April, William S. Hart made his first visit to the cottage.

As rain lightly fell, at the door to Siringo's leaking cabin stood the tall screen Westerner himself. The same long figure, minus his holsters, who had played Blaze Tracy, who stalked out of the smoking entrance of the burning saloon in *Hell's Hinges*, now filled Siringo's small doorway. The admiration was mutual: Bill Hart had been inspired by Siringo's *A Texas Cowboy; or, Fifteen Years on the Hurricane Deck of a Spanish Pony*. That was fine by Charlie, who approved of the romantic story Hart was putting on film. Hart had his production company in West Hollywood and was completing his own ranch in the Santa Clarita valley outside the city, in Newhall, where he collected historical weapons and Western paintings by his friends Charlie Russell and James Montgomery Flagg. In 1922, the year Charlie left his ranch for California, Hart had even published a briskly selling children's book told by his popular on-screen horse, Fritz, and illustrated by Flagg.[12]

Born in Newburgh, New York, Hart rode well from boyhood years in the West, where he told the newspapers the Sioux had taught him warrior skills: "With those rugged sons of the West, I learned to ride horseback, shoot with deadly accuracy and to hunt and track wild game."[13] His father had been a miller who traveled in search of sites for water power and flour mills, and Bill saw a lot of the country before returning east as a young man. He remembered a Wisconsin native woman who instructed him in Sioux sign language he would later use in movies.*

"The bigness of the West makes men quiet," Hart wrote. "They seldom talk unless they have something to say."[14] Siringo

---

* The actor Iron Eyes Cody, interviewed for Kevin Brownlow's superb history of the silent movies for Thames Television, *Hollywood* (1980), was actually Italian American but played Native parts for decades (most famously in the 1970 "Crying Indian" Ad Council campaign). But he learned enough to critique Hart for using Sioux sign language in his films, "like the women did" (one non-Native calling out another for his lack of authenticity).

Siringo guiding actor Bill Hart around the California replica of Caldwell, Kansas, during the filming of *Tumbleweeds*, 1925.
Seaver Center for Western History Research, Los Angeles County Museum of Natural History

was a chatty exception. Although he deferred to Siringo, Hart was only nine years younger than the elder Texas cowboy, having come to Hollywood as a successful Broadway actor at age fifty, ancient for a beginning screen star, hoping to make authentic Westerns.

While visiting Siringo's cabin, Hart offered to pay for repairs to the leaking roof. Charlie proudly declined, but late that summer of 1925, Hart hired him to advise for seven weeks on his movie about the Oklahoma land rush, *Tumbleweeds*, giving "pointers" to the director about a historical event Charlie had seen roll past him on an assignment. Hart hoped his expensive film would meet the moment for Western historical epics.

While it may have been his finest work, it failed at the box office in 1925. Hart's refusal to cut his epic from eight reels to five had led to United Artists booking fewer theaters, as alleged in a long-running lawsuit Hart ultimately won. But in the meantime, the film's failure would lead to Hart's second and final retirement, depriving Siringo of his chief connection for further film work, although many in Hollywood were still happy to run their own frontier scenarios by Charlie for his blessing.

Instead of getting his own movie deal, Siringo drew the interest of an East Coast publishing house, Houghton Mifflin, in 1926. It was a chance, once again, to tell his life story and his part history of the Wild West. Houghton had published works by his friends Henry Knibbs and Eugene Rhodes, and Knibbs had suggested the idea of a new Siringo book to the publisher. It had been long enough since his last attempt, Charlie explained to his potential new editors, that he could finally recount his best detecting experiences unabridged. They discussed putting together his old titles, including *A Cowboy Detective*, to make a new autobiography.

31

"The Shrine of Shakespeare"

Thereafter his life, lived mostly in New Mexico and California, was
meager and splattered, some of it spent in writing, perhaps more of
it spent in contesting a power that suppressed what he had written.
Carrying them in a satchel, he peddled his own privately printed books.

—J. Frank Dobie

One Sunday in January 1927, a caravan of Westerners
had started out from Hollywood for a short afternoon
drive through the fragrant towns of Glendale, Eagle
Rock, and Pasadena north to Altadena, at the edge of the mountains. When the group rolled down Morton Avenue, a runty old
man in a light-colored suit and red kerchief was out front to meet
his friends, holding his loaded steel cane that he was said to flour-
ish more than lean on.

Siringo had moved to the three-room "den" in Altadena in
1926 at the urging of his son by his second marriage, Lee Roy,
who recommended the town where he lived and the slightly
higher altitude of the Verdugo Mountains. Siringo agreed it
might improve his poor health, especially his chronic bronchitis.
Although often absent as a father, he sought the support of his
children as his strength faded. Nonetheless, Charlie removed any
mention of his son or Lee Roy's mother, Lillie, from his latest life
story, telling his Houghton editor that such biographical facts
were "not connected with my work as a detective" and so of no
interest to the reader.[1]

The main reason for the January visit by his friends, what the writers and cowboy artists and cameramen along that day were hoping to see, was the reunion of two plainsmen who had not met for forty years since both were working on the Cherokee Strip. At the time Siringo left Caldwell, Kansas, Gordon W. Lillie had been an interpreter for *Buffalo Bill's Wild West*. With his wife, May, managing as well as doing some horseback shooting, Lillie had started his own Western revue, *Pawnee Bill's Historic Wild West*, and in 1908 reunited with his showman mentor for a joint traveling production called *The Two Bills' Show*.

Lillie had long worn the Codyesque long mustache, sweeping hair, and buckskins, like a stocky understudy who could easily play Buffalo Bill, if Cody himself ever gave up the role. But that day at Siringo's place in Altadena, Pawnee Bill was dressed in a dark civilian suit and cowboy hat as he told some wide-ranging stories to the other guests, including tales about Charlie once serving as Caldwell's marshal, which Siringo delighted in hearing and claimed to have forgotten but did not deny.

The other famous Westerner traveling out to Siringo's that Sunday was Emmett Dalton, who had once nearly died along with his outlaw brothers at Coffeyville. On this day, Emmett was visiting at the little house of a man who had known at least as many real criminals as he had.

In addition to the reunion, the visitors were there to hail the upcoming launch of Siringo's new book about the West, *Riata and Spurs: The Story of a Lifetime Spent in the Saddle as Cowboy and Detective*. After touring the house and drinking some and sharing stories, the men posed for pictures out in the yard, one a group of eleven, and others including just Emmett, Pawnee Bill, and Siringo, who brought the spirit of Billy the Kid into the group by holding the rifle that had wounded the Kid during his escape from the Lincoln County jail. The backyard portraits from the day were perfectly suited for the rogues' gallery that lined Charlie's wall.

That March, Houghton Mifflin gave a party at the Hotel Alexandria in downtown Los Angeles celebrating *Riata and Spurs*. The Alexandria was popular with movie people; it was there that the biggest stars in Hollywood—Douglas Fairbanks, Charlie Chaplin, Mary Pickford, and D. W. Griffith—had publicly signed the papers creating United Artists, the studio that produced Bill Hart's *Tumbleweeds*.

"Coffee and pistols for a large number will be in order this evening at the Alexandria," previewed the *Los Angeles Times*, promising that both Billy the Kid guns would be present—the rifle that grazed him and Billy's own sidearm—as well as the skull of a buffalo that once jumped over Charlie's head as he crouched after shooting it.

Backyard portrait of Siringo (with rifle that wounded Billy the Kid) and a dark-suited Pawnee Bill, 1927.
Newberry Library

Seated along a table on the Alexandria's ballroom stage, Bill Hart was joined by Siringo's friend and physician Dr. Henry Holt, the writer W. C. Tuttle, the author and explorer James W. Schultz, the writer Henry H. Knibbs; the Lakota leader and author Luther Standing Bear; and Siringo, who had brought his promised speaking props. As Houghton Mifflin was sponsoring the party, the publisher's western representative, Harrison Leussler, was also onstage.

For the recent fiftieth anniversary of the Battle of the Little Bighorn, Hart had "spent many days and nights" memorizing a short speech in what he called "Sioux" to address an audience that included a surviving chief, White Bull, who recalled the dusty fighting in which Custer and his men met their end.

As Hart rose to speak on the stage, he opted to make his tribute to Siringo also in "Sioux," his remarks rendered back into English by Luther Standing Bear, who had also translated Hart's speech at the Little Bighorn.*

Not to be outdone, Siringo chatted onstage with one of his cowboy panelists in "Indian sign." He next stoked the crowd's excitement by telling about his long-ago meeting with Billy the Kid, holding Billy's pistol, borrowed for the evening from Bill Hart. This presentation especially impressed the writer for the *Los Angeles Evening Express*: "Suddenly, as he talked along, he whipped out with a speed that made everyone gasp, the Pistol of the Kid, now the property and the favorite gun of Bill Hart. Siringo looks like a whisp beside the giant movie star, but when he glances up your heart stands still."[2]

After living so many years under aliases, on this night he could be the unapologetic center of things as himself. "I was never in danger," he had recalled of his time among the Wild Bunch, "for they never knew who I was." Tonight, everyone knew.

Bookstore orders so far were encouraging, and on publication in April, the book sold some thirty-five hundred copies. It

---

* Hart never specifies mastering a particular dialect. But in his autobiography (*My Life East and West* [Houghton Mifflin, 1929], p. 349), he claims his accent was so authentic that Native speakers "covered their mouths" in astonishment.

also drew long tributes in newspapers around the country. But perhaps most pleasing to Charlie was the admiring note that arrived from Will Rogers, whose galleys of *Riata and Spurs* had finally caught up with him: "Somebody in some town gave me the proof sheets of your book and wanted to know what I think of it. What do I think of it? I think the same of it as I do the first Cowboy Book I ever read: 'Fifteen Years on the Hurricane Deck of a Spanish Pony.' Why, that was the Cowboy's Bible when I was growing up." He added a remembrance: "I camped with a herd one night at the old L.X. Ranch, just north of Amarillo in '98 and they showed us an old forked tree where some Bronk had bucked you into. Why, that to us was like looking at the shrine of Shakespeare is to some of these 'deep foreheads.'" Rogers had recently revisited the LX and lamented that the corral was now "full of oil wells."[3] Siringo had the Rogers passage copied to promote the book and told Bill Hart the quote would make "a send-off that can't be beaten."[4]

But a month after publication, a letter arrived for J. D. Philips at Houghton Mifflin's Chicago office. It came from the Washington Street desk of John A. Brown, representing Pinkerton's National Detective Agency. He cited the previous successful injunctions won by his employers against "a so-called cowboy detective," incensed to learn that stories and names excised from Siringo's earlier memoirs by court order were included in his definitive new book. Brown forwarded a copy of the previous Superior Court of Cook County, Illinois, decree against Siringo and the W. B. Conkey company, explaining that Houghton should compare their book's contents to *A Cowboy Detective*. There was no statute of limitations on agency secrets even for genial old cowboys writing sunset memoirs. All these years later, much of what Siringo had learned and done undercover remained unprintable to the agency, which guarded its clients, no matter how gamy.*

Charlie was out of the loop and still hopeful of big sales during what followed: Philips sent Brown's letter to Ferris Greenslet, editor in chief, at Houghton Mifflin's main office, at 2 Park Street in Boston. Greenslet was blindsided, since the charming cowboy author had assured the company these legal questions were years in the past. Nevertheless, he posted a terse letter that evening defending their book: "In our edition name Pinkerton occurs only on pages 123 and four, 134, 217, 26, 49, and 63. See no legal ground for injunction." Perhaps naively, he added an appeal that their author "is old and ill and case ought to be settled on grounds of common sense."[5]

When Houghton Mifflin's Chicago representatives visited Brown's office on June 14, they continued the appeal to mercy. The superintendent of Pinkerton's own Chicago office, Lowell Spence, who had once identified Harvey Logan's exhumed body, summarized Brown's meeting in an intercompany memo: "The publishers . . . claimed that they were publishing Siringo's book more as a matter of sentiment than anything else; that Siringo is down and out. Living in California near the seashore and had enlisted the aid of some film actor such as Bill Hart, etc. in assisting him."[6]

This provoked a definitive cable from Pinkerton's New York office to its Chicago branch: WE HAVE NO SYMPATHY FOR SIRINGO ONLY VIEWPOINT IS TO STOP PUBLICATION AND SALE. A similar cable went from Brown to Houghton's office manager, B. M. Ticknor, in Boston on June 21, invoking: COMPLETE VIOLATION OF INJUNCTION ORDER IN USE OF MY CLIENT'S NAME AND BUSINESS SECRETS.

---

* The Pinkerton archives at the Library of Congress are layered not just with Charlie's detective accomplishments but with much evidence of the agency's legal struggle to silence him. Siringo's case has its own set of folders.

CLIENT DEMANDS THAT YOU STOP ALL PUBLICATION AND SALE OF RIATA & SPURS.[7] Ticknor responded to Brown the same day: WE GREATLY REGRET SITUATION THAT HAS DEVELOPED WOULD IT NOT BE ENTIRELY SATISFACTORY IF WE MAKE BOOK OVER REMOVING ANY REFERENCE OBJECTIONABLE TO YOUR CLIENT PLEASE WIRE REPLY.[8]

Brown in turn wired his client's request that Ticknor appear in New York to plead the publisher's case: IF NOT COURT PROCEEDINGS FOLLOW.[9] Ticknor complied, attending a New York meeting where he promised no more copies would be distributed and that the second edition just printed would be destroyed. According to the Pinkerton general manager's account of the discussion, "[Ticknor] is considering re-writing the story eliminating references to us. If he finds he can write such a story, that will be interesting, with these eliminations, he will submit it to us for our approval, but the chances are he will find that when he cuts out what is covered by the injunction, he will have nothing left."[10] Many in the agency hoped Siringo's latest book would die altogether.

Charlie read about Brown's return to action only in July, when a letter from the publisher explaining printing delays referenced "exceptions" being made by the Pinkerton agency. After learning the worst, Siringo wrote to Alois Renehan, who had expressed concern that the troubled *Cowboy Detective* might be incorporated into his new work. Charlie confessed his plans were now in disarray, and rather than highlighting his unique life the book might be his ruination, adding to the pile of debt instead of helping him to dig out. In mid-July, Siringo was thrilled to be the guest of Will and Betty Rogers. He brought along the troubling letter from his publisher and dazedly showed it to Rogers, who was furious and promised to send a cable to the agency on Charlie's behalf. If he made another appeal for mercy for an old cowboy, it had no effect.

Under fire, Houghton Mifflin purged and reworked the book, but instead of substituting fictional names, as Siringo at first suggested, the editors favored replacing the detective sections entirely with the manuscript Siringo had hoped would be his follow-up work, "Bad Man Cowboys of the Early West" (already rejected by Yale University Press). His case histories were stripped out, the first edition was pulled, and the "Bad Man" manuscript replaced the many sections describing his Pinkerton adventures, from pages 120 to 268, saving one book but costing him the next. Siringo's dreams of earning thousands in sales were dashed as Houghton Mifflin had to make expensive rewrites and new printings.*

Of course, when he finally needed one, Siringo would choose an old cowboy friend to be his doctor, their shared frontier adventures as important as any other expertise. Now in his seventies, as his health slid he was in the care of Dr. Henry Hoyt, whom he had known when both worked for the LX Ranch in the Texas Panhandle in the late 1870s.

The Minnesotan had first hung his shingle in the mining camp of Deadwood in the Black Hills before he reached the Staked Plains in November 1877, where he ran out of medical work, and Siringo helped him learn to be a cowboy. After leaving Texas for New Mexico on a horse sold to him by Billy the Kid himself, Hoyt kept the bill of sale signed by the Kid for the rest of his life. He later became chief surgeon for the Great Northern Railway lines and of the US Volunteers, recounted in his 1929 book of his Western experiences, *A Frontier Doctor.*

Hoyt had journeyed to California, where he set up business in Long Beach and, in 1921, wrote to his old friend Siringo

---

* The unexpurgated, troublemaking first edition of *Riata and Spurs* is worth a couple hundred dollars to collectors.

that he should leave Santa Fe and come out to Hollywood to "get in the game. With your expert horsemanship, quick gun work, etc., etc. A lot of former cowboys have made good all right."[11] Now a bald, spectacled physician in a high collar, in the spring of 1927 he advised Charlie to move again to be closer to him, where he might treat his declining health and repay the man who taught him how to lasso. Charlie had complied, leaving Altadena and resettling in Long Beach in early May, near enough to Hoyt for several sessions per week. Since the early 1920s, when a doctor at Yale reported success treating pneumonia with alternating currents of electricity, the field of "diathermy" had taken a step toward the legitimate. Hoyt had recently ceased doing what were called "gland" treatments in favor of electrical diathermy to stimulate Charlie's blood. He also treated him for diabetes.

But Hoyt's own health failed after only a month of treating Siringo, and the doctor went back home to Saint Paul to recuperate. Siringo moved again, ending up in a Grand Canal apartment in Venice, California, near where his niece lived and ran a hot-dog-cart business. There, in an "over-heated den," the Western writer J. Evetts Haley tracked him down for a talk about early Panhandle days but ended up also hearing about his latest battles with the Pinkertons. "Old Charlie told me that the Pinkertons objected not to what he said about them but merely to the revelation of their methods of detective work."[12] The royalties he had expected had been eaten by the expensive revisions made to please the Pinkertons, and his condition continued to decline. He moved into a room belonging to his niece, but the winter on the water further aggravated his lungs.

"Charlie is a slender, brown-skinned man, quiet of manner, full of fun, and he has a remarkable memory," wrote his friend Henry

Herbert Knibbs in his *Los Angeles Times* review in May 1927, titled "A Ulysses of the Wild West":

> Weather and rough trails have aged him beyond his years, and yet he has retained the heart of a boy. . . . The word "detective" is a rather clammy sort of word. Charley Siringo wasn't that kind of a detective. Although he worked for the Pinkertons, he was really an itinerant officer of the law, often doing what local officers were paid to do, but didn't. He couldn't be bribed, and he wouldn't be scared, and he didn't get killed. And it is the eighth wonder of the world that he wasn't killed.[13]

His death instead would come quiet and alone, but he faced it with a cowboy hopefulness nearly to the end. Moving again to suit his lungs, Siringo returned to his old block in Hollywood, this time in a new apartment building owned by the family of his friend Jack Cole, the Colehurst. At the corner of Vine and Santa Monica, he had nearby everything he needed and a fair number of his friends, including Bill Hart.

Hart soon stopped by the apartment to invite Charlie to visit his newly finished Horseshoe Ranch in Newhall, and Cole drove him out one Sunday. The ride north through sagebrush hills to Hart's private road took less than an hour. They passed a bunkhouse to round the hillside on which he had built his large Spanish colonial revival house, where he now lived with his younger sister and his dogs, surrounded by the Western artworks of friends and his collection of rare frontier weapons.

It seemed a cowboy's paradise. The front windows looked across the Santa Clarita valley, and the town of Newhall was still sparse enough that all its homeowners could be listed on a single piece of paper hung in the hallway's telephone booth.

Charlie might have been satisfied merely to live in Hart's bunk-house as a kind of plainsman raconteur, entertaining parties of Hollywood folk and riding Hart's horses over the hills of his enviable view.*

Siringo returned instead to a life that J. Frank Dobie called "meager and splattered" at the end. He was still writing, trying to interest Houghton Mifflin in a new book of frontier episodes, to be called "Flashes from a Cowboy's Pen," after he failed to get a magazine to serialize them. Reading a sample, though, his editors declined to commit before seeing much more of the book.

But when he learned in July that his lawyer and friend Al Renehan had recently died in Santa Fe, he gave up writing alto-gether and seemed resigned for the end.[14] Siringo reluctantly left Hollywood once again and returned to Altadena, where two converted rooms in the house of his son would become his last den. As his health collapsed, his friend Henry Hoyt was called in to see him out of this life, and his years of bronchitis ended in a coronary.

Will Rogers and Bill Hart were each away in New York when news came of the death of Charlie Siringo on October 18, 1928. They sent a joint telegram:

ANOTHER AMERICAN PLAINSMAN HAS TAKEN THE LONG TRAIL. MAY FLOWERS ALWAYS GROW OVER HIS GRAVE.[15]

Siringo was buried in Inglewood Park Cemetery in Los Angeles after a ceremony with some Westerner friends and fam-ily. (His daughter and son by different marriages never met again in later years.) He might have liked a send-off more like his friend

---

* Hart would later will his ranch to the county of Los Angeles, where it can be seen today, more or less as it was, bunkhouse and dog cemetery and home with its Charlie Russells intact, plus a small grazing bison herd.

Wyatt Earp received several years later in Los Angeles, with Bill Hart and his rival cowboy star Tom Mix as pallbearers, the screen West helping bury the Wild West it romanticized. Instead his grave was unmarked until 1991, when it was upgraded by a fan to its current black stone in the ground, still too small to fit verses by Badger Clark Jr. that Charlie once hoped to include on his headstone:

> *When my old soul hunts range and rest*
> *Beyond the last divide,*
> *Just plant me on some strip of West*
> *That's sunny, lone and wide.*
>
> *Let cattle rub my headstone round,*
> *And coyotes wail their kin,*
> *Let hosses come and paw the mound,*
> *But don't you fence it in.*

Siringo's headstone in Inglewood Park Cemetery, added by a fan in 1991.
Donetia Meshack / Inglewood Park Cemetery

Epilogue:
Memories

Forty miles outside Los Angeles, at La Agoura Rancho, Charlie had worked happily as a consultant on Hart's last picture, *Tumbleweeds*. For seven weeks he helped the filmmakers re-create the Cherokee Strip land rush he had seen launched from Caldwell in 1893. He had a boot in each world—the remembered West and its Hollywood memory—during his time on set, as he watched the galloping drama of the settlers charging across the plains.

If Hart had done as he was asked by United Artists and edited *Tumbleweeds* down from eight reels to five, he might have gotten a wider distribution for his epic, which might have had a fighting chance at the box office. Instead, *Tumbleweeds* would be Hart's final film, whether because the studio distributed it half-heartedly, as the actor would successfully claim in court, or he was simply past his peak playing bachelor plainsmen, and the movie was too long.

But had he cut it as they demanded, he certainly would have had to remove snippets such as the strange old cowboy who appeared for several murky seconds in the Caldwell House saloon. His brief turn in the bar scene raised more questions than it answered, but he remained in the final cut, a sentimental cameo granted by a friend.

Since coming to Hollywood, Siringo had seen many Westerns depicting or stretching frontier events he had himself survived. But five months after filming, he saw the movie he had helped make, in a downtown theater. In February 1926, the film had its western premiere at the new Forum Theatre on West Pico in Los Angeles, an impressively pillared, terra-cotta movie palace large enough to occasionally put on skating exhibitions. Hart appeared onstage for several showings of *Tumbleweeds* during its opening week, lecturing crowds about his experiences in the West.

Charlie Siringo went to the Forum that week for a matinee showing of "a new Western play that was said to be fine," he wrote Hart afterward.[1] At the climactic moment, he again watched the settlers rush to stake their claims, hundreds of covered wagons rolling in a massive race for territory with at least as many Hollywood cowboys riding full speed, even a man wobbling across the grasses on a high bicycle; a wagon driven by a widow approached a cliff just as Bill Hart's charging horse turned it safely from disaster.[2]

The film had left Charlie "boiling over with enthusiasm," he explained to Hart, and his friend with him in the theater, a sometimes "cold-blooded" former cowboy named William Hawks, was "stirred up to a high pitch" by what he saw, as was a nearby young girl, who insisted on staying for the evening show. Siringo reminded Hart of his frontier credentials, "I ought to be able to judge a true-to-life Western play, as I have been in the saddle, and on the scene of action, since 1867, from the Gulf of Mexico to the British possessions on the north. Furthermore, I was familiar with nearly all the cow trails and water holes on the Cherokee Strip during the cattle days."

He had been mesmerized seeing versions of the history he had lived put on-screen. "But for a thriller which penetrates through to the heart, the Tumbleweeds has got it skinned a mile, each way from the center." The closing scene had brought tears to his old eyes.

What Siringo did not mention was that, less than an hour into the picture, he had seen something truly unusual: himself, far bigger than life, moving on the theater screen. The saloon set of Caldwell House had been built incorporating his own remembrances of Caldwell, Kansas, the kind of dark, raucous place with which he was too familiar. There he was on the high-spirited night before the big land rush, a bony old man under a tall hat, seated in a corner of the crowded saloon, playing an instrument just beyond the frame. The lights brought a gleam to his dark cowboy face. Then, just when the movie crowd might start wondering about this weathered gent fidgeting in the bar, the cowboy was gone.

Acknowledgments

The bones of this book were contained in a five-thousand-word Siringo profile generously published by Patricia Calhoun in *Westword* in 2018. Patty also ran my shorter pieces on Black cowboys and the Texas bulldogger Bill Pickett and on early confidence men and mine salting in Colorado. Sections of the book on the exploits of Wild Bill Hickok or the dangers of dime novels for travelers out west were articles I wrote for Dwyer Murphy at *CrimeReads*. The passage on Emmett Dalton comes from my *Medium* piece on the Dalton gang.

The book project itself, though, owes everything to the literary and historical appetites, professional patience, and editing skills of my terrific editor and friend at Grove Atlantic, George Gibson. George has believed in the idea of a Siringo book for a number of years, seeing him as a figure whose astonishing personal story could flesh out a larger history of the Old West he traveled. From the American Revolution to the D-Day landings, George publishes what passionately engages him, and so I am proud and grateful that he thought this project worth the time and trouble to see our cowboy through his historical journey.

Many thanks also to Grove Atlantic's esteemed president and publisher, Morgan Entrekin, for giving the book such a distinguished literary home. Thanks again to Ed Breslin for placing the book there.

A much older debt is due my father, the historian Geoffrey Ward, a fan of things Western since at least the fourth grade, when he and his best friend, Robert Strozier, were sent to buy a class gift for a grieving child in Chicago and naturally chose a pair of pearl-handled Hopalong Cassidy cap guns in leather holsters. My father has never been too busy for talk about the West, its heroes and its horrors. During the first throes of my own boyhood interest, he indulged me with a subscription to the Time-Life *History of the Old West*, whose gold-tooled, faux-leather volumes I pulled from our mailbox (*The Scouts*, *The Expressmen*, *The Miners*, *The Gunfighters*) as if delivered by stagecoach. If my Siringo book makes it into the bookcase with any of the Western works my father has enjoyed since his long-ago mission with Bob, I will be truly glad.

I wish I could share this book with two other fans of the Old West: my late father-in-law, Roland Calhoun, an Illinois-born member of the army's last mounted cavalry in Arizona, who later bought a former homesteader's cabin in Montana, where my wife, Katie Calhoun, and her siblings have spent most of their summers; and my late Brooklyn neighbor Patrick Kenny, always willing to recommend Western films in the driveway and lend something from his collection.

As a boy, I wondered watching *Butch Cassidy and the Sundance Kid* about the nameless horsemen chasing the outlaws across the stony Southwest, provoking Butch's famous line, "Who *are* those guys?" But I didn't get interested in a particular one of those relentless riders until much later. It is largely for the pleasures of writing about Siringo's years spent tracking the Wild Bunch that this book was attempted.

I came to Siringo while researching a book (*The Lost Detective*) on Dashiell Hammett's transition from young Pinkerton operative to crime writer, sifting through old operative reports, wanted posters, and code books at the Library of Congress's Pinkerton archive. Although the name Hammett did not appear in those files, Charles Siringo's repeatedly did, sometimes in regard to the Wild Bunch train robberies but mostly having to do with the Pinkerton campaigns to shut down the books he kept publishing about his agency work. I was interested not only in his undercover adventures as a cowboy detective but also his compulsion to keep telling his story—as if he saw himself as a writer before he ever started as a Pinkerton, which turned out to be the case.

It was the alternating heroism and vehemence in the agency's papers regarding Siringo that intrigued me and led to my photocopying many pages in hopes of pursuing his story sometime in the future. I was fortunate I did. Months after I began to research Charlie and his West, the Library of Congress (and everything else) shut down due to the pandemic. But I had a stash of Pinkerton materials squirreled away to tide me over until I could return.

Starting out, I ordered a wall-size print of the 1867 *Traveller's Map of the State of Texas* (beautifully reproduced by the Texas General Land Office) to plot out the Lone Star history I was learning on my study wall, closer to the Hudson than the Brazos. For a non-Texan, the podcast interview series *Cowboy Crossroads*, hosted by the Texas poet and musician Andy Hedges, gave me a wide entry point to a cast of living experts; his fellow Texas poet, songwriter, and storyteller Andy Wilkinson graciously recommended a curriculum starting with classics of the field like *Trail Drivers of Texas* and *Prose and Poetry of the Livestock Industry.* A membership to the Texas State Historical Association filled in some other gaps.

In Denver's Hermitage Bookshop I bought the valuable first edition of Siringo's *Riata and Spurs* (1927), with all Charlie's best stories laid out as they were before the last Pinkerton legal actions; this edition was useful in weighing his various versions of events over the five memoirs. In following Siringo's adventures around the West, a researcher has to reckon with these books' varying strengths and weaknesses, written at different times and under different levels of scrutiny. One thing that's consistent is he seems to exaggerate more when borrowing someone else's tales he had not witnessed (such as the lynching of Henry Brown or alleged digging up of Billy the Kid to account for his fingers) than in relating his own stories, which he can folksily downplay in frontier style more than modesty.

At the Arizona History Museum in Tucson, an old edition of Charles Kelly's *The Outlaw Trail* on the sale bookshelf took me down the path with Butch and Sundance through the outlaw gap of the Red Wall and beyond. The Grizzly Claw in Seeley Lake, Montana, sold me a cowboy cappuccino as well as "Professor" Thomas Dimsdale's *Vigilantes of Montana*, with its evocations of mining-camp life and firsthand accounts of the dark work of vigilance committees. The New York Public Library was useful, as it so often is, for steering me toward holdings I did not know I wanted—such as lawyer John A. Brown's account of his years-long campaign to squelch Siringo's writings, recounted in an issue of the *Westerner Brand Book.*

My luckiest find was discovering new writing by Charlie Siringo himself—his anonymous newspaper columns about life in Caldwell, Kansas, that he wrote as "Dull Knife" for the *Sumner County Standard* in neighboring Wellington in the spring and summer of 1885. (At the same time he was privately writing his first book.) A computer search of Siringo's name in Newspapers. com took me to a strenuous denial that the column's writer and Siringo were one and the same. When I read all of Dull Knife's columns, their tone and subject were strongly familiar.

I was fortunate to visit the William S. Hart ranch outside Los Angeles in February 2020. A volunteer in cowboy dress named John Smith gave the tour to my daughter and me, as patient as he was knowledgeable about silent Westerns and cowboys and Hart's considerable collection of Western art. But even while closed to the public, many institutions and their employees continued to answer queries: Thanks to John M. Cahoon at the Seaver Center for Western History Research, which has the Siringo–Hart correspondence; Loretta Deaver, reference librarian of the Manuscript Division of the Library of Congress; and Inglewood Park's Donetia Meshack, who advised on burial terminology and gave me an updated photo of Charlie's grave. My friend the writer Allen Barra, author of a fine study of Wyatt Earp, graciously read part of the book. Cathy Smith, Archives Administrator of the Haley Memorial Library and History Center in Midland, Texas, turned up interesting writings on Siringo by J. Evetts Haley and furnished several photos used in the book.

Finally, I should acknowledge some of the authors whose books were especially helpful (in addition to Siringo's): J. Frank Dobie, David Dary, Howard Lamar, Kevin Brownlow, E. C. "Teddy Blue" Abbott, Michael Wallis, Philip Ashton Rollins, Christopher Knowlton, Charles Kelly, J. Anthony Lukas, H. W. Brands, J. Evetts Haley, Ben E. Pingenot, Thom Hatch, Orlan Sawey, Mark Lee Gardner. Not mentioning them here would feel like failing to thank your hosts.

Selected Bibliography

Abbott, E. C. "Teddy Blue," and Helena Huntington Smith. *We Pointed Them North: Recollections of a Cowpuncher*. (1939.) Univ. of Oklahoma, 1955.

Adams, Andy. *The Log of a Cowboy: A Narrative of the Old Trail Days*. Skyhorse, 2014.

Avrich, Paul. *The Haymarket Tragedy*. Princeton Univ., 1986.

——. *Sacco and Vanzetti: The Anarchist Background*. Princeton Univ., 1991.

Bailey, Jack. *A Texas Cowboy's Journal: Up the Trail to Kansas in 1868*. Edited by David Dary. Univ. of Oklahoma, 2006.

Ball, Larry D. *Tom Horn: In Life and Legend*. Univ. of Oklahoma, 2014.

Barra, Allen. *Inventing Wyatt Earp: His Life and Many Legends*. Carrol and Graf, 1998.

Bible, Karie, Marc Wanamaker, and Harry Medved. *Location Filming in Los Angeles*. Images of America / Arcadia, 2010.

Blum, Howard. *The Floor of Heaven: A True Tale of the Last Frontier and Yukon Gold Rush*. Broadway, 2011.

Branch, Douglas. *The Cowboy and His Interpreters*. Cooper Square, 1976.

Brands, H. W. *Dreams of El Dorado: A History of the American West*. Basic, 2019.

Brownlow, Kevin. *The War, the West, and the Wilderness*. Knopf, 1979.

Cary, Diana Serra. *The Hollywood Posse: The Story of a Gallant Band of Horsemen Who Made Movie History*. (1975.) Univ. of Oklahoma, 1996.

Clavin, Tom. *Dodge City: Wyatt Earp, Bat Masterson, and the Wickedest Town in the American West*. St. Martin's Griffin, 2017.

Darrow, Clarence. "Darrow's Speech in the Haywood Case." *Wayland's Monthly* 90 (Oct. 1907), 115.

Dalton, Emmett. *Beyond the Law*. Pelican, 2009.

———. *When the Daltons Rode*. Pelican, 2012.

Dary, David. *Cowboy Culture: A Saga of Five Centuries*. Univ. Press of Kansas, 1981.

———. *Red Blood and Black Ink: Journalism in the Old West*. Knopf, 1998.

De Vaca, Alvar Núñez Cabeza. *The Journey and Ordeal of Cabeza de Vaca*. Dover, 2011.

Dimsdale, Prof. Thomas J. *Vigilantes of Montana*. TwoDot / Globe Pequot, 2003.

Dobie, J. Frank. *The Longhorns*. (1941.) Univ. of Texas, 1985.

———. *The Mustangs*. (1934.) Univ. of Nebraska, 2005.

Durham, Philip, and Everett L. Jones. *The Negro Cowboys*. (1965.) Bison, 1983.

Farrell, John A. *Clarence Darrow: Attorney for the Damned*. Doubleday, 2011.

Fehrenbach, T. R. *Lone Star: A History of Texas and the Texans*. Collier, 1968.

Frazier, Ian. *Great Plains*. Penguin, 1989.

Fulton, Maurice G. *History of the Lincoln County War*. Univ. of Arizona, 1968.

Gardner, Mark Lee. *To Hell on a Fast Horse: The Untold Story of Billy the Kid and Pat Garrett*. Morrow, 2011.

Garrett, Pat F. *The Authentic Life of Billy the Kid*. (1882.) Indian Head, 1994.

Gilbert, Elizabeth. *The Last American Man*. Penguin, 2002.

Glasrud, Bruce A., and Michael N. Searles (eds.). *Black Cowboys in the American West*. Univ. of Oklahoma, 2016.

Gordon-Reed, Annette. *On Juneteenth*. Liveright, 2021.

Haley, J. Evetts. *Charles Goodnight: Cowman and Plainsman*. (1936.) Univ. of Oklahoma, 1949.

Hart, William S. *My Life East and West*. Houghton Mifflin, 1929.

Hatch, Thom. *The Last Outlaws: The Lives and Legends of Butch Cassidy and the Sundance Kid*. New American Library, 2013.

Horan, James D. *Desperate Men: The James Gang and the Wild Bunch*. (1949.) Bison, 1997.

Horn, Tom. *Life of Tom Horn: Government Scout and Interpreter, Written by Himself*. Univ. of Oklahoma, 1964.

Hoyt, Henry F. *A Frontier Doctor*. Houghton Mifflin, 1929.

Hunter, J. Marvin (ed.). *The Trail Drivers of Texas*. Frontier Times Museum, 1920.

Hyslop, Stephen G. *The Old West*. National Geographic, 2015.

Kelly, Allen. *Bears I Have Met and Others*. Dodo, 1903.

Kelly, Charles. *The Outlaw Trail*. Devin-Adair, 1959.

Knowlton, Christopher. *Cattle Kingdom: The Hidden History of the Cowboy West*. Houghton Mifflin, 2017.

Krech, Shepard, III. *The Ecological Indian*. Norton, 1999.

Lamar, Howard R. *Charlie Siringo's West: An Interpretive Biography*. Univ. of New Mexico, 2005.

Leerhsen, Charles. *Butch Cassidy: The True Story of an American Outlaw*. Simon and Schuster, 2020.

Love, Nat. *The Life and Adventures of Nat Love*. Univ. of Nebraska, 1985.

Lukas, J. Anthony. *Big Trouble: A Murder in a Small Western Town Sets Off a Struggle for the Soul of America*. Touchstone, 1997.

Mackay, James. *Allan Pinkerton: The First Private Eye*. Castle, 2007.

Maverick, Mary A. *Memoirs of Mary A. Maverick*. Alamo, 1921.

McCoy, Joseph G. *Historic Sketches of the Cattle Trade of the West and Southwest*. Ramsay, Millet, and Hudson, 1874.

O'Neal, Bill. *West Texas Cattle Kingdom*. Images of America / Arcadia, 2013.

Paterson, Richard. *Butch Cassidy: A Biography*. Bison, 1998.

Peavy, Charles D. *Charles A. Siringo: A Texas Picaro*. Steck-Vaughn, 1967.

Pingenot, Ben E. *Siringo: The True Story of Charles A. Siringo, Texas Cowboy, Longhorn Trail Driver, Private Detective, Ranger, New Mexico Ranger, and Author*. Texas A&M Univ., 1989.

Pinkerton, Allan. *The Mollie Maguires and the Detectives*. Dover, 1973.

Prassel, Frank Richard. *The Western Peace Officer: A Legacy of Law and Order*. Univ. of Oklahoma, 1972.

Riffenburgh, Beau. *Pinkerton's Great Detective: The Amazing Life and Times of James McParland*. Viking, 2013.

Rollins, Philip Ashton. *The Cowboy: An Unconventional History of Civilization on the Old-Time Cattle Range*. (1922.) Univ. of Oklahoma, 1997.

Sawey, Orlan. *Charles A. Siringo*. Twayne, 1981.

Shores, Cyrus Wells "Doc." *Memoirs of a Lawman*. Edited by Wilson Rockwell. Sage, 1962.

Siringo, Charles A. *A Cowboy Detective: A True Story of Twenty-Two Years with a World-Famous Detective Agency*. Bison, 1988.

——. *History of "Billy the Kid."* Univ. of New Mexico, 2000.

——. *A Lone Star Cowboy: Being Fifty Years in the Saddle as Cowboy, Detective, and New Mexico Ranger.* Chas. A. Siringo, Santa Fe, 1919.

——. *Riata and Spurs: The Story of a Lifetime Spent in the Saddle as Cowboy and Detective.* Houghton Mifflin, 1927.

——. *The Song Companion of A Lone Star Cowboy: Old Favorite Cow-Camp Songs.* Chas. Siringo, 1919.

——. *A Texas Cowboy; or, Fifteen Years on the Hurricane Deck of a Spanish Pony.* (1885.) Penguin, 2000.

——. *Two Evil Isms: Pinkertonism and Anarchism.* Steck-Vaughn, 1915.

Slotkin, Richard. *Gunfighter Nation: The Myth of the Frontier in Twentieth-Century America.* Harper, 1992.

Smith, Duane A. *The Trail of Gold and Silver: Mining in Colorado, 1859–2009.* Univ. Press of Colorado, 2009.

Starobin, Paul. *A Most Wicked Conspiracy: The Last Great Swindle of the Gilded Age.* Public Affairs, 2020.

Stiles, T. J. *Jesse James: Last Rebel of the Civil War.* Vintage, 2002.

Stillman, Deanne. *Blood Brothers: The Story of the Strange Friendship between Sitting Bull and Buffalo Bill.* Simon and Schuster, 2017.

Stoll, William, as told to H. W. Whicker. *Silver Strike: The True Story of Silver Mining in the Coeur D'Alenes.* Little, Brown, 1932.

Time-Life Books (ed.). *The Wild West.* With a foreword by Dee Brown. Warner, 1993.

Twain, Mark. *Roughing It.* Penguin, 1983.

Wallis, Michael. *Billy the Kid: The Endless Ride.* Norton, 2007.

——. *The Real Wild West: The 101 Ranch and the Creation of the American West.* St. Martin's Griffin, 1999.

Wanamaker, Marc, and Robert F. Nudelman. *Early Hollywood.* Images of America / Arcadia, 2007.

Ward, Geoffrey C. *The West: An Illustrated History.* Little, Brown, 1996.

Webb, Walter Prescott. *The Great Plains.* Grosset and Dunlap, 1931.

White, Richard. *Railroaded: The Transcontinentals and the Making of Modern America.* Norton, 2011.

Wright, Lawrence. *God Save Texas: A Journey into the Soul of the Lone Star State.* Knopf, 2018.

Younger, Cole. *The Story of Cole Younger, by Himself.* (1903.) Minnesota Historical Society, 2000.

Notes

Prelude: A Cowboy Adrift

1. Charles A. Siringo, *Riata and Spurs* (Houghton Mifflin, 1927), 272.

1. A Plain Damn Fool

1. Lee Shippey, "Lee Side of L.A.," *Los Angeles Times*, Dec. 5, 1927, 22.
2. Montgomery's life is featured in the wonderful history of early Hollywood stunt riders by his daughter, Diana Serra Cary, *The Hollywood Posse: The Story of a Gallant Band of Horsemen Who Made History* (Univ. of Oklahoma, 1996). Jack Montgomery made his first visit to the café in 1920 and got a tip to go out the next day to the Edendale ranch the cowboys called Mixville, where he was hired to double for Tom Mix himself—rare work, since Mix was an actual cowboy and veteran of Wild West shows who prided himself on performing his own stunts and had ridden into saloons not only in movies but in life.
3. Louella Parsons, "Making of Feature Western Films Presages Better Times for Heroes of 'Horse Opera,'" *San Francisco Examiner*, Apr. 17, 1927, 49. Parsons is credited as "Motion Picture Editor of Universal Service."
4. J. Frank Dobie, *Guide to Life and Literature of the Southwest* (Southern Methodist U. Pr., 1952), 119.
5. Orrie W. Robertson, "A Whisper of the Wild and Wooly West," *Los Angeles Times*, June 19, 1927, 130.

6. J. Evetts Haley, "Charlie Siringo, Cowboy Chronicler," *Shamrock*, Spring 1962, 7.

2. A Fatherless Boy

1. Charles A. Siringo, *A Texas Cowboy* (Penguin, 2000), 4.

2. David Woodman, Jr., *Guide to Texas Emigrants* (M. Hawes, 1835), 30–31 (available at Rare Book and Texana Collections, Dallas Public Library, Texashistory.unt.edu). Woodman was a New England writer who may have never seen the Texas wonders he extolled.

3. Ibid., iv.

4. *Buffalo Commercial Advertiser*, Jan. 27, 1851.

5. Howard R. Lamar, *Charlie Siringo's West* (Univ. of New Mexico, 2005), 4.

6. *Louisville (KY) Daily Courier*, Dec. 12, 1854, 2.

7. *Republican Banner* (Nashville), June 4, 1856, 2.

8. "Another Murder," *Texas Republican* (Marshall), Mar. 28, 1857, 2.

9. "A Camel in a Rage," *Marshall (TX) Messenger*, June 21, 1877, 1.

10. Siringo, *A Texas Cowboy*, 8.

11. *Louisville Daily Courier*, quoting *Washington States*, Nov. 21, 1859, 1.

12. Siringo, *A Texas Cowboy*, 9.

13. As H. W. Brands and others have pointed out, although Antonio López de Santa Anna's Mexican government was autocratic and worthy of resentment, it was the lack of enforcement of a previous agreement, allowing the colonists' importation of their enslaved workers, that worried them most.

14. Thomas H. Krenek, "Sam Houston," *Handbook of Texas*, Texas State Historical Association, https://www.tshaonline.org/handbook/entries/houston-sam; Brands, *Dreams of El Dorado*, 111–115.

15. Charles A. Siringo, *A Lone Star Cowboy* (Chas. A. Siringo, Santa Fe, 1919), 1.

16. Siringo, *A Texas Cowboy*, 13.

17. Ibid., 15.

18. Ibid., 9.

19. T. R. Fehrenbach, *Lone Star* (Collier, 1968), 394, says seventy thousand, but Ralph Wooster (rev. Brett J. Derbes, 2021), "Civil War," *Handbook of Texas*, Texas State Historical Association, says between seventy thousand

and ninety thousand, as the census of 1860 counted ninety-two thousand eligible males in the state.

20. Fehrenbach, *Lone Star*, 395. Writing in the 1960s, Fehrenbach says Texas freedmen were "cast adrift," either as a judgment of the speed of Emancipation or of the later failings of Reconstruction. See also Annette Gordon-Reed's excellent title essay in her collection *On Juneteenth* (Liveright, 2021), 145.

21. J. Marvin Hunter (ed.), *The Trail Drivers of Texas* (Frontier Times Museum, 1920). This oral history compiled for the Trail Drivers' Association in 1920 remains a defining source for first-person stories from the trail. George W. Saunders was a president of the association. Philip Durham and Everett L. Jones in *The Negro Cowboys* (Bison, 1983) later figured that Black cowboys had made up a quarter of the total. Their figure is repeated by Albert S. Broussard in his preface to *Black Cowboys in the American West*, ed. Bruce A. Glasrud and Michael N. Searles (Univ. of Oklahoma, 2016).

3. Mavericking

1. Howard R. Lamar, *Charlie Siringo's West* (Univ. of New Mexico, 2005), 60; also J. Frank Dobie, *The Mustangs* (Univ. of Nebraska, 2005), 376.

2. "Hunting Wild Horses," *San Marcos (TX) Free Press*, Apr. 13, 1878.

3. Philip Ashton Rollins, *The Cowboy* (Univ. of Oklahoma, 1977), 1.

4. Christopher Knowlton, *Cattle Kingdom* (Houghton Mifflin, 2017), 32.

5. Charles A. Siringo, *A Texas Cowboy* (Penguin, 2000).

6. Charles A. Siringo, *A Lone Star Cowboy* (Chas. A. Siringo, Santa Fe, 1919), 2.

7. *Memoirs of Mary A. Maverick* (Alamo, 1921), 48.

8. David Dary, *Cowboy Culture* (Univ. Press of Kansas, 1981), 139.

9. *Memoirs of Mary A. Maverick*, 123–24. This book contains a useful supplement by George Maverick on the derivation of the term. While blaming the wandering unbranded steers on Jack, it also includes distressed letters from cattlemen after Sam Maverick moved back to San Antonio. The supplement is an excerpt of a very long letter George Maverick published in the *St. Louis Republic*, Nov. 16, 1889, correcting the account of the term contained in *The Century Dictionary*.

10. Ibid.

11. Ibid., 126.

12. Siringo, *A Texas Cowboy*, 38–39.

13. "Maverick," *Brenham (TX) Weekly Banner*, Feb. 18, 1886.

14. Siringo, *A Texas Cowboy*, 38–39.

4. River Cities

1. Charles A. Siringo, *A Texas Cowboy* (Penguin, 2000), 24.

5. Shanghai

1. Charles A. Siringo, *A Texas Cowboy* (Penguin, 2000), 41–42.

2. "The Fisk School," *New Orleans Republican*, June 18, 1870, 1.

3. Charles A. Siringo, *A Lone Star Cowboy* (Chas. A. Siringo, Santa Fe, 1919), 10.

4. *San Francisco Call*, Jan. 6, 1901.

5. David Dary cites this story in *Cowboy Culture* (Univ. Press of Kansas, 1981), 255, attributing it to Chris Emmett's *Shanghai Pierce* (Univ. of Oklahoma, 1953), 7.

6. This passage is well known, but my source is Dary, *Cowboy Culture*, 106–7.

7. Siringo, *A Texas Cowboy*, 41–42.

8. Howard R. Lamar, *Charlie Siringo's West* (Univ. of New Mexico, 2005), 53–54.

9. J. Frank Dobie, "Charlie Siringo, Writer and Man," introduction to William Sloane Associates's 1950 reprint of Siringo's *A Texas Cowboy*, xvii. Dobie found Jim Heller still working on a ranch in Brazoria County, Texas, in 1931. Among the other things Heller said about Siringo was, "That first book of his told things just like they was."

6. Shorthorns

1. Charles A. Siringo, *A Texas Cowboy* (Penguin, 2000).

2. Ibid., 41.

3. Ibid., 42.

4. Ibid., 46.

5. Ibid., 49.

6. Ibid., 50.

7. Charles A. Siringo, *Riata and Spurs* (Houghton Mifflin, 1927), 14.

8. Howard R. Lamar, *Charlie Siringo's West* (Univ. of New Mexico, 2005), 62.

9. *Tri-Weekly Nebraska Republican* (Omaha), Nov. 5, 1862, 3.

10. Stephen G. Hyslop, *The Old West* (National Geographic, 2015), 166–169.

11. Richard White, *Railroaded* (Norton, 2011); H. W. Brands, *Dreams of El Dorado* (Basic, 2019); Geoffrey C. Ward, *The West* (Little, Brown, 1996), 446; Hyslop, *The Old West*.

12. McCoy, quoted in Walter Prescott Webb, *The Great Plains* (Grosset and Dunlap, 1931), 220.

13. David Dary, *Cowboy Culture* (Univ. Press of Kansas, 1981), 174.

14. Webb, *The Great Plains*, 218. Webb's classic history provides year-by-year tables of the northern migration of Texas herds.

15. Christopher Knowlton, *Cattle Kingdom* (Houghton Mifflin, 2017), 141.

16. "Ellsworth: The Great Cattle Market of the West," *Kansas Daily Commonwealth* (Topeka), July 1, 1873.

17. *Rocky Mountain News* (Denver), reprinted as "Life among Long-Horns," *Galveston (TX) Daily News*, July 2, 1875.

18. Joseph G. Rosa breaks down all of Hickok's gunplay in his fact-based investigation, *Wild Bill Hickok, Gunfighter: An Account of Hickok's Gunfights* (Univ. of Oklahoma, 2003). Considering how much his audience wants to have the lore confirmed, Rosa's several Wild Bill books are impressively scrupulous, allowing contradictory witnesses to the same event and recreating the scene of each with architectural renderings.

19. "Shooting Affray," *Abilene (KS) Weekly Chronicle*, Oct. 12, 1871; the Hickok-Coe gunfight is expertly covered by Joseph G. Rosa (author of *They Called Him Wild Bill* [Univ. of Oklahoma, 1974]), in "Wild Bill in Abilene," Dickinson County (KS) Historical Society blog, http://dkcohistory.blogspot.com/2011/03/wild-bill -in-abilene.html. See also Bob Boze Bell, "Wild Bill's Last Fight," *True West*, Oct. 2014.

20. Dary, *Cowboy Culture*, 210–11.

7. Chisholm

1. David Dary, *Cowboy Culture* (Univ. Press of Kansas, 1981), 188.

2. J. Evetts Haley, *Charles Goodnight* (Univ. of Oklahoma, 1949), 251.

3. Charles A. Siringo, *A Texas Cowboy* (Penguin, 2000), 52.
4. Charles A. Siringo, *A Lone Star Cowboy* (Chas. A. Siringo, Santa Fe, 1919), 29.
5. Howard R. Lamar, *Charlie Siringo's West* (Univ. of New Mexico, 2005), 63–64.
6. Siringo, *A Lone Star Cowboy*, 23.
7. *Galveston (TX) Daily News*, Sept. 22, 1875, 2.
8. Siringo, *A Lone Star Cowboy*, 35.
9. *Galveston (TX) Daily News*, Sept. 21, 1875, 1.
10. Siringo, *A Texas Cowboy*, 67.

8. Wichita

1. *Wichita (KS) Eagle*, July 15, 1875, 2.
2. A. Huffmeyer, "Catching Antelope and Buffalo on the Trail," in J. Marvin Hunter (ed.), *The Trail Drivers of Texas* (Frontier Times Museum, 1920), 120.
3. E. C. "Teddy Blue" Abbott and Helena Huntington Smith, *We Pointed Them North* (Univ. of Oklahoma, 1955), 67. One time on night watch, Abbott endured a hailstorm so intense his group of cowboys had to remove their saddles to protect their heads.
4. Charles A. Siringo, *A Lone Star Cowboy* (Chas. A. Siringo, Santa Fe, 1919), 41.
5. Ibid., 42–43.
6. Ibid., 43.
7. Ibid., 47.
8. Ibid., 49.
9. Charles A. Siringo, *A Texas Cowboy* (Penguin, 2000), 71.
10. Ibid., 72.
11. Siringo claims in several books that he bore scars of the toll taker's buckshot in his leg, but it somehow strikes me as gilding the storytelling lily.
12. *Wichita (KS) Eagle*, reprinted as "That Affray," *Leavenworth (KS) Daily Commercial*, Nov. 1, 1873, 4.
13. *Kansas City (MO) Journal*, reprinted as "On the Cattle Trail," *Leavenworth (KS) Times*, June 17, 1873, 2.

14. In Mar. 1873, a report appeared that "a gentleman from Texas, whose brother the wild one had sent to the spirit land, came up to Kansas to have a shot at William. He shot the wild William so dead that he never quivered." After seeing the shock of his own death in his favorite paper, Hickok wrote the editor of the *St. Louis Democrat*:

> Wishing to correct an error in your paper of the 12th,
>
> I will state that no Texan has, nor ever will "corral William." I wish you to correct your statement on behalf of my people.
>
> Yours as ever,
>
> J. B. Hickok
>
> P.S. I have bought your paper in preference to all others, since 1857.

15. "Assassination of Wild Bill," *Black Hills Weekly Pioneer* (Deadwood City, Dakota Territory), Aug. 5, 1876, 4.

16. Siringo, *A Texas Cowboy*, 75.

17. Orlan Sawey, *Charles A. Siringo* (Twayne, 1981), 48.

18. Siringo, *A Texas Cowboy*, 77.

19. Ibid., 79.

20. *Columbus (OH) Republican,* July 20, 1876, 6.

21. Charles A. Siringo, *Riata and Spurs* (Houghton Mifflin, 1927), 34.

22. Ibid., 34.

9. "Stinkers"

1. Charles A. Siringo, *A Lone Star Cowboy* (Chas. A. Siringo, Santa Fe, 1919), 62.

2. Quoted in "The Great Bovine Market of the World," *Dodge City (KS) Times*, Sept. 7, 1877.

3. Siringo, *A Lone Star Cowboy*, 62.

4. David Dary, *Cowboy Culture* (Univ. Press of Kansas, 1981), 221.

5. *New York Times*, reprinted in *San Marcos (TX) Free Press*, July 6, 1878, 6.

6. Announcement for sheriff, *Dodge City (KS) Times*, Oct. 13, 1877.

7. Tom Clavin, *Dodge City* (St. Martin's Griffin, 2017), 147–55.

8. *Dodge City (KS) Times*, Sept. 29, 1877, 4.

9. Charles A. Siringo, *A Cowboy Detective* (Bison, 1988), 316.

10. Although Siringo told this story several times, the most thorough account is in *A Cowboy Detective*, 315–19.

11. Ibid., 318.

10. Panhandle

1. *Texas Rural Register and Immigrants' Hand-Book*, quoted in J. Evetts Haley, *Charles Goodnight* (Univ. of Oklahoma, 1949), 276.

2. "Pan-Handle Country," *Galveston (TX) Daily News*, Aug. 31, 1877, 2; *New York Herald*, reprinted as "Mackenzie's Expedition," *Galveston Daily News*, Oct. 22, 1874.

3. Edward Campbell Little, "The Battle of Adobe Walls," *Pearson's Magazine*, Jan. 1908.

4. Charles A. Siringo, *A Lone Star Cowboy* (Chas. A. Siringo, Santa Fe, 1919), 74.

5. Ibid., 73.

6. "Pan-Handle Country," *Galveston (TX) Daily News*. Aug. 31, 1877, 2.

7. Siringo, *A Lone Star Cowboy*, 67–68.

8. Margaret Sheers, "The LX Ranch in Texas," *Frontier Times* (ed. J. Marvin Hunter), Feb. 1952; also see H. Allen Anderson, "LX Ranch," *Handbook of Texas*, Texas State Historical Association, https://www.tshaonline.org/handbook/entries/lx-ranch.

9. Michael Wallis, *Billy the Kid* (Norton, 1997), 207. Wallis points out that what attracted the Kid to Tascosa may have been its toleration for trading in stolen horses.

10. Henry F. Hoyt, *A Frontier Doctor* (Houghton Mifflin, 1929), 61–62.

11. Charles A. Siringo, *A Texas Cowboy* (Penguin, 2000), 85.

12. Hoyt, *A Frontier Doctor*, 65.

13. Orlan Sawey, *Charles A. Siringo* (Twayne, 1981), 56.

14. Siringo, *A Lone Star Cowboy*, 81.

15. A famous herd seen in Arkansas by Colonel Francis Dodge was later "found to be 50 miles wide and to occupy five days in passing a given point on its way north," writes the curator of All about Bison (allaboutbison.com). "To make an accurate estimate of the numbers seen would be impossible, but Mr. Hornaday, by a conservative calculation, estimates that Col. Dodge must have seen 480,000 and that the herd comprised half a million buffaloes."

16. Siringo, *A Lone Star Cowboy*, 92.

17. Goodnight published several remembrances of Quanah Parker, quoted in Haley, *Charles Goodnight*, 312.

11. Squatters

1. Charles A. Siringo, *A Lone Star Cowboy* (Chas. A. Siringo, Santa Fe, 1919), 109.

2. Ibid., 94–95.

3. Charles A. Siringo, *A Texas Cowboy* (Penguin, 2000), 102.

4. Michael Wallis, *Billy the Kid* (Norton, 1997), 224.

5. Henry F. Hoyt, *A Frontier Doctor* (Houghton Mifflin, 1929), 90.

6. Mark Lee Gardner, *To Hell on a Fast Horse* (Morrow, 2010), 114. Outside of Garrett's own book, with its well-documented flourishes, Gardner's is the best account of Billy the Kid and Pat Garrett I have read, both accurate and stirringly told.

7. Ibid., 124.

8. Ibid., 130. Some sources leave the quote at that; Garrett claimed Bowdre then whispered, "I'm dying."

9. Charles A. Siringo, *History of "Billy the Kid"* (Univ. of New Mexico, 1920), 103. While much of Siringo's biography of Billy the Kid deals in lore, the letter from Jim East he quotes has general authenticity.

10. Siringo, *A Texas Cowboy*, 124, 126–27.

11. In his first telling (*A Texas Cowboy*), Siringo has Manuela staying in the house of rancher Pete Maxwell, where he says the dance also was and where Billy was killed days later. Yet in his last telling (*Riata and Spurs*), he says he accompanied her to her two-room adobe house. Mark Lee Gardner has her living in a room at the old Indian hospital in town. Siringo's first account lines up well with the later chronology of that week, so I lean toward it.

12. Charles A. Siringo, *Riata and Spurs* (Houghton Mifflin, 1927), 90.

13. Editorial, *Tennessean* (Nashville), Sept. 29, 1881, 2.

14. Pat Garrett, The *Authentic Life of Billy the Kid* (Indian Head, 1994), 219. Garrett's account of the manhunt is wonderful—ground zero for all subsequent scholarship—but before that starts he leaves the story to his collaborator Ash Upson, who embraces much of the lore. On page

139, the narrative finally switches to first-person as Garrett firmly takes the reins.

15. Ibid., 220.

12. Mamie

1. Howard Lamar, *Charlie Siringo's West* (Univ. of New Mexico, 2005), 137; and Charles A. Siringo, *A Texas Cowboy* (Penguin, 2000), 170.

2. The publication of Siringo's *A Lone Star Cowboy* (Chas. A. Siringo, Santa Fe, 1919) allowed David D. Leahy to tell this story in his column "The Shillelah," *Wichita (KS) Beacon*, Jan. 28, 1920. I have no reason to doubt Leahy's version, as he admired Siringo, who was still alive when the review ran. It makes more sense than Siringo's account of his rather instant romance with Mamie.

3. Charles A. Siringo, *A Texas Cowboy* (Penguin, 2000), 171.

4. Douglas Lober, "Caldwell, Kansas and the Cattletown Solution" (unpublished senior essay ms. at Yale, 1982, cited in Lamar, *Charlie Siringo's West*, 121.)

5. Siringo, *A Texas Cowboy*, 172. In later versions, Siringo recalls dramatically turning over his herd when several days out on the trail, but I go with his original telling.

6. Item in *Caldwell (KS) Advance*, Sept. 13, 1883, 3.

7. Douglas Branch, *The Cowboy and His Interpreters* (Cooper Square, 1976), 24.

8. Advertisement in *Caldwell (KS) Journal*, found by J. Frank Dobie in the Kansas State Historical Society, Topeka, and quoted in his magnificent introduction to Siringo's *A Texas Cowboy* (Sloane, 1950), xxix. (Also quoted by Ben Pingenot, *Siringo* [Texas A&M Univ., 1989], 13.)

9. Descriptions of all these phrenologists and their tours come from contemporaneous accounts of 1884–85 in Kansas newspapers such as the *Manhattan Nationalist*, *Lawrence Daily Journal*, *Topeka Mail*, and *Burlington Republican*.

10. Prof. Randleman, Phrenologist, "A Letter to the Students," *Daily Kansas Herald* (Lawrence), Mar. 26, 1884.

11. Charles A. Siringo, *A Cowboy Detective* (Bison, 1988), 13.

12. Ibid.

13. Details of the failed Medicine Lodge robbery and subsequent lynching of Marshal Brown and his co-conspirators are drawn chiefly from town

newspapers of that week, especially the eyewitness accounts in the *Medicine Lodge (KS) Cresset*, May 8–14, 1884; the *Barber County (KS) Index*, whose offices shared the building with the stricken bank; and the *Caldwell (KS) Daily Standard*, in whose extra editions Siringo finally unburdened himself about Brown and Wheeler and the Kid.

14. *Caldwell (KS) Daily Standard*, May 8, 1884, 3.

15. Ibid.

16. Orrie W. Robertson, "A Whisper of the Wild and Wooly West," *Los Angeles Times*, June 19, 1927, 130.

13. Dull Knife's Return

1. Charles A. Siringo, *A Texas Cowboy* (Penguin, 2000), 4.

2. All Dull Knife's weekly Caldwell Flashes columns are from the *Sumner County Standard* (Wellington, KS), spring and summer of 1885. I discovered the columns (unknown to previous biographers) by chance. A computer search of Siringo's name in Newspapers.com took me to a strenuous denial that the column's writer and Siringo were one and the same. I then read all of Dull Knife's columns and found their tone and subject strongly familiar.

3. Siringo, *A Texas Cowboy*, 172.

14. Human Nature

1. Charles A. Siringo, *A Lone Star Cowboy* (Chas. A. Siringo, Santa Fe, 1919), 225.

2. "The New York Strikes," *Daily Inter Ocean* (Chicago), May 1, 1886, 4.

3. Paul Avrich, *The Haymarket Tragedy* (Princeton Univ., 1984), 197–215.

4. "A Hellish Deed," *Chicago Tribune*, May 5, 1886, 1.

5. Charles A. Siringo, *A Cowboy Detective* (Bison, 1988), 12.

6. Ibid., 17.

7. "Pinkerton Man Joins the Anarchists to Betray Them," *Austin (TX) American-Statesman*, July 27, 1886, 1.

8. Charles A. Siringo, *Riata and Spurs* (Houghton Mifflin, 1927), 126.

9. Siringo always spells the superintendent's name "Eams," as do some biographies. But Beau Riffenburgh does not, in *Pinkerton's Great Detective*

(Viking, 2013), his biography of the man who replaced Eames, James McParland. And the name appears in newspapers of the times as "Eames," as well as in the Chicago census, as far as that goes.

10. Charles A. Siringo, *Two Evil Isms* (Steck-Vaughn, 1915). It is sometimes hard to judge the veracity of this bitter tell-all Siringo wrote on the heels of his legal battles over *A Cowboy Detective*. It is a vengeful piece of writing and definitely poisoned things further with Pinkerton's. Needless to say, the agency sued him again, and successfully.

15. Wayfaring Stranger

1. Charles A. Siringo, *Riata and Spurs* (Houghton Mifflin, 1927), 127.
2. *Grand Junction (CO) News*, Feb. 5, 1887, 2.
3. Charles A. Siringo, *A Cowboy Detective* (Bison, 1988), 30.
4. Ibid., 32.
5. Ibid., 35.
6. Charles A. Siringo, *Two Evil Isms* (Steck-Vaughn, 1915), 18.

16. Cheyenne

1. Quoted in Charles A. Siringo, *A Cowboy Detective* (Bison, 1988), 519.
2. *Denver Republican*, Oct. 15, 1887.
3. Charles A. Siringo, *A Texas Cowboy* (Penguin, 2000), 192.
4. Christopher Knowlton, *Cattle Kingdom* (Houghton Mifflin, 2017), xviii.
5. Details of Gunn's shooting from an examination reported in the *Lusk (WY) Herald*, as reprinted in the *Nebraska State Journal* (Lincoln), Jan. 26, 1887.
6. Charles A. Siringo, *A Lone Star Cowboy* (Chas. A. Siringo, Santa Fe, 1919), 162.
7. Information on McCoy's escape attempts from various newspaper reports: "Jailbreakers Foiled," *Deseret Evening News* (Salt Lake City, UT), Aug. 11, 1887; "A Jail Escape," *San Francisco Examiner*, Oct. 5, 1887; "Four Bad Men Make Their Escape," *Long Island (KS) New Leaf*, Oct. 13, 1887.
8. Siringo, *A Lone Star Cowboy*, 163.
9. Charles A. Siringo, *Riata and Spurs* (Houghton Mifflin, 1927), 132.
10. Siringo, *A Cowboy Detective*, 65.

17. The Great Detective

1. Cyrus Wells "Doc" Shores, *Memoirs of a Lawman* (Sage, 1962), 165.
2. Beau Riffenburgh, *Pinkerton's Great Detective* (Viking, 2013), 183.
3. Charles A. Siringo, *A Cowboy Detective* (Bison, 1988), 69.
4. Ibid. Of course, this book was heavily revised to suit the agency, so Siringo's text reads "W. L. Dickenson," not "Pinkerton."
5. Nathan Ward, *The Lost Detective* (Bloomsbury, 2015), 93. The form, held by the Library of Congress, is quoted in a footnote.

18. Salting a Mine

1. The miners were August Rische and George Hook. David Lavender, "How to Salt a Gold Mine," *American Heritage*, Apr. 1968.
2. Mark Twain, *Roughing It* (Penguin, 1983), 221.
3. "How They Salt a Mine," *St. Louis Post-Dispatch*, Dec. 9, 1888, 21. See also "Romance in Mining," *Morning Oregonian* (Portland), Mar. 4, 1888, 1; "Salting a Mine," *Leaf-Chronicle* (Clarksville, TN), 3.
4. Lavender, "How to Salt a Gold Mine."
5. Ibid. See also Duane A. Smith, *The Trail of Gold and Silver* (Univ. Press of Colorado, 2009).
6. Charles A. Siringo, *A Cowboy Detective* (Bison, 1988), 71.
7. Ibid., 71.
8. Ibid., 77.
9. Ibid., 83.
10. Ibid.; see also Howard R. Lamar, *Charlie Siringo's West* (Univ. of New Mexico, 2005), 150–51.

19. "A Strange Country"

1. *Reno (NV) Weekly Gazette*, Apr. 23, 1889; May 16, 1889. See also *Nevada State Journal*, May 17, 1889. Some biographies borrow the aliases for Peltier and Price that Siringo used in *A Cowboy Detective*, calling them "Pelling" and "Prinz." The Pinkerton revisions did some scholarly damage. The account in the first edition of *Riata and Spurs*, however, has the correct names. Charles A. Siringo, *Riata and Spurs* (Houghton Mifflin, 1927), 142–43.

2. Charles A. Siringo, *A Cowboy Detective* (Bison, 1988), 92–93.

3. Ibid., 94.

4. Ibid., 101.

5. Siringo, *Riata and Spurs*, 147.

6. Siringo, *A Cowboy Detective*, 105.

7. Ibid., 109.

8. Ibid., 106.

9. Siringo, *Riata and Spurs*, 149.

10. *Springfield (MO) Daily Leader*, Aug. 11, 1890.

11. *Caldwell (KS) Advance*, Aug. 21, 1890. In all his books, Siringo says Mamie's death occurred during the winter, and others have taken his word in their own writings. But how, then, to reconcile the August 1890 newspaper accounts of her death? It seems she died in the summer, and the event may have been remembered as a bleak, wintry event.

12. Siringo, *A Cowboy Detective*, 115.

13. Ibid., 116.

14. Ibid.

15. Ibid.

20. White Caps

1. *Santa Fe Daily Sun*, reprinted in *La Voz del Pueblo*, Feb. 14, 1891, 4.

2. *Santa Fe Daily New Mexican*, Feb. 6, 1891.

3. Charles A. Siringo, *Two Evil Isms* (Steck-Vaughn, 1915), 32.

4. Charles A. Siringo, *A Cowboy Detective* (Bison, 1988), 118.

5. Charles A. Siringo, *Riata and Spurs* (Houghton Mifflin, 1927), 154.

6. Ibid., 155.

7. Siringo, *A Cowboy Detective*, 132.

8. Ben Pingenot, *Siringo* (Texas A&M Univ., 1989), 31.

21. "Oh, Mr. Allison, Run for Your Life"

1. J. Anthony Lukas, *Big Trouble* (Touchstone, 1997), 101. Although Lukas unaccountably gets Siringo's age wrong, this remains a sprawling, tragic masterpiece, which has even more in it every time I consult it.

2. Charles A. Siringo, *Riata and Spurs* (Houghton Mifflin, 1927), 158.

3. *Idaho Daily Statesman* (Boise), "Damaging Testimony: A Detective's Experience among the Coeur d'Alene Miners," Sept. 22, 1892, 1.

4. John Hays Hammond, "Strong Men of the Wild West," *Scribner's Magazine*, Feb. 1925, 122.

5. Ibid.

6. Charles A. Siringo, *A Cowboy Detective* (Bison, 1988), 139.

7. Hammond, "Strong Men of the Wild West," 122.

8. *Idaho Daily Statesman*, "Damaging Testimony."

9. Though the author obviously comes at it from the mine owners' side, William Stoll's *Silver Strike: The True Story of Silver Mining in the Coeur D'Alenes*, as told to H. W. Whicker (Little, Brown, 1932), gives a lively account, dovetailing with Siringo's own.

10. *Idaho Daily Statesman*, "Damaging Testimony."

11. Siringo, *Riata and Spurs*, 162–63.

12. Ibid., 164.

13. Stoll, *Silver Strike*, 207.

14. Siringo, *Riata and Spurs*, 165.

15. Siringo's note is quoted in Stoll, *Silver Strike*, 213. Siringo's operative correspondence would have gone to the client, as was Pinkerton policy.

16. Siringo, *Riata and Spurs*, 169–71.

17. Ibid., 170.

18. Siringo, *A Cowboy Detective*, 174.

19. *Idaho Daily Statesman*, "Damaging Testimony."

20. Charles A. Siringo, *Two Evil Isms* (Steck-Vaughn, 1915), 108. While this was a work of revenge against the Pinkertons and is full of bitter hyperbole meant to embarrass Siringo's former employer, it has many heartfelt-sounding passages, including the regretful one about the coal miners, which continues: "While I only reported facts, I consider it a disgrace to tell the truth, knowing that the truth will retard justice to a class of men who take their lives into their own hands every time they enter a dirty coal mine."

21. Siringo, *Riata and Spurs*, 183.

22. Charles A. Siringo, *A Lone Star Cowboy* (Chas. A. Siringo, Santa Fe, 1919), 229–30.

22. For the Taking

1. "Clint Butts Making an Arrest Related to the Great Cincinnati Train Robbery," *Hancock Democrat* (Greenfield, IA), Oct. 26, 1865, 3.

2. Coverage of the robbery from the *Hartford (CT) Courant*, Jan.–May 1866.

3. William Pinkerton, *Train Robberies, Train Robbers, and the "Holdup" Men*, address to International Association of Police Chiefs (Jamestown, VA, Nov. 1907), available at Internet Archive, https://archive.org/details/trainrobberiestr00pinkrich.

4. "Bandits Held the Train Up," *Salt Lake Herald*, June 3, 1899, 1.

5. While a recent Butch biography (Charles Leerhsen, *Butch Cassidy* [Simon and Schuster, 2020], 304) says the leader that day was "Butch, of course," I am more comfortable with the accounts of Thom Hatch (*The Last Outlaws* [New American Library, 2013], 350) and Charles Kelly (*The Outlaw Trail* [Devin-Adair, 1959], 374), who are each skeptical despite their admiration for Cassidy's leadership. My witness account of a "small man, almost under size" climbing into the cab also comes from *Salt Lake Herald*, June 3, 1899.

6. "Bandits Held the Train Up," *Salt Lake Herald*.

7. According to Charles Kelly (*The Outlaw Trail*), Woodcock was knocked unconscious against the safe and could not recall its combination, necessitating further dynamite. Another book claims there were two safes in the car, but news reports (containing testimonies of the mail and express clerks) and photos in Pinkerton files do not bear this out.

8. Wyoming law dispatch, quoted in "Big Man Hunt Organized," *El Paso (TX) Herald*, June 17, 1899.

9. "The Hole-in-the-Wall," *Anaconda (MT) Standard*, June 28, 1899.

10. Ibid.; "Sam Carey, Bad Man," *Daily Inter Ocean* (Chicago), June 25, 1899.

11. "Detective Hans Talks about the Hole-in-the-Wall Country," *Anaconda (MT) Standard*, June 18, 1899.

12. Ibid.

13. James D. Horan, *Desperate Men* (Bison, 1997), 218. A number of early lawmen (and writers) understandably thought Butch's original name was George. It was Robert, as was his namesake grandfather's. But he did change it to "George Cassidy" in 1892 (per Howard R. Lamar, *Charlie Siringo's West* [Univ. of New Mexico, 2005], 370).

23. To the End

1. James D. Horan, *Desperate Men* (Bison, 1997); Charles Kelly, *The Outlaw Trail* (Devin-Adair, 1959). Although it indulges in ridiculous dialogue, Horan's popular book, originally published in 1949, is based on original Pinkerton documents, many of which were stored, while Horan worked, in his own house. Kelly's book is also old, but it is thorough on the trail systems and hideouts, all of which Kelly knew firsthand and describes like a veteran guide.

2. "Butch Cassidy Still Alive," *Salt Lake Herald*, May 17, 1898.

3. "Orders Implements of War," *Salt Lake Herald*, Mar. 20, 1898, 8.

4. Charles A. Siringo, *Riata and Spurs* (Houghton Mifflin, 1927), 209.

5. Ibid., 185.

6. Ibid.

7. Ibid., 193.

8. Ibid., 238.

24. Alma

1. William French, *Recollections of a Western Ranchman* (High Lonesome, first American copyright 1928), as quoted in Charles Kelly, *The Outlaw Trail* (Devin-Adair, 1959), 250.

2. For my account of the Folsom robbery and aftermath, I have relied chiefly on Kelly's *The Outlaw Trail* and newspaper accounts.

3. Pinkerton Archive, Wild Bunch/Cassidy Boxes 85–93, Library of Congress (LOC), Washington, DC. Although Siringo later referred to "McGinnis" as "Bob" in *Riata and Spurs* (Houghton Mifflin, 1927), the correspondence he would have seen at this time, like the query to the warden from Pinkerton's, clearly says "William McGinnis."

4. "Hanging of Tom Ketchum Is a Fearful Sight," *Lamar (CO) Register*, May 1, 1901.

5. Kelly, *The Outlaw Trail*, 256–57. Kelly doesn't take everything French says as truth, but here he confirmed it with Coates.

6. Siringo, *Riata and Spurs*, 219.

7. James D. Horan, *Desperate Men* (Bison, 1997), 260–61. Horan does err on the side of the colorful, and his is a Pinkerton-sanctioned work, but the bones of his story (dates, weather, personnel) are built on the actual agency reports. The LOC archives are littered with his early drafts.

25. The Phantom Limb

1. Thom Hatch, *The Last Outlaws* (New American Library, 2013), 195–96.
2. Charles A. Siringo, *Riata and Spurs* (Houghton Mifflin, 1927), 238.
3. Ibid., 239.
4. Ibid., 245.
5. Ibid., 248.
6. Ibid., 250.
7. In 2011, Fort Worth, Texas, historians restored credit for the discovery to Detective Charley Scott: Richard Selcer and Donna Donnell, "Last Word on the Famous Wild Bunch Photo," *Wild West*, Dec. 2011.
8. Thom Hatch gives the most balanced roundup of the various Etta Place theories; *The Last Outlaws*, 169.
9. DiMaio remembrance from "F.P.D Reports," Sept. 17, 1941, Pinkerton Archive, Criminal Files, Box 89, Folder 7, Library of Congress, Washington, DC.
10. Lowell Spence identification of Logan, recounted in a letter dated Oct. 27, 1939, is from Pinkerton Archive, Criminal Files, Box 88, Folder 6. A death portrait in the National Archives also shows a figure which, allowing for the shaved mustache, could be Curry.
11. "Detective Who Fought Wild West Desperadoes Now Hollywood Citizen," *Los Angeles Times*, Apr. 12, 1925, 43.

26. The Fiery Pools

1. "Wentz Mystery May Be Cleared within Brief Time," *Philadelphia Inquirer*, Oct. 25, 1903, 1.
2. Charles A. Siringo, *A Cowboy Detective* (Bison, 1988), 400.
3. Ibid., 400.
4. Ibid., 407.
5. Ibid., 437.
6. "Wentz Body Went to Pieces When Handled at Inquest," *Viriginia Pilot* (Norfolk), May 11, 1904, 1.
7. Associated Press, "Killing Is Accidental: Decision Came as Surprise" and "Son Was Murdered," *Times Dispatch* (Richmond, VA), May 12, 1904.
8. Charles A. Siringo, *A Cowboy Detective* (Bison, 1988).

27. "Dean of Black Sleuthdom"

1. Charles A. Siringo, *Two Evil Isms* (Steck-Vaughn, 1915), 84–85.

2. John A. Farrell, *Clarence Darrow* (Doubleday, 2011), 146–47.

3. Siringo, *Two Evil Isms*, 95.

4. J. Anthony Lukas, *Big Trouble* (Touchstone, 1997), 584.

5. "Two Men Who Have Helped Make History in the West," *Idaho Daily Statesman* (Boise), July 5, 1907 . It is hard to know how far to trust this anecdote, since, strictly speaking, Siringo never rode with Curry, but Sheriff Meldrum and Siringo told this story to the *Daily Statesman* reporter. If lore, it is at least firsthand lore.

6. Lukas, *Big Trouble*, 584.

7. "Tale of a Pinkerton Plot," *New York Times*, Apr. 29, 1907, 5.

8. *Bill Haywood's Book: The Autobiography of Big Bill Haywood* (International, 1929), 214. Haywood's life story as a labor leader is ghostwritten but sounds pugnaciously like the man himself. It ends with his escape to Lenin's Soviet Union, where he died in 1928, the same year as Siringo.

9. "Darrow's Speech in the Haywood Case," *Waylan's Monthly*, Oct. 1907, 78 (available in the Clarence Darrow Digital Collection, Univ. of Minnesota Law Library, http://moses.law.umn.edu/darrow2/index.html).

10. *Bill Haywood's Book*, 215.

11. Siringo, *Two Evil Isms*, 96.

12. Charles A. Siringo, *Riata and Spurs* (Houghton Mifflin, 1927), 263.

28. Ghosts

1. Charles A. Siringo, *Riata and Spurs* (Houghton Mifflin, 1927), 263–64.

2. Charles A. Siringo, "The Cowboy Outlaw," *Wide World Magazine*, Aug. 1921, 349–51.

3. "Morenci Bank Robbed," *Graham Guardian* (Safford, AZ), Sept. 8, 1910. This account also reports $3,200 stolen, less than Siringo claimed later.

4. *Arizona Daily Star* (Tucson), Oct. 9, 1910, 13.

5. "Train Robbers Escape on Eve of Trial," *Arizona Republic* (Phoenix), Mar. 22, 1908.

6. "In Re: Siringo," *Westerners Brand Book* 16, no. 12, 90–91. Transcript of John A. Brown's appearance before Western enthusiasts at Chicago's Normandy House.

7. Ibid.

8. Charles A. Siringo, *Two Evil Isms* (Steck-Vaughn, 1915), 108.

9. Charles A. Siringo, *A Cowboy Detective* (Bison, 1988), preface.

29. Last Chances

1. "The Last Buffalo," *Effingham (KS) Times*, Aug. 4, 1888, 1.

2. Charles A. Siringo, *A Texas Cowboy* (Penguin, 2000), 155.

3. *Fort Worth (TX) Daily Gazette*, Dec. 25, 1886, 2.

4. "Lessons in Cody's Last Buffalo," *Los Angeles Herald*, Dec. 26, 1910, 4.

5. The story about selling copies on the trip is from Ben Pingenot, *Siringo* (Texas A&M Univ., 1989), 76.

6. Charles A. Siringo, *Riata and Spurs* (Houghton Mifflin, 1927), 269.

7. Howard R. Lamar, *Charlie Siringo's West* (Univ. of New Mexico, 2005), 266–67; Pingenot, *Siringo*, 76.

8. Pingenot, *Siringo*, 81.

9. Ibid., 79. Pingenot quotes Siringo letter from Oct. 17, 1914.

10. "In Re: Siringo," *Westerners Brand Book* 16, no. 12, 90–91.

11. Pingenot, *Siringo*, 80.

12. "Pinkerton's Game to Grab Man Blocked," *Day Book* (Chicago), Apr. 26, 1915.

13. "Siringo May Mark Famous Old Chisholm Trail of Texas Longhorn and Puncher," *Santa Fe New Mexican*, Mar. 24, 1915.

14. *Wichita (KS) Eagle*, quoted in *Topeka (KS) Daily Capital*, Sept. 19, 1915, 5.

15. Charles A. Siringo, *A Lone Star Cowboy* (Chas. A. Siringo, Santa Fe, 1919), 37.

16. Pingenot, *Siringo*, 95.

17. "How Detective McParland Broke Up Two Great Reigns of Terror," *New York Herald*, May 25, 1919, 72.

30. Hollywood

1. "Hart's Doorstep Cowboy's Goal," *Los Angeles Evening Express*, Mar. 28, 1922; "Prairie Jack Edwards Arrives in Salt Lake," *Salt Lake Telegram*, Mar. 9, 1922; see also "Casper Cowboy Rides to Hollywood," *Great Falls (MT) Tribune*, Apr. 2, 1922; *Des Moines (IA) Tribune*, Aug. 2, 1922. If Prairie Jack's

dangerous ride was actually a paid publicity stunt, I have not been able to prove it.

2. The Sunny Slope was finally sold by a special master at auction on Mar. 31, 1924, to one of Charlie's loan-holders, Alonzo Compton, for $1,465, a little over half of what Charlie had paid to print a paperback version of *A Cowboy Detective*. Ranch sale cited in Ben Pingenot, *Siringo* (Texas A&M Univ., 1989), 191n10.

3. Kevin Brownlow, *The War, the West, and the Wilderness* (Knopf, 1979), 380–81. Changing standards made it impossible to defame someone's ancestors, is how Brownlow characterizes the court's finding.

4. George Shaffer, "Cowboy Colony Shoots 'Em Up in Hollywood," *New York Daily News*, May 2, 1927, 26–27.

5. Al Jennings and Will Irwin, *Beating Back* (Musson, 1915), 46.

6. This appealing story is made somewhat more credible by the fact that both men tell it. "Al Jennings Returns Bill Hart's Kindness," *Wichita (KS) Daily Eagle*, Jan. 12, 1919.

7. Within weeks of the Coffeyville showdown, *Coffeyville Journal* editor David S. Elliott had a commemorative booklet out, *Last Raid of the Daltons: A Reliable Recital of the Battle with the Bandits at Coffeyville, Kansas*, featuring a Homeric account of the battle and engraved portraits of all the principals, dead and living, good and bad. The reprint by the Coffeyville Historical Museum (1892) can still be purchased online. It remains the finest brief account of the battle and its significance.

8. The best history of this era and its movies remains Brownlow's *The War, the West, and the Wilderness*, as well the Thames Television series it inspired (written and co-directed by Brownlow), *Hollywood* (1980). In his wonderful books and documentary series, Brownlow treats film history like real history worthy of our serious attention, not just a recitation of stars and moguls.

9. In a letter, Charlie refers to his upcoming work in "Nine Scars Make a Man," but its name in IMDb (International Movie Database) and elsewhere is *Ten Scars Make a Man*. It is listed as a lost film on IMDb.

10. Charles A. Siringo, *Riata and Spurs* (Houghton Mifflin, 1927), 275.

11. Eugene Manlove Rhodes, in his own profile of his friend Siringo two years later in *Sunset* (June 1927), would include a correction of Hammond's report of Siringo's death: "I asked Siringo about this [being dead], and he denies

it. He is an appallingly truthful man and I, for one, am inclined to believe him."

12. William S. Hart, *My Life East and West* (Houghton Mifflin, 1929); Karl K. Kitchin, "Art for Bill's Sake," *St. Louis Post-Dispatch Sunday Magazine*, June 1, 1919, 5.

13. Kitchin, "Art for Bill's Sake."

14. Hart, *My Life East and West*, 37.

31. "The Shrine of Shakespeare"

1. Ben Pingenot, *Siringo* (Texas A&M Univ., 1989), 117.

2. "Chat with Ex-Cowboy, Hailed as Great Literary Find, Recalls Wild West Days," *Los Angeles Evening Express*, Apr. 11, 1927, sec. 3, pp. 1, 4.

3. Pingenot, *Siringo*, 121.

4. Ibid.

5. The most complete account of the back-and-forth of the editorial process between the Pinkerton lawyers and Houghton Mifflin and, eventually, Charlie appears in Pingenot's faithful biography, which cites Houghton Mifflin company records. Pingenot, *Siringo*, 127.

6. John Brown telegrams are all from Pinkerton Archive, Box 61, administrative folder of Siringo legal correspondence, Library of Congress, Washington, DC.

7. Pingenot, *Siringo*, 128.

8. Pinkerton Archive, Box 61, administrative folder.

9. Ibid., Brown cable to Ticknor, June 23, 1927.

10. Ibid., Pinkerton letter from Albert Rossetter, June 25, 1927.

11. Pingenot, *Siringo*, 101.

12. J. Evetts Haley, "Charlie Siringo, Cowboy Chronicler," *Shamrock*, Spring 1962.

13. *Los Angeles Times*, May, 29, 1927, 24.

14. Pingenot, *Siringo*, 149. Pingenot writes that Charlie began feeling he had "run the race and the end of the course was in sight" after news of Renehan's death.

15. Howard R. Lamar, *Charlie Siringo's West* (Univ. of New Mexico, 2005), 301.

Epilogue: Memories

1. Siringo to Hart, Feb. 27, 1926, William S. Hart Papers, Seaver Center for Western History Research, Natural History Museum of Los Angeles County, GC 1012, Box 8.

2. Most accounts of the film quote three hundred wagons and a thousand riders. It appears to be hundreds, but those sound like round publicity numbers cited in *Photoplay*.

Index